Reading Capitalist Realism

The New American Canon

The Iowa Series in Contemporary Literature and Culture

SAMUEL COHEN, series editor

Reading Capitalist Realism

Edited by

ALISON SHONKWILER & LEIGH CLAIRE LA BERGE

University of Iowa Press   Iowa City

University of Iowa Press, Iowa City 52242
Copyright © 2014 by the University of Iowa Press
www.uiowapress.org
Printed in the United States of America

Design by Omega Clay

The University of Iowa Press is a member of Green Press
Initiative and is committed to preserving natural resources.

Printed on acid-free paper

ISBN: 978-1-60938-234-6, 1-60938-234-X (pbk.)
ISBN: 978-1-60938-263-6, 1-60938-263-3 (ebk.)
LCCN: 2013952707

CONTENTS

ACKNOWLEDGMENTS

I would like to thank A. K. Summers for wit and argument, Franklin Summers for the point of view of Franklin Summers, Elizabeth Freeman for unstinting intellectual generosity, series editor Samuel Cohen for enthusiasm and early support, Andrew Hoberek for timely counsel, two manuscript readers for key interventions, and editor Elisabeth Chretien for her patient assistance in guiding this book through publication. —A. S.

Like my co-editor, and for identical reasons, I would like to thank two anonymous reviewers from the University of Iowa Press, together with Samuel Cohen and Elisabeth Chretien. I would also like to thank the Affective Publics group at The University of Chicago, my wonderful New Faculty Speaker Series colleagues at Saint Mary's University and Dalhousie University, and finally, Dehlia Hannah, for using the phrase "capitalist realism" in jest before I knew it was real. —L. C. L.

Reading Capitalist Realism

A Theory of Capitalist Realism

ALISON SHONKWILER & LEIGH CLAIRE LA BERGE

Capitalist realism is both an old and a new concept for literary studies. Realism, after all, has long been considered the aesthetic mode
most intimate to capitalism. It is this intimacy that in the view of its
admirers generates realism's depth and incisiveness of critique. It is
what in the equally compelling view of its detractors fatally compromises the realist project, producing the very subjects and objects that
the mode claims to document. Where literary critics on both sides
would most likely agree, however, is on the redundancy of the prefix
"capitalist." All realism is already capitalist.

Meanwhile, in the political and economic realm the term "realism" has had an altogether different career. The exhortation to "be
realistic" is now part of the ideological enforcement process of neoliberalism. The appeal to the logic of fiscal "common sense," has been
amplified into the moral urgency of reducing spending and trimming
deficits for entire economies. As politicians pursue austerity in the
name of getting one's household in order, "realism" becomes a one-
sided moral regime that focuses on reduction on the social side of
the ledger while ignoring excesses of growth on the corporate and
military side. Given that the realist imperative ignores precisely the
debt expansion and financial machinations on which the past four
decades of capitalist accumulation have depended, one could not be
blamed for the suspicion that any political call to fiscal realism is an
ideologically dubious one. Slavoj Žižek once quipped that the fantasy of every capitalist is to have capitalism without capitalism: For
me, monopoly control of territory! For everyone else, free trade and
open markets. For me, guaranteed profits! For everyone else, the assumption of risk.[1] And yet the presence of a realistic common sense

remains powerful and for many, including on the left, politically difficult to resist, even if the result were to be the veritable collapse of the social sphere. Whenever "realism" is defined as that which is measurable within a system of capitalist equivalence, then everything *not* measurable according to this standard becomes, by simple definition, unaffordable and unrealistic.

The term "capitalist realism" has been used to describe the contemporary condition in which all social and political possibility is seemingly bound up in the economic status quo. Mark Fisher, in his 2009 book *Capitalist Realism*, uses the term to characterize "the widespread sense that not only is capitalism the only viable political and economic system, but also that it is now impossible even to *imagine* a coherent alternative to it."[2] Fisher's claim that "capitalist realism is therefore not a particular type of realism; it is more like realism in itself" (4), thus refers to the abovementioned expansion of realism beyond any particular ideological precinct to become, essentially, the sum of all ideology of the present. Realism, as described by Fisher, is not a representational mode or aesthetic. It is instead a general ideological formation in which capitalism is the most real of our horizons, the market-dominant present that forms the limits of our imaginaries. Thus Fisher argues, echoing similar statements from Fredric Jameson and Žižek, that it is easier to imagine the end of the world than the end of capitalism.

Capitalist realism, in our view, is a theoretical concept that demands further elaboration. The concept's potential lies in its ability both to address the limitations of postmodernism and to connect the postmodern (or post-postmodern, such as it may be) more powerfully to the features of our contemporary political economic moment. The aim of this volume is to open up the term in its political, economic, and aesthetic dimensions while accepting the larger intention of Fisher's project: to provide a language and terminology for what comes *after* a Jamesonian critique at its most totalizing, suffocating, and yet unassailably correct. One example suffices to remind us of the tone and sense of finality of Jameson's 1984 essay "Postmodernism, or the Cultural Logic of Late Capitalism": "The new expansion of multinational capital ends up penetrating and colonizing those very precapitalist enclaves, Nature and the Unconscious, which offered footholds for critical effectivity. . . . This whole extraordinarily demoralizing and depressing global space is the "moment of truth" of postmodernism."[3] Capitalist realism presumes that things have gotten worse. A quarter of a century further into the dialectic of financialization and commodification, capitalism has intensified its claim on its established terrain and further foreclosed upon imaginable alternatives.

A full tour through the history of the term would include stops in art and literary criticism as well as through the Cold War discourse of Realpolitik and the ways in which international political pragmatism has been used to justify the domestic neoliberal "practicalities" of fiscal austerity, pension restructuring, privatization, and union suppression.[4] We focus here on the most contemporary resonances. We write this Introduction in the wake of the most substantial economic crisis to visit the capitalist world-system in some eighty years. Even before the subprime mortgage crisis, the bank bailouts, and the rise of protest movements on the right and left, critics and journalists were calling attention to the inequities and unevennesses of the global neoliberal regime.[5] We are now witnessing a flourishing across different media of realisms attentive to these conditions: in literature, in television and film, and in the vast amount of reportage and documentary work produced in response to the financial crisis itself. Perhaps the most basic question we begin with is whether our current forms of representation are equipped to comprehend and historicize what Ernst Mandel was one of the first to call late capitalism and what David Harvey and Giovanni Arrighi, among others, have argued is a new historical phase of accumulation: the roughly forty-year period in which, as Arrighi claims, "something fundamental seems to have changed in the way capitalism works."[6] Harvey and Arrighi both date this change to the early 1970s. Harvey argues that the "crisis" of overaccumulation of this period was never resolved but instead displaced through financial reorganization in a series of temporal and spatial fixes. Arrighi, using the historical model of a *longue durée*, represents the financial expansion of the late twentieth century as only the latest of a series of systemic cycles of accumulation alternating between phases of material and financial ex-

pansion. In Marxist terms, the causes come back to crises of accumulation and overproduction, the search for new pathways of growth in
the face of a declining rate of profit, and, failing that, doubling down
and squeezing harder on existing profit sources—whether through
speculation and finance or through the downward global pressure on
wages (what Harvey, following Marx, calls the "rate of exploitation").
Michael Hardt and Antonio Negri describe the new capitalist order
as "intensive" rather than "extensive." Its open and fluctuating networks of power deepen and intensify already-existing sites of capitalist valorization instead of expanding imperially through cartographic
space. Jeffrey Nealon uses this argument of intensification to diagnose the "mutation" in the postmodern that inaugurates the logic of
what he calls the "post-postmodern."[7] Whether or not they agree on
a definable end or "after" to the postmodern, Marxist, post-Marxist,
and other critics have shared the sense of a break or change in economic production that is seen to demand a corresponding response
in accounts of cultural production. It is this logic of "intensification
and generalization" that many critics identify as the point of connection between capitalism and the forms of representation that are attached to it. A bevy of new concepts has been provided to understand
the transition, as well as benchmarks to periodize it, from the early-
1970s collapse of fixed exchange rates, to the rise of global, flexible
accumulation, to, most recently, such forms of financialization as the
securitization of assets and the expansion of debt.[8]

Our volume works within this periodization, and its essays borrow
from all these analytics. Perhaps the most crucial political-economic
term is "neoliberalism." Although capitalist realism shares an articulation with neoliberalism, it is not coterminous with it. If postmodernism names a depressing moment of truth produced by the loss of
spatial-temporal coordination, neoliberalism names those aspects of
globalization that, under the auspices of the market, limit social functioning and naturalize structures of inequality. Its rise dating in most
accounts from the early to mid-1970s, neoliberalism typically refers
to an economic and political paradigm in which freedom is conceived
almost entirely in market terms, as the ability to operate unhampered
by state regulation or political interference, even as the production

of the conditions of market organization and construction of citizenship that complements it are often seen as the state's "proper" function. The central features of the neoliberal state, besides privatizing wealth, deregulating markets, and reducing social spending, include preoccupation with supporting the interests of an unfettered global financial system and, as recent critics have extensively argued, taking advantage of crises to advance market-based, free-trade-oriented, and even financially imperialist agendas. One need not even necessarily accept David Harvey's capsule description of neoliberalism as a "programmatic" restoration of capitalist class hegemony, under the guise of the promise to the masses of increased individual freedoms, to concede a drastic shift in the past four decades toward greater concentrations of wealth in the hands of an elite few, with those few "controlling power over large sections of the economy."[9]

Periodizing Capitalist Realism

As a term, "capitalist realism" is intended to capture a relationship that neither postmodernism nor neoliberalism adequately encompasses. Mark Fisher's critique of postmodernism as an analytic or a periodization is not that it is (or was) incorrect but that it no longer contains the referential capacity required for contemporary analysis. He explains that "some of the processes that Jameson described have become so aggravated and chronic that they have gone through a change in kind" (7). These processes have become spatially and temporally intensified—always the method of capital.[10] Thus when Jameson in 1984 claimed that the "Unconscious" had been captured by circuits of multinational capital, he surely couldn't have predicted (nor could anyone else) that epidemics of "bipolar disorder" would sweep through whole preschool populations and require—of course—new, expensive, brand-name pharmaceuticals for treatment.[11] Postmodernism is not *enough* to describe this neoliberal scene. Fisher suggests that capitalist realism might be. Postmodernism could still remember precapitalist enclaves with enough nuance to produce a nostalgia for them; it could still look to the Eastern bloc for a site of economic otherness. Indeed, whether de facto Eastern communism offered a viable alternative or not, its existence provided a trope for the Western, democratic left and functioned as a generative site for the discursive production of an outside. What was lost with its decomposition was a site, however fictitious, for the imagination of another world. That the imagined reality of that other world was, in retrospect, a fantasy only shows the necessity of using fantasy to imagine other alternatives. Yet, according to Fisher, that content of fantastic imagination is ceaselessly metabolized by capitalist realism. And indeed, if it is easier to imagine the end of the world than the end of capitalism, this must be at least partly because capitalist representation now specializes in previews of the apocalyptic: from its compendium of possible, upcoming disasters to narrative re-creations of recent ones.[12]

For capitalist realism or any similar theoretical concept to be of service to the present it must articulate (1) the violence produced by a capitalism that constantly seeks to expand its sources and strategies of accumulation; (2) the lived economic, social, and affective instabilities of an entrepreneurial risk society; and (3) how these are together transformed into a widely accepted brand of Gramscian "common sense," in which an inequitable, winner-take-all system of casino capitalism has seemingly achieved popular consent. Hence we arrive at some of the limitations of the term "neoliberal" for describing the *realization* of market imperatives at an ideological level. If neoliberalism appears to describe a structural basis or referent for the account of postmodernism as a cultural dominant (though in fact the global expansion of market logic is no less cultural than anything else), and might seem to function as a complement to Jameson's articulation, this term too suffers from inadequacies: first, to account for the role of representation and belief in *producing* that which becomes reality; second, to register capitalism's ability to double down upon those sites of reality to insist that "there is no alternative." Capitalist realism denotes the site upon which the limit of the imaginary is constructed. It insists on the circulation between imagination and reality, the ways in which this relationship is produced and disavowed.

In an interview in this volume with the political theorist Jodi Dean, Fisher claims that "capitalist realism is the pathology of the left" because it sustains and amplifies the "corrosion of social imagination." But if for Fisher the term signifies resignation and exhaustion, we believe it is possible to energize it critically. Capitalist realism need not only represent ideological closure and defeat. It can also operate theoretically and critically to describe the relationship between accumulation and representation in the present. Against those who would insist that capitalist realism does not describe an aesthetic form, and that the concept's strength lies precisely in exceeding the limitations of a representational or aesthetic theory, we counter that it is possible to have it both ways. The effectiveness of the concept is that it emphasizes the economic while insisting at the same time on the political and representational dimensions of capitalism. After all, capital represents and is represented. It is within this system of economic representation that we are interpellated as economic subjects of various sorts: as consumers, producers, and debtors, and as spectators and as casualties. Like any contest, therefore, this contest of representation is open to potential transformation.

For this volume the question becomes, How can such struggles of representation be informed by the *literary*? Representational realism, in the sense in which we aim to develop it here, is not an aesthetic afterthought to a political and economic ideology of privatization and wealth protection; in other words, this is not simply a localized application, in the literary realm, of the more generalized, market-driven aesthetic of "realism" that Fisher theorizes. While capitalist realism is a concept that has been developed outside literary theory, we suggest that it offers a powerful means to connect the transformation of these modes of accumulation to changes in the effort to interpret and historicize that transformation. We thus begin this project by asking how the "realism" that functions as an ideological marker in political and economic discourse relates to the realism of narrative production. How might the realism of lowered expectations—in the affective register, what Lauren Berlant has called "cruel optimism"—be measured or identified by literary criticism?

Representations

There can be no doubt that the economic events of the last five years have generated space for the creation of new economic knowledge and representation. How will the present be represented back to us and what role will these representations have in generating new critiques and understandings of the credit crisis, the Great Recession, and the mass occupations that have followed? In a recent issue of *Bookforum*, Christian Lorentzen predicts that "in the fall of 2013 or 2014, if not before, we'll probably be reading a novel about Occupy Wall Street. What would such a book look like, and what would it tell us about money? You can bet the narrator will be omniscient and the telling panoramic."[13] If Lorentzen's prediction is correct, the economic novel's repeated recourse to realism expresses a desire for the most thorough possible indexing of capitalism to the present. Here is one likely site to identify one of the motivating cruxes of the capitalist realist project: the effort to expose and make legible the conditions that have been produced by so-called illegible abstractions of finance capital, particularly the vehicles of securitization and risk management of the early 2000s, such as credit default swaps and derivatives. Conversely, it might be a project of capitalist realism to reveal through representation whether this perceived financial complexity is not just one more strategy of accumulation.[14]

Nonetheless, our objective is not to anticipate a genre of Zuccotti Park fiction, however it may develop or whatever formal features it may exhibit. Indeed, the most pertinent fictions of post-crisis resistance may turn out not to refer to the Occupy movement at all, let alone to recall a panoramic 1980s Wall Street novel by Tom Wolfe. Whether or not contemporary fiction writers nostalgically seek to reprise a nineteenth-century Balzacian realist framework, there is no doubt that the realisms of today do not operate in the same world of conditions and demands as a nineteenth-century novel and cannot make the same kinds of claims to truth. Even viewed from entirely within a literary-historical context, modes of realism today are not clearly or straightforwardly alignable with the realisms of previous literatures.

Thus, when Joshua Clover, for instance, argues in this volume that narrative realism has lost its privileged relationship to capitalism and its purchase on the representation of it, this returns us precisely to the question of how to discuss realism's ongoing claims to explain the world around us. It is to ask to what extent this realism is still defined by an investment in scenes of the everyday, an accumulation of detail, and/or the moral encounter of the individual with social forces. It is to ask whether realism's critical intervention—whatever it might ever have been—has been entirely turned over to journalism, where many accounts of the financial crisis seek, at a forensic level of detail, to narrate the sequential unfolding of various financial operations, or to film, whose own medium seems structurally better able to grasp mimetically the quotidian operations of Wall Street such as charts, numbers, infographics, and the like. And yet surely both journalism and film are likewise limited by the same complicities and inadequacies that cause literary realism to be, as Jameson argues, ontologically committed to the status quo as such.

In other words, while it is today increasingly recognized that capitalism requires retheorization to account for its ever-evolving scenes of enclosure and indebtedness, it is less widely insisted that realism, too, demands renewed scrutiny for its relevance and complicity in capturing these scenes. Our own scrutiny of realism in what follows of this Introduction takes two paths: first, reflection on what revisions may be demanded by our literary genealogies, including the familiar realism–modernism–postmodernism account; and second, consideration of whether capitalist realism can be said to constitute a new formal mode rather than an elaboration or appropriation of earlier modes.

Joe Cleary suggests in his recent essay "Realism after Modernism" that modernism should be reconceived not as a break with realism, as standard accounts have had it (although there is no doubt that modernism represented a crisis of representation within it), but instead as an "attempted sublation of realism into more spatially and cognitively expansive forms" (261). The recent special issue of *MLQ*, "Peripheral Realisms," in which Cleary's essay appears is a powerful step toward this revision of literary realism away from a London–Paris axis toward the expanded point of view of capitalist world-systems.[15] In their introduction, Jed Esty and Colleen Lye claim that "we need, but lack, comprehensive theories and historical atlases of twentieth-century realism" on a global scale. Their focus on realisms from the periphery might be seen as an effort to reorient criticism from a Eurocentric modernism—with its privileging of the literary criteria of ambiguity, hybridity, and irony, for instance—and to recognize the continuing purchase of realist concepts such as class consciousness, social totality, and historical transition, as "part of a wider remapping of the literary world system now" (280).[16]

While an expanded global *scale* offers a way to revise the realism-modernism dialectic, so too does an expanded notion of accumulation and production. Like the editors of "Peripheral Realisms," we see realism to be a moment we find ourselves in not *again* but *still*. Whereas Esty and Lye address realism's supposed failure to grapple with problems of alterity, we expand on its relationship to austerity: namely, the ways in which realism is imbricated in a generalized crisis of accumulation. We argue that the relationship between capitalist realism and narrative and visual representation demands recognition of their mutual imbrication in current conditions of crisis and contradiction.

To make this argument is not to jettison the well-accepted dialectics of literary development from realism to modernism and from modernism to postmodernism. Nor is it to reject the model of "cultural dominants" and the corresponding generic and modal signatures that each contains, such as realism's free indirect discourse as contrasted with modernism's first-person narrators, or modernism's Weltschmertz as ceding to postmodernism's schizophrenia. What might capitalist realism add to this narrative? As postmodernism cedes its legacy and organizing forms to capitalist realism, a new desire for objectivity and mimetic certainty emerges with the new, self-reflexive knowledge that the certainties of realism are things to be bought and sold. Ultimately, capitalist realism might describe the logical conclusion of these processes: how realism undergoes the precise processes of capture and subsumption into the circuits of capital that it claims to represent.

To emphasize this internalization of production as a process is not the same as to ask about conditions of production in an older sense, as in the question "Who paid for modernism?"[17] It is instead about the ways in which the "reality" of production is incorporated into and interacts with modes of representation—some new, some familiar.

Here it will be useful to enumerate some of the features of capitalist realism as we see them and how they function in relation to each other, as well as to acknowledge its conceptual risks.

First, capitalist realism is unstable in regard to its own mode. Whereas earlier realisms laid claim, however problematically, to a stability of mode and perception, the capitalist realist mode interrupts and disorganizes itself, through its incorporation of other genres and through its desire to show the processes of its own commodification. This claim can be demonstrated not through a deconstructive reading of texts, in which their internal logics are shown to be in tenuous relation, balanced on a fragile stability, but rather through attention to plot, structure, and production processes. As a methodology, capitalism realism demands an engagement with specific economic forms such as the commodity, money, and finance, as well as organized economic processes such as production and consumption.

Two examples from this volume help to demonstrate the instability of mode as revealed at the level of production. The first comes from an analysis of *The Wire*, the David Simon television series widely upheld as perhaps the most trenchant recent example of a "new realism." Indeed, even realist crank extraordinaire Jonathan Franzen commented in a 2009 interview that had he "seen *The Wire*" he wouldn't have been so critical in 1996 of the future of American realism and the realist novel in particular.[18] *The Wire* is a great realist production. But *The Wire* is not a novel; it is a television series. As a text conceived, written, produced, and directed for television, it has different formal possibilities than one conceived as a novel. Perhaps the outpouring of critical response to the show demonstrates, more than anything else, that critics need to venture outside the medium of the realist novel in order to offer a critique of it. Moreover, we question whether Simon's realist series is devoted to resuscitating realism or to disaggregating it. In her essay in this volume on *The Wire*, Leigh Claire La Berge argues that the show, which spent its first four seasons realistically detailing the failure of social institutions, from the labor movement to the school system, ultimately turns its critical lens on realism itself. The fifth and final season of *The Wire* renders realism, too, a failed institution, by introducing the unrealistic, indeed the melodramatic, plotline of a fictitious serial killer whose sensational violence allows the viewer to disavow what had previously constituted the show's realism, namely, its representation of economic violence. It is through the gradual sale of its own realism at the level of plot that *The Wire* questions whether it was ever realist at all at the level of mode.

In an even more direct example of capitalist realism's operation at the level of production process, J. D. Connor, in an essay on the film *Déjà Vu*, looks at the race in the film industry to secure state and municipal tax credits to lure film production to specific locales. This race is internalized into film's own productive apparatus, Connor argues, demonstrating how Hollywood "adopted a post-crisis mode of production" before the actual crisis. Connor's piece suggests that critics working within the capitalist realist mode may help to locate new instantiations of forms of value, ones that call into question some of our most trusted political-economic categories in the study of culture. Is seeking out cheap labor through tax credits an example of commodification, as defined by Marx as production for the market by wage labor? Or is it an example of financialization, as defined by Arrighi as the ascension of a financial imperative over other forms of economic organization? These two terms have often been used indistinguishably by critics, with the implicit understanding that the second follows from the first. But we argue that these are different processes, captured and negotiated differently by cultural forms.

Whereas the internalization of *production* may be identifiable in the example of film tax credits, or the relationship between race, money, and seriality in *The Wire*, it may be less obvious elsewhere at the level of *mode*. In the novel we see various levels of mediation become possible. In the texts discussed in this volume, the destabilization and subsumption at the level of mode often transpires through genre. Thus, for instance, in his essay in this volume Andrew Hoberek argues that realism now invariably tends toward generic categories: "It is almost as though the realist novel, so closely tied to a particular form of capitalism and the kinds of social mobility it enabled, must turn to genre fiction to represent forms outside of it, whether the residual feudal hierarchies that lingered into capitalism's heyday or the hierarchies of money that characterize an emergent post-capitalist capitalism." The turn to allegory in a novel such as *The Reluctant Fundamentalist*, for example, like *The Wire*'s turn to melodrama, opens up a middle ground on which realism both represents and cannot represent forms of global capital indexically. Timothy Bewes locates a similar generic reorientation in his reading of J. M. Coetzee's *Elizabeth Costello*, which he argues switches between realist and allegorical terms. Meanwhile, Alissa Karl diagnoses an impulse to narrative totalization within neoliberal capitalism that is exposed as both obsolete and persistent. Reading James Kelman's *How Late It Was, How Late* and Ali Smith's *Hotel World*, Karl argues that the "neoliberal novel" doesn't abandon narrative totality but simultaneously invokes it and undermines it through indeterminacy and contradiction. This double movement, we might say, flags the instability of the capitalist realist mode. As a mode without a fixed point *either* inside or outside the process of representation, it does not commit itself to offer ballast against the instability of the capitalism it represents. Terms and features that appear to stabilize turn out to do so at best provisionally, limitedly, and/or incoherently.

In response to the question whether capitalist realism is something *new* rather than an elaboration of previous modes, moreover, we answer that it is both. To identify a difference of mode requires not only isolating the narrative features of realism but also contending with the changed situation of literature and literary production more generally. A useful example is Paul Dawson's recent argument on the return of omniscience in contemporary fiction in the UK and US.[19] The reappearance of the "ostensibly outmoded" omniscient narrator in Dawson's account responds specifically to the late-twentieth-century decline of literature's cultural authority. It is not as if contemporary omniscient narrators have suddenly reclaimed the "moral and epistemological certainties" of their eighteenth- and nineteenth-century counterparts; instead the narrator borrows authority from the public persona of the author, who thus stands to the narrator in a kind of proxy relationship. In certain instances, therefore, the contemporary author functions as a kind of extradiegetic character. Whether or not contemporary omniscience rises to the level of a new form, it is constituted through an entirely specific cultural history of the present that can never be simply understood as a repeat performance.

Following this line of argument, it becomes possible to see not only omniscient narration but other techniques and preoccupations of the classic realist mode—its mimetic and documentary registers, its assumptions about actuality, its aspirations to social totality, its uneasy rivalry with allegory, its strategies of surveillance, spectatorship, and ethnographic "othering"—as taking on different significance in the present. Realism's claims to capture the real are, more than ever, indicative of a contest over the stabilization of a financially productive reality.

Second, in our view, capitalist realism is neither an updating of socialist realism nor simply a neoliberal inversion of it. If nineteenth-century bourgeois fiction was the height of a purportedly "stable" version of realism, then socialist realism represented the officially sanctioned, twentieth-century turn toward a new literature of the worker and of revolutionary consciousness. Yet, as the painters Vitaly Komar and Alexander Melamid and the anthropologist Alexei Yurchak have made clear, the irony of socialist realism was that its "real" was so highly idealized that it forfeited its mimetic and indexical coordination altogether.[20] Nonetheless, it represented itself as splitting off from the elitism and decadence of modernism, and as reshaping literary values for the benefit of the "ordinary" worker. Western criticism's privileging of literary modernism during the Cold War period was a de facto acknowledgment of the split. But like the modernist avant-gardism that is itself defined by its rejection of the economic sphere, socialist realism is so deeply framed and organized by its opposition to capital that it too might be said to be capitalist.[21] Ironically, today the socialist-realist project may remain politically relevant through its ability to cast into relief the idealizations to which other, Western, and supposedly less "political" realisms are no less susceptible.

Here is where it is most useful to understand capitalist realism as *both* an ideological formation (as Fisher describes it) and a mode. As an ideological formation, it describes the pervasive logic of capitalism in the present. As a mode, however, it potentially conjoins both conservative and critical impulses—on the one hand retaining the conservatism of representational realism in its commitment, as Jameson puts it, to the status quo, while on the other hand modeling the very transformative capitalist processes of commodification and financialization that it records. In contrast to socialist realism, then, capitalist realism traverses the terrain between the ideological and the critical.

But could not this same work be performed under the auspices of *neoliberalism*? Indeed, critics including Walter Benn Michaels and Jeffrey J. Williams use this term to describe contemporary literary formations. Michaels, for instance, argues that questions of identity and recognition tend to dominate over questions of economic distribution in contemporary fiction, to the detriment of a full recognition of the neoliberal tradeoff between the two. By resisting representation of economic difference, he argues, contemporary novels "naturalize the unimaginability of any alternative to neoliberalism and so make[ ] it easier for us to accept the inequality neoliberalism has produced."[22] Although Michaels here usefully calls attention to the politics of what fiction ignores, he only goes so far as to define the neoliberal novel in the negative for what it doesn't do. Defining a category by its failure to critique structures of class inequality does not produce a positive set of features by which to rule a text *in* rather than *not out*. Williams, more specifically, describes the neoliberal novel in terms of a new mode of "resignation." In contrast to the postmodern mode of conspiracy and surveillance, the neoliberal mode marks a turn in the machinations of power, a recognition of the ruling rich, by shifting "from moral allegory to a resigned realism."[23] In this view Jonathan Franzen's *The Corrections* and *Freedom* actively demonstrate and support a fatalistic idea that "we can only successfully solve problems through private means and individual action" (94). The neoliberal novel, for Williams, becomes a way of recasting Lionel Trilling's "liberal imagination" of the 1950s as the "plutocratic imagination" of the present in which the "real action occurs among the rich" (95).

Contemporary fiction is indeed highly varied in its critique of the neoliberal order. What capitalist realism can highlight are the rival dynamics of this critique at work. Whereas the postmodern emphasizes indeterminacy and ontological uncertainty, capitalist realism acknowledges the limitations of critique—even as it constantly seeks new avenues for it. Under capitalist realism the postmodern skepticism toward systems and paranoia about agency control give way, certainly not to a restored faith in systems but to a recognition of the ruling order of capitalism as both more banal and more encompassing. This is not to say that the metasystems under scrutiny are no longer sinister (terrorism and violence are implicated in *The Reluctant Fundamentalist* and in the similar neoliberal finance-dominated worlds represented in novels such as *Kapitoil* and *A Young Man's Guide to Capitalism*)[24] but that the contest of representation is heightened through processes of being alternately internalized and externalized by the text.

Michael Hardt has suggested that in a classically liberal regime, the state controls the market, but in a neoliberal regime, the market controls the state.[25] We might transform that aesthetically into the claim that in liberalism the market was represented; in neoliberalism, the market represents. In our theorization, again, capitalist realism as a process tends toward miscegenation between the categories of accumulation and representation. At its logical extreme, capitalist realist criticism elaborates a tension already present within many conceptions of the realist mode: the point at which realism simultaneously records and undergoes the economic processes of commodification and financialization.

Third, in our view, capitalist realism calls into question *what realism is*. Our attention to the shifting ground of capitalism demands renewed attention to the stability of realism, to the dialectic between historical processes and aesthetic efforts to capture them. Realism is repoliticized. It was always political, of course, but now the stakes are raised again, calling attention to the ways in which capitalism impoverishes our imagination while simultaneously claiming that impoverishment cannot be imagined otherwise. Matthew Beaumont, in the introduction to *Adventures in Realism* (2007), argues against limiting our definitions even of the nineteenth-century novel to "passive, positivistic" models, a stance that seems to invite developing more dynamic models of literary realism as a historical process.[26] Yet, at the same time, Beaumont dismisses what he calls "common sense" notions of realism and resists what he sees as the tendency to collapse the term into its "most degraded meaning" (9). Common sense is tied to the "crassest ideological assumptions about reality" in this view and therefore represents a default conservatism that theorists of realism should decisively reject.

But the politics of "common sense," much like the exhortation to "be realistic," are tied up with the very recognition of what constitutes the political and are thus hardly dismissible. And even when realism is understood exclusively in literary terms, it is no less in the thick of the "degraded" politics business. We maintain that the ironic coupling of our term "capitalist realism" can represent exactly the challenge of theorizing it for the left imaginary without granting literary realism a naïve authority to demystify capitalist processes of accumulation, or to de-reify the real. "Capitalist" and "realism" describe a phenomenon that is neither confined to the literary nor separable from it. The literary and the economic *both* operate on *both* sides of the phrase. "Capitalism" as a system cannot exist apart from modes of representation, and the realist mode (however else it is defined) is invested in an economically situated conception of history.

Jameson has called the theorization of realism a "contradictory project." He argues that it is a "contradiction which can, however, be reformulated in a productive way, as a tension to be solved and resolved over and over again in a series of fresh innovations" (Beaumont, 261). Realism, in this sense, is the ground zero of representational politics. It is indeed, as its critics charge, a mode of increments, reformism, and stability. But paradoxically its commitment to the absolute uniqueness of what *is* renders it perhaps the most expansive, capacious, and easily adaptable mode. Perhaps to assess the politics of realism's claims to truth—wherever and whatever they might be—one must begin with an even simpler, recent formulation from Jameson: "We may even wonder whether the most useful 'definition' of *realism* may not lie in the capacity of a text to raise the issue of realism as such within its own structure, no matter what answer it decides to give."[27]

* * *

The essays collected here engage with fiction, nonfiction, film, and literary and cultural criticism. They conceive the present as a moment of flourishing realisms and flourishing capitals in order to interrogate how the two work together. Although the intimacy of these new realisms to capitalism cannot be in doubt, the contributors to this volume reveal their ambivalence toward the term "capitalist realism" as a critical tool. For some critics, indeed, the very intimacy and proximity of realism to capital reifies the categories on which capital is dependent and thus ossifies the critical project of interpretation. But even where critics disagree about the usefulness of the term, they demonstrate the demand for some level of mediation between forms of representation and the neoliberal insistence on "common sense"—even if they question the literary as a site for such mediation.

We begin with an interview between Mark Fisher and political theorist Jodi Dean, in which they discuss capitalist realism's potential as a theoretical tool. Their different positions on the affective dimension of capitalism, in particular, are useful in theorizing how capitalism becomes viewed as an inevitable ("irresistible") force rather than a socially and politically transformable one. Dean emphasizes the rewards and gratifications capitalism offers; Fisher, the attachment between circuits of pleasure and boredom. With capitalist realism, for Fisher, "we're faced with an entertainment that doesn't really entertain alongside a populism which really isn't popular." The homogeneity and predictability of capitalism make necessary an aesthetic critique—one that should be directed *at* capitalist realism—to show that capitalism is not nearly as pleasurable as it makes itself out to be.

The essays in the first section of the book, "Novelistic Realisms," take up the uneven transformations of realist narrative, in light of what Hoberek calls in his essay the absence or impossibility of a "fully functioning realism." As in the example of *The Reluctant Fundamentalist* mentioned above, Hoberek argues that realism's formal crisis can be identified through the "breakdown in the novel's historical capacity to translate fact into some sort of socially useful truth." Fiction such as Lorrie Moore's *A Gate at the Stairs* and Jess Walter's *The Financial Lives of the Poets*, the novels Hoberek examines here, connect anxiety over the breakdown of individual responsibility to a crisis of contract. Specifically, adultery stands in for this crisis of fulfilling social and economic obligations under a current capitalism that Hoberek claims "is no longer capitalistic." Through his readings of these novels, he argues that the fundamental question that haunts all capitalist transactions—how can value be produced through an equal exchange?—has now been absorbed and retheorized into novelistic space through an allegorization of contract itself. If contract is the fiction whereby an inequality is secured and rendered commensurable, Hoberek reveals how novelistic fiction has become a site of critique of this particular capitalist logic.

Alissa G. Karl describes the aesthetic modes by which fictions mediate between the bodies of individuals and the bodies of entities such as nation-states. Arguing that the broken bodies in James Kelman's novel *How Late It Was, How Late* and Ali Smith's *Hotel World* represent the incongruous effects of an atomized and disposable labor force, Karl presents the novels as critiquing the ways in which neoliberalism discards those parts of the social body that cease to have value or come to represent excessive capacity. The neoliberal novel, in Karl's formulation, does not resist representation of the nation but incorporates the rival impulses of nation making and nation breaking to challenge the assumption that the nation-state is obsolete.

In an essay on Russell Banks's global fictions, Phillip E. Wegner reads *The Darling* in light of changing national and geopolitical situations. Suggesting that the events of 9/11 render certain episodes from Banks's earlier novels newly improbable, Wegner argues that the status of the *event*—as defined by philosopher Alain Badiou, the improbable impossibility that nonetheless is real—affects our notion of possible intervention in the world and our imagination of radical change. As earlier strategies of realism are demonstrated to be less viable by social, cultural, and geopolitical changes, the result, according to Wegner, is a "baleful new sense of capitalist realism" with its own impossibilities that constrict our being-in-the-world as subjects. In each of the essays of this section, then, the transnational and post-imperial are newly articulated within a new genre: novelistic capitalist realism.

The second section of the book, "Genres of Mediation," addresses the commodification of visual and nonfictional narrative genres under neoliberalism and some of its aesthetic ramifications. We have already mentioned La Berge's analysis of *The Wire* and Connor's analysis of the film *Déjà Vu* as examples of the way the commodification and production of the text becomes an interruptive aspect of the capitalist realist mode. *The Wire*, La Berge contends, disarticulates and deconstructs not only its realism but the problem of realism itself. Connor, meanwhile, citing Deleuze's account of the eruption of money as an event *within* the postwar history of film, links the emergence of the time-image to the cinema's internalization of its own relationship to money. Connor argues that under the "free trade" auspices of competition for film-industry locations and industry tax breaks, films become self-allegorizations of their own conditions of production—specifically the combination of time, space, labor, and capital required for every individual film project. This formal-financial coordination of the medium represents another giving over to the logic of capitalist equivalence.

The fact that these two essays—our two most specifically political-economic—are outside the scope of the literary proper is suggestive of the challenge that remains in reconceptualizing mediation for more traditionally literary works and genres. The final essay of this section, by Caren Irr, examines the realism of nonfiction writer and journalist William Vollmann and addresses some of these challenges. In his writing about the poor, Irr argues, Vollmann exposes the double bind of documentary realism, a genre that, in seeking to treat its subjects on a level of equality with that of the writer/observer, risks evacuating the very political categories that might be used to redress poverty. Vollmann's ethic of radical equality with the poor and the homeless people he writes about requires a commitment to "ceaseless self-scrutiny." But this self-destabilizing stance as an observer also commits him to an existential individualism from which no structural critique can be made. Skeptical of the apoliticism of Vollmann's approach, Irr contrasts it with Jacques Rancière's analysis of how the poor expose the paradox of equality in modern democracy. Ultimately, she cautions, the emerging project of capitalist realism cannot avoid the representational dilemma between ethical and political approaches. The commitment to documentary realism and the commitment to critique of capitalism must figure out a way to represent ethically while not foreclosing the possibilities of structural and collective politics.

Our third section, "After and Against Representation," provides a set of theoretical explorations that question whether the act of literary representation itself is not already a compromised project. Michael W. Clune takes the occasion of Fisher's mention of William Gibson's *Neuromancer* to develop a more sustained discussion of the novel, while critiquing the methodological tendency of literary critics to treat fiction as realistic—or even as aspiring to realism. The transformative power of fiction lies in its *anti-mimetic* capacities, Clune claims, not its degree of attachment to actuality. By no stretch of the imagination, then, can literature be used as functional evidence of social or economic reality. Literature produces the stretch *of* the imagination required to envision a world of new possibilities. To read *Neuromancer* "anti-mimetically," in this vein, is to discover the discrepancies, not the continuities, between market reality and market fiction. For Clune, the unique contribution of the literary for thinking critically about capitalism can only be established once we see non-realistic images of the market as an imaginative resource rather than as necessarily "ideological and degraded."

Timothy Bewes subjects "representation" to even deeper theoretical scrutiny, arguing that recent discussions of reification by Axel Honneth and Kevin Floyd have fundamentally misconceived the Lukacsian form of this concept. Bewes posits that reification is to be understood neither as a form of misrepresentation nor even as the development over time of a falsification. Instead it refers to the pre-existing logic under which instantiation under capitalism only ever takes place—a logic, as Bewes puts it, "that defines the ontological propensities of capitalism itself." In this argument, to ask if representation is ever possible without reification would require separating the "theory and practice of representation" from what Bewes formulates as "the logic of the instance."

But if capitalism instantiates (as opposed to representing), then what are the consequences for literature, or the critical functions available to literary representation? Indeed, all the essays of this third section might be understood to revolve around the question, In what capacity can literature be said to represent without instantiating? Bewes's answer would seem to suggest that no realism that also instantiates would be enough to critique capital. Briefly discussing J. M. Coetzee's novel *Elizabeth Costello* as an example of a text that calls the scene of representation into focus through its oscillation between realist and allegorical modes, he argues that only in the movement between theory and example—or in other words, between representation and a model of representation—can the reifying instant possibly be challenged.

Finally, Joshua Clover returns us to the premises of this volume by arguing provocatively that the literary theorization of capitalist realism should be called to a halt. Capitalist realism, he insists, is "neither an aesthetic mode, nor a strategy of representation" but a "displacement of such matters . . . as increasingly frivolous." If the only *real* of capital according to Marx is value, then the only *realism* of capital is the working out of the law of value through all its contradictions. The only overcoming of this realism, in other words, would be the overcoming of capitalist valorization itself, the achievement of some form of production beyond value. The only redress for capitalist realism, in short, is communism. With his thrust against the very concept of capitalist realism, however, Clover also reminds us of the constitutive historical tensions of the concept in the first place: on one hand, the effort to understand the *processes* of realization that constitute the real; on the other, the recognition of what Richard Dienst calls, in an afterword to this volume, the continuing "strength of the contemporary capitalist world-picture."

Our volume, *Reading Capitalist Realism*, is an attempt to make sense of new realisms whose intimacy to capital cannot be in doubt and whose critics feel ambivalent toward their very deployment of the term. Ultimately, exploring what a theory of realism may encompass in our moment of neoliberal triumph and leftist tenuousness is not about simply adding terms or recuperating old ones but coming to understand their relationships in newly dialectical fashion. In spite of the critical ambivalence in this volume, therefore, we maintain that the irony of the phrase "capitalist realism" is a means of thinking through the doubling and disidentification of intensities and sites of valorization required to theorize the term for literary studies. In the spirit of Žižek's criticism of the fantasy that there can be capitalism without capitalism, we insist that recognizing capitalism *with* capitalism is the only way to account for the enclosures of capital, the scenes of indebtedness it produces, and its ability to form the most real of our horizons.

NOTES

1   Louis Menand, "Faith, Hope, and Clarity," *The New Yorker* (September 16, 2002).

2   Mark Fisher, *Capitalist Realism: Is There No Alternative?* (London: Zero Books, 2009), 2.

3   Fredric Jameson, *Postmodernism, or, The Cultural Logic of Late Capitalism* (Durham, NC: Duke University Press, 1991), 49.

4   German artist Gerhardt Richter used it in 1963, partly in jest, to distinguish his realist photo-paintings from the commercialism of Pop Art at the "Demonstration for Capitalist Realism" art show in Dusseldorf. American political scientist Scott A. Greer employed the term independently that same year in his monograph *Metropolitics* to describe the peculiar urban culture of American cities and urban planning approaches to them. *Metropolitics: A Study of Political Culture* (New York: Wiley and Sons, 1963). Literary scholar Richard Godden has described the "capitalist realist" effect of Hemingway's prose descriptions of material objects. Godden, *Fictions of Capital: The American Novel from James to Mailer* (New York: Cambridge University Press, 1990), 50. Slavoj Žižek calls Arthur Hailey the "first great author of 'capitalist realism,'" referring to his 1960s best sellers *Hotel, Airport,* and *Cars,* and nominates Michael Crichton (*Prey, Disclosure, State of Fear*) as Hailey's latest heir. Žižek, *In Defense of Lost Causes* (London: Verso, 2008), 52.

5   For perhaps the most sweeping embrace of this horizontal capitalism, see Thomas L. Friedman, *The Lexus and the Olive Tree: Understanding Globalization,* rev. ed. (New York: Picador, 2012). For a more critical appraisal, see Joseph E. Stiglitz, *Globalization and Its Discontents* (New York: Norton, 2003).

6   Giovanni Arrighi, *The Long Twentieth Century: Money, Power, and the Origins of Our Times* (London: Verso, 1994), 1. See also David Harvey, *The Condition of Postmodernity: An Enquiry into the Origins of Cultural Change* (Cambridge, MA: Blackwell, 1990).

7   Jeffrey T. Nealon, *Post-Postmodernism: Or, the Cultural Logic of Just-in-Time Capitalism* (Stanford, CA: Stanford University Press, 2012).

8   On financial circulation, see Edward LiPuma and Benjamin Lee, *Financial Derivatives and the Globalization of Risk* (Durham, NC: Duke University Press, 2004). On debt, see the work of Richard Dienst, *The Bonds of Debt* (London: Verso, 2011), and David Graeber, *Debt: The First 5,000 Years* (Brooklyn, NY: Melville House, 2011).

9   David Harvey, *A Brief Introduction to Neoliberalism* (New York: Oxford University Press, 2006), 34.

10   The spatial is what Fisher, using Deleuze, describes as a site of "enclosure"; the temporal, as a site of indebtedness. For an elaboration of this logic, see also the more recent Maurizio Lazzarato, *The Making of the Indebted Man: An Essay on the Neoliberal Condition*, trans. Joshua David Jordan (Amsterdam: Semiotext(e), 2012).

11   See Marcia Angell's excellent *The Truth about the Drug Companies: How They Deceive Us and What to Do about It* (New York: Random House, 2005).

12   One could include here the whole genre of apocalyptic film and fiction, from scenes of global warming–induced planetary annihilation to nuclear winters.

13. The rest of the quotation reads:

> If half the action takes place in and around Zuccotti Park—where the hardened core of the cast squats, drumming, deliberating, echoing announcements—the rest will be scattered about the newsrooms, boardrooms, barrooms, and bedrooms of Manhattan, with excursions to Williamsburg or Long Island City or Hoboken, maybe even Staten Island, convenient by ferry, and surely suburbs to the north such as Greenwich, cradle of the 1 percent. But beyond journalistic attention to the protests' throbbing center and the fissures extending up the avenues, how to dramatize it all?

Christian Lorentzen, "Fictitious Values: Boom and Bust in Twenty-First-Century Lit," *Bookforum* (June–August 2012), http://www.bookforum.com/inprint/019_02/9453.

14   Leigh Claire La Berge, "The Rules of Abstraction: Methods and Discourses of Finance Capital," in "Fictions of Finance," ed. Aaron Carico and Dana Ornstein, special issue, *Radical History Review* (forthcoming).

15   Joe Cleary, "Realism after Modernism," in "Peripheral Realisms," ed. Jed Esty and Colleen Lye, special issue, *Modern Language Quarterly* 73:3 (September 2012).

16   Esty and Lye also note: "Though postcoloniality and postmodernism have given way to alternative modernities and global modernisms, the ten-

dency to read against realism has in fact traveled rather eas
model to the other" (274).

17 Paul Delany, "Who Paid for Modernism?," *The New Economic ᴜ, ...*
    Studies at the Intersection of Literature and Economics, ed. Martha Wood-
    mansee and Mark Osteen (London: Routledge, 1989), 335–351.

18 See Christopher Connery and Jonathan Franzen, "The Liberal Form: An
    Interview with Jonathan Franzen," *Boundary 2* 36:2 (June 20, 2009),
    31–54.

19 Paul Dawson, "The Return of Omniscience in Contemporary Fiction." *Nar-
    rative* 17:2 (May 2009), 143–161.

20 JoAnn Wypijewski, ed., *Painting by Numbers: Komar and Melamid's Scien-
    tific Guide to Art* (Berkeley: University of California Press, 1998). Alexei
    Yurchak, *Everything Was Forever, Until It Was No More: The Last Soviet
    Generation* (Princeton, NJ: Princeton University Press, 2005).

21 See Susan Buck Morss's *Dreamworld and Catastrophe* for the deep inti-
    macy between the projects of socialist and what we would call capitalist
    realism, particularly in the visual realm. *Dreamworld and Catastrophe:
    The Passing of Mass Utopia in East and West* (Cambridge, MA: MIT Press,
    2002).

22 Walter Benn Michaels, "Model Minorities and the Minority Model: The
    Neoliberal Novel," *Cambridge History of the American Novel*, ed. Leonard
    Cassuto et al. (New York: Cambridge University Press, 2011), 1028.

23 Jeffrey J. Williams, "The Plutocratic Imagination," *Dissent* 60:1 (Winter
    2013), 95.

24 Teddy Wayne, *Kapitoil* (New York: Harper, 2010); Peter Mountford, *A
    Young Man's Guide to Capitalism* (Boston: Houghton Mifflin, 2011).

25 Michael Hardt, "Militant Life," *New Left Review* 64 (July–August 2010).

26 Matthew Beaumont, *Adventures in Realism* (Malden, MA: Wiley-Blackwell,
    2007).

27 Fredric Jameson, "Antinomies of the Realism-Modernism Debate," *MLQ*
    73:3 (September 2012), 477.

We Can't Afford to Be Realists

A Conversation with Mark Fisher and Jodi Dean

JODI DEAN: With your account of capitalist realism, you took an idea that Slavoj Žižek got from Fredric Jameson and made it completely fresh. Žižek said that it was easier to imagine the end of the world than the end of capitalism. But whereas for Žižek this observation is basically depoliticizing, or symptomatic of a depoliticization that he, at the time, oscillated between confirming and critiquing, you make it into a critical wedge, a category for criticism. When you started writing *Capitalist Realism*, were you aware of the ways you were upgrading and extending the concept or did that come later, through the writing?

Further, could you say something about how you understand the concept working? I find myself using it in a couple of different ways, but not completely sure if you agree with both or either. On the one hand, "capitalist realism" designates a general ideological formation, that of late neoliberalism, wherein all illusions and hopes for equality have been shed. On the other, it is a more specific ideological weapon, an argument wielded against those who might try to challenge capitalist hegemony. Do you find one of these renditions closer to your argument than the other?

MARK FISHER: I think both of the senses of capitalist realism that you describe are valid. But perhaps the use of capitalist realism as a specific weapon is necessary only when capitalist realism as a general ideological formation fails, as it has started to fail since 2008.

One way of thinking about capitalist realism is as a belief that capitalism is the only viable political-economic system—that other systems may be desirable, but capitalism is the only one that works.

Another way of getting to capitalist realism is thinking of it as an attitude in relation to all this—a feeling of resignation: there's no point struggling, we just have to adapt. But there are problems with conceiving of capitalist realism in either of these two ways because they suggest individual psychology, when what we are talking about is more like a transpersonal psychic infrastructure. It's ideological, not in the sense that it directly persuades people of the truth of its propositions, but more because it convinces people that it is an irresistible force. I mentioned in the book the example of managers who implement neoliberalizing changes in the workplace, while saying, "I don't believe in any of this stuff, but this is just the kind of thing we have to do now." Ideology I think operates at two levels here: the first is the acceptance and propagation of the belief that neoliberalism can't be fought; the second is the notion that adapting to neoliberal domination is just a question of pragmatic survival, not political at all. Ideology is of course at its strongest when it appears as non-political, just the way things are. When capitalist realism is at its most powerful, it always generates this depoliticizing effect.

JD: I like very much your emphasis here on the affective dimension of capitalist realism. One of the most difficult challenges facing the contemporary left is the resignation you mention. People have a hard time gearing themselves up to protest, to engage in long-term battles in a variety of terrains, because they think that, ultimately, it won't really matter. We will lose. We will be co-opted. Capital will adapt (it always does). And if we win, it will be even worse—the ultimate lesson of the twentieth century is that anything other than capitalism is death. Enter Stalin and Mao.

MF: We have to bear in mind something that you have brought out very well in your own work—that what we are talking about is really a retreat of the left, not really depoliticization per se. It's our politics that are missing, not politics as such. Capitalist realism is a pathology of the left. It's no accident that many of the experiences I recount in the book happened while I was working as a teacher during the high pomp of New Labour, because the concept of capitalist realism is really about what underlay the New Labour project. Both New Labour and the Clinton administration in the US were about coming to terms with a "new realism." As we all now know, their arrival didn't signal the end of right-wing domination but the hegemonic consolidation of neoliberalism.

But capitalist realism isn't only about capitulation to neoliberalism —it's also about the corrosion of social imagination. To say it's easier to imagine the end of the world than the end of capitalism is not only to say that we think it is very improbable that any alternative to capitalism will arise; it's also to say that we cannot yet even imagine what a post-capitalist society would look like. The old Thatcherite idea that "there is no alternative to neoliberalism" can be heard as an ontological claim—it isn't just that neoliberalism is preferable to other political programs; it's that nothing else is now even conceivable. This has come into focus as opposition to capital has built since the bank crises. Faced with the Occupy movement, capital's defenders argue that there is no positive alternative to capitalism being articulated here. We need to take that seriously; it isn't sufficient to complain and petition, we do need a sense of what we want. Yet we can't expect to be able to come up with this kind of vision immediately; we shouldn't underestimate capitalist realism's capacity to impede social imagination.

JD: I think you are right that we should not underestimate capitalism's ability to impede the left imagination. I worry that we see this in the anarchist tendencies in the Occupy movement. What I have in mind are the sorts of positions that emphasize the autonomy of local actions, saying things like "Anything is open to what anyone wants to do"—that doesn't seem to me to be any different from what we have. People can already make signs, organize demonstrations, distribute pamphlets—the real challenge is bringing together a large number of people in effective collective action. Or, the real challenge is figuring out what to do together that will really make a difference. Another example: I recently heard an activist talk about a new approach to banking. He described the tasks of his working group as trying to find a transparent, sustainable, profitable, and attractive banking model, one that consumers would want. To my ears, he sounded like just another entrepreneur, one who wanted a responsible capitalism, as if Occupy were basically a movement for capitalism with a human face. Capitalist realism seemed to have structured his subjectivity so completely that his only way to conceive of any alternative was as a better consumer product. Or, differently put, the corrosion of the social imagination was the corrosion of the capacity to think collectively.

Your discussion of capitalist realism, then, is a way of getting at the neoliberal subject, at how an economic and political formation that emphasizes free choice, personal responsibility, and competition gives a certain shape to the subjectivity even of those who ostensibly reject it, a shape that is rather stunted, meek, and compliant and that ultimately doesn't see much hope in collective political action. The left subject of capitalist realism, in other words, believes that capitalism is inevitable, finds capitalism itself to be a source of energy and innovation, embraces individualism and consumerism, and eschews collective action—all because of its acquiescence to a certain "inevitability" (and, of course, the reverse is true as well—this sense of inevitability is itself an effect of the believing, embracing, and eschewing). In Lacanian terms we could say that this subject cedes its desire.

Do you accept this description of a certain affective attachment to capitalism, one that isn't dreary at all but which sees capitalism as offering all sorts of novelties and pleasures, albeit guilty ones (and I should add that I'm thinking here about a chat we had in London in December 2010)? I say this because in *Capitalist Realism* your description of capitalism tends to emphasize how dreary, conformist, and boring it is. I read the critique, then, as one that holds out the promise of more intensive delights, as it were, such that your argument highlights an aesthetic critique. In contrast, I'm suggesting that for many folks in the US and UK, even in the face of debts, foreclosure, unemployment, austerity, and a general proletarianization of our lives, there are still lots of goodies—YouTube, Facebook, lots of different kinds of music, sports on television, cheap imported clothes, abundant snack food—and that these goodies, these little nuggets of pleasure, attach us to capitalism. We don't want to give them up. So

I tend to emphasize a combination of "Sacrifice is necessary; these treats are rooted in a system that is fundamentally barbaric as it installs extreme inequality and inequality; it is ultimately a hideous sort of blackmail where we have given up equality and solidarity in exchange for entertainment and communication" and "It doesn't matter if we want these goodies anymore, the system is in crisis and collapsing all around us, so we can't have them anyway." What do you think?

MF: I don't think that the dreariness and the little nuggets of pleasure are opposed to one another—rather I think they are the same thing seen from different angles . . .

JD: [interrupts] Oh, right, that's very good.

MF: . . . the result of the continual consumption of tiny nuggets of pleasure is an overall dreariness. In his book *Retromania* (2011) the music critic Simon Reynolds notes that over the last decade or so, everyday life has speeded up, but culture has slowed down. The very fact that people are constantly plugged into the drip-feed of digital stimulus means that the conditions for groundbreaking cultural production—certain kinds of withdrawal, certain spaces for reflection, the capacity for absorption—are no longer there. In *Retromania*, Reynolds describes the same sense of temporal inertia that I confront in *Capitalist Realism*. We're now so accustomed to retrospection and pastiche that we no longer notice them. Almost nothing now escapes the prophetic account of postmodern culture that Jameson developed in the 1980s. It's now plain that, for all capital's rhetoric of novelty and innovation, culture has become increasingly homogenized and predictable.

It's no accident either that, at the same time as entertainment and pleasure have become so easily available, depression is on the rise, particularly amongst the young. That's what I was trying to get to in my discussion of hedonic depression in *Capitalist Realism*: the inability to go beyond the pleasure principle doesn't produce perpetual pleasure, but an endless insomniac drift. Isn't our experience after spending an evening clicking through social networks or YouTube links precisely that of the simultaneity of pleasure and boredom? The boredom associated with the Fordist era is finished. There is no space for it: the smartphone plugs all the gaps where that boredom could grow. But the insomniac urge to click through links is not straightforwardly pleasurable either. Instead, the signature mood attached to this kind of digital drift is a mixture of fascination and boredom: we're bored at the same time as we are fascinated. I find the analysis of drive that you have presented in your discussion of communicative capitalism persuasive: the pleasures of communicative capitalism are lures which keep us hooked on drive as such. Drive as such is not aimed at this or that pleasure; it's not manifested in attachment to a particular content, it's more about the impulse to click itself. Even the desire for pornographic content appears somewhat quaint when compared with the blind implacability of this drive. I think my emphasis would be on how we are to direct this drive differently, whereas you believe that drive has to be circumvented entirely?

JD: Yes, well, sort of. I say "sort of" because it's not a matter of the total elimination or suppression of one or the other; it's a matter of dominance or degree. There is still desire in communicative capitalism although the "social link" or more general discursive-material habitat is characterized by drive. What I have in mind is the installation and maintenance of the gap or lack necessary for desire—and this is not a matter of redirecting the drive but of rupturing it.

When I first read Badiou, I quickly and reactively fixated on "names" and "naming" and was all like, "No, awful, this is calling for a new master," blah, blah, blah. But then over time (partly from reading Žižek, partly because of reading and conversing with Bruno Bosteels and Peter Hallward), I started to realize how my reaction was failing to grapple with the way names, or the discourses names may structure, are crucial for stopping the endless play of signification, the relentless deferral of meaning and dispersion of possibility characteristic of drive's repetitive circuits. Of course, a term, name, concept, discourse can't completely fix meaning or determine possibilities. But it can provide a momentary and provisional shape that can orient thinking and galvanize action. (We have examples of this kind of temporary stabilization all the time. What happens, though, is that those on the left freak out because of what might be excluded and those on the right consciously, deliberately, and evilly repeat and/or distort them—contemporary ideological warfare in a complex media environment.) So I started to think that what was absent from our current setting was these sorts of names.

Well, so far so good, this is just another way of describing the setting of drive as a kind of force of loss or loss itself as force. But what if our relation to this loss were not just to insist constantly on it, to repeat it, time and time again, but instead to think of it as the lack constitutive of desire? What might that tell us? It tells us that what's missing is common and collective (I get at some of this in *Blog Theory* [2010] via Debord and Agamben on the spectacle and the way the spectacle returns to us a kind of collectivity in an inverted form). Moving from nugget to nugget, issue to issue, trend to trend, bill to bill in the circuit of drive is an effect of the absence of collectivity, whether in terms of common meaning, common goals, common resources, or common projects. My book *The Communist Horizon* (2012) introduces some of this, but it's really just the beginning of a larger project on communist desire as the other of and answer to capitalist drive. The way you've described the depressive, inert flip side to the crazy mania of drive resonates for me as it makes apparent the fact that something is missing, there is an absence. What's missing is the gap necessary for desire. A crucial component for a better left politics, then, is making this gap apparent, felt, undeniable—we could even say occupying it.

MF: I would want to resist the move of opposing desire, broadly speaking, to capital. Having to choose between equality and solidarity on the one hand and desire and entertainment on the other is an aspect of capitalist realism itself. For capitalist realism wants to claim that desire is compatible only with capitalism, that desire, ultimately, is the serpent which will destroy any non-capitalist system. That's why I would want to insist on the dreariness of late capitalist culture, and why the aesthetic critique of capitalist realism is so crucial. With capitalist realism, we're faced with an entertainment that doesn't really entertain alongside a populism which isn't popular.

JD: I love your last line, but I don't think I'm convinced. I think we both reject the articulation of capitalism with desire and agree that cutting through, thoroughly destroying, capitalism's seeming monopoly on the incitement, cultivation, and delimiting of desire matters. The thing is, I think the goodies we get really are entertaining—like the Broadway show by the guys who do South Park, *The Book of Mormon* (I haven't seen it), or the ads for banks and cell phones that look like flash mobs but aren't—several hundred people are singing and dancing in a train station—totally wonderful. I cry every time I see it. Likewise, populism is real. Sure, there are folks who try to manipulate it, but consistently in the US there is about a quarter of the population who are benighted racist homophobes perpetually more worried about the government taking their money than they are about the capitalists who take their futures. So it seems to me that it's important to separate desire and drive, that is to say, to emphasize what is missing so as to incite desire, a desire for collectivity that takes back what has been made private and makes it all of ours in common. One would acknowledge that capitalism provides entertainment, and that it does so unequally (who can access it), unfairly (via exploitation), and at too high a cost (lives, futures, the environment, and desire itself).

MF: Not all of the features of really existing cyberspace have any necessary relation to capitalism. There's nothing intrinsically capitalist about something like YouTube, for instance. In fact, doesn't YouTube vindicate Hardt and Negri's claims that capital is essentially parasitic? The impulse behind YouTube is a co-operative one; capital is not the precondition for YouTube, or if it is, it is only in a very contingent way. Alongside the intensification of commodification and capitalist subjectivity in cyberspace, we're also seeing a massive tendency toward decommodification and new modes of collectivity.

Nevertheless, I think that you're right that some kind of withdrawal from current libidinal circuits will of course be necessary—and inevitable, given that, as you say, the system may not be able to deliver these kind of treats for much longer. Jameson puts this very well in *Valences of the Dialectic* (2009) when he anticipates an "abstinence from commodities" (384) but warns of "how difficult it may be to relinquish the compensatory desires and intoxications we have developed in order to make the present livable" (384). Again, though, I'd prefer to think of this commodity abstinence not as a withdrawal from desire per se, but as the opportunity for different kinds of desire to emerge. Is your position that we should embrace abstinence as such?

JD: I share your skepticism about a politics of withdrawal. I live on the edge of the "rust belt" in the US, an area where capital withdrawal has resulted in increases in poverty and unemployment and decreases in population. Also, in the wake of the financial and economic crises, it seems like lots of people are forced to withdraw from their previous consumption habits—another instance where commodity abstinence isn't immediately politically liberatory. As you suggest with your reference to Jameson and decommodification, the present capitalism isn't well understood in terms of the commodity. Better is to think in terms of competition and rents (which is why I would still insist on thinking of YouTube as capitalist even as it clearly shows how easy it is to cut off the capitalist head and let the productive body live on). No, rather than abstinence, I am thinking more of discipline. The kind of discipline through which people make themselves into collectives.

Maybe this is a good segue to utopianism. In *First as Tragedy, Then as Farce* (2009), Žižek says that there is a utopian core in neoliberal capitalism—the idea that this is the best system. Would you say that this is the other side of your more dystopian capitalist realism, perhaps the capitalist side or the side of the ruling class?

MF: This is complicated—because on the face of it capitalist realism can be characterized by its repudiation of any utopianism. That repudiation is what the "realism" consists of. What we saw on the parliamentary left was an abandonment of anything that could be construed as utopian, a rhetorical performance of pragmatic adaptation to a narrowly conceived model of the possible. But if there is an ineradicable utopian core to neoliberalism, then this reveals the differences between capitalist realism and neoliberalism. Neoliberalism has succeeded because it was capable of subordinating the left to capitalist realism, but the two tendencies are not identical. Where capitalist realism is anti-utopian, neoliberalism does have a utopian dimension. One of the puzzling things about neoliberal ideologues is to what extent they actually believe this utopianism, or whether it is just a mask for ruling-class self-interest. Someone like Blair was a genuine enigma in this respect.

One lesson we can draw from the persistence of the utopian is that a purely pragmatic, "realistic" politics is not actually possible. There will never come a point at which capital will unmask and say without qualification, "OK, capitalism is necessarily exploitative and rapacious, live with it." There are elements of this with capitalist realism, but they are offset by the utopian claims of neoliberalism.

JD: Actually, I think that capital *is* saying that, and precisely because this undeniable and rapacious core is exposed in the current collapse of neoliberalism. So various European officials are pushing cuts and austerity, saying that European states can no longer afford to live the way they've been living, which means the further withering away of the achievements of working class struggle and basic welfare state provisions. In the US—and this has been apparent in the campaigns for the Republican presidential nomination for the 2008 and 2012 elections—there has been a tendency to see who can be the harshest, most macho, most *realistic*, most willing to let people die on the streets if they can't pay for their own health care. It's almost as if the neoliberalism we've had in the US and the UK was the "kinder, gentler" form, and now we are going to get the extreme versions that they had in Latin America and Africa.

MF: Yes, that's true, but I think those appeals to harsh realism can only be sustained by the belief that there is something good about capitalism—or at least that capitalism is the least bad system, that everything else would be worse. Capitalism is good because it is based upon the "reality" of "human nature"; that is why capitalism allegedly "works" and no other system does. But there's still some kind of claim that capitalism is *preferable* to the alternatives; it's not just a matter of triumphalist crowing that capital will win no matter what.

JD: I've been wondering whether accompanying capitalist realism there is a democratic realism that proceeds as if democracy is the only term for a better politics (even as it is the name of the politics we have). It affirms and supports capitalist realism's inevitability, its reduction of action to that of individuals, its restricted schema of value and valuation. Direct action, particularly as it requires coordinating the activities of large numbers of people, seems a way to break out of some of the restrictions of realism—it shows that other ways are possible.

MF: I think this depends on how we construe the democratic. Your own work has exposed the limitations of the dominant model of the democratic. But we could conceive of direct action not as opposed to the democratic, but as a properly democratic expansion of the highly circumscribed channels of "capitalist parliamentarianism." With the decline of the workers' movement, we've seen parliamentary politics subordinated to the interests of business. We can either say that this is where so-called democratic systems will always end up, or argue that this is a perversion of democracy—a perversion which, plainly, cannot be counteracted within the terms of the system itself, but only by the kinds of popular action that are taking place at the moment. For me, it's a strategic mistake to concede democracy to the enemy. It allows the left to be smeared as apologists for totalitarianism. I think it's better to argue that only post-capitalism can deliver democracy—that we are on the side of progress and enlightenment, while capital is on the side of barbarism.

Direct action is ambivalent. There are forms of direct action which still seem to be testaments to the power of capitalist realism. People feel the need to take direct action because they have lost faith in *in*direct action. But isn't politics about indirect action, what Lazzarato calls "action at a distance"? Often, it seems that we take direct action because we no longer believe that systemic change is possible. The paradox, though, is that systemic change is only likely to come about when direct action is taken. But that presupposes—as I would want to argue—that much of the significance of direct action lies beyond its direct effects. For me the crucial thing about direct action is whether it breaks out of the petitionary mode or not. Is it about appealing to capital as big Other, or is it about demonstrating the irrelevance of that big Other? We don't need to protest; we need to constitute a counterforce.

JD: Why do you say post-capitalism rather than communism? And, why do you think it's important to worry about how our enemies will smear us—they will do that no matter what we do. So why not assert that communism is the side of progress and enlightenment? That a collective approach to common resources and responsibilities is the only alternative to capitalist barbarism?

MF: Well, it's a question of not making things easier for those who want to smear us. Part of the success of capitalist realism has been its association of the non-capitalist with the totalitarian—incredibly, people are still writing articles with arguments like "If you don't like capitalism, go and live in North Korea." The preference for the term "post-capitalism" over "communism" is motivated by the same thought. We need to think about the memetic potentials of particular terms here—it isn't the philosophical meaning that a term has which is crucial, it is its power to propagate. We're competing with branding consultants and advertisers: they would reject a word like "communism" because of the amount of conceptual laundering that you have to do to disassociate it from the very bad connotations it has acquired. I'm not saying that there are no conditions in which the term could be used, but I think we need to create a new context for it, a new conceptual constellation in which it can appear. The benefit of the concept of post-capitalism is that it doesn't bring with it a heavy legacy of bad associations. On the contrary, the term "post-capitalism" is empty; it makes demands on us to fill it. It also avoids any primitivist temptation: what we're struggling for is not a return to the pre-capitalist agrarian, but the emergence of something new, something that hasn't taken shape yet, something that can build on the modernity that capitalism constructs and thwarts at the same time. What I also like about post-capitalism is that it presupposes our victory: asking what post-capitalism will be like forces us to think about what it will be like when we have won.

PART I *Novelistic Realisms*

Adultery, Crisis, Contract

ANDREW HOBEREK

In an August 2007 *Boston Globe* column on the burgeoning subprime mortgage crisis, the journalist and economic commentator Robert Kuttner asserted that "irresponsibly speculative lenders should be prohibited from selling mortgages in the secondary market, even if they can find a consenting adult foolish enough to buy them."[1] And in a January 2009 story on the failure of Gemstone, a subprime mortgage operation set up by Deutsche Bank, the *New York Times* reporter Vikas Bajaj wrote that "the German bank counters that M&T executives entered into the investment as consenting adults, and that they knew, or should have known, the risks they were taking."[2] If the rhetoric of consenting adults participates in the project of ideological damage control that followed the crisis—casting it as the product of bad individual decisions, rather than of capitalism as a system—it does so via a curiously sexualized metaphor. Although Kuttner questions this individualizing rhetoric by suggesting that regulatory constraints should perhaps be imposed upon lenders' ability to take advantage even of consenting adults, he joins Deutsche Bank (or at least Bajaj's characterization of its position) in describing investors as analogous to people who were old enough to consent to, and thus to some degree responsible for, their sexual activities.

Far from being coincidental, this metaphorical invocation of responsibility within an illicit and damaging transaction resonates strongly with the way in which adultery installed itself, at around the same time, at the center of the American zeitgeist. In the late nineties, at the height of the Clinton-Lewinsky scandal, Laura Kipnis could already note that "adultery has become the favored metonym for all broken promises, intimate and national, a transparent sign for tawdriness and bad behavior."[3] But in the late aughts adultery became a metonym for something even more specific: not promise, but contract. Just as the mortgage crisis was flowering into the greatest economic downturn since the Great Depression, media coverage of extramarital affairs on the part of such figures as John Edwards, Tiger Woods, New York governor Eliot Spitzer, South Carolina governor Mark Sanford, and Sandra Bullock's husband Jesse James became ubiquitous and inescapable. This coverage was not only a media-generated sideshow designed to distract attention from more pressing economic issues (although it certainly was that); it was also a displaced register of these issues. The media's fascination with this particular wave of adultery by politicians and celebrities, and the intense rage unleashed around their infractions, was in fact related to the ongoing travails of the US economy, insofar as these stories of adultery provided a site for people to express their anger at the violation of the contract form putatively central to capitalism but in fact increasingly outmoded within its current incarnation. As a violation of contract with particularly deleterious effects on the home, adultery served as an apt symbolic stand-in for not only the transformation of capitalism in general but the effects of the mortgage crisis in particular.

Politicians like Edwards and Sanford made particularly good subjects of this narrative insofar as they straddled the line between private and public responsibility, and their transgressions thus implied damage not only to the people with whom they had contracted (their wives) but also to a broader public (their constituents, their parties). Crucially, though, commentary on the Tiger Woods scandal also carried this resonance of public guilt and accountability. Marney Rich Keenan's opinion piece for the *Detroit News* two weeks into the coverage, for instance, focused not on the scandal itself but on how it had been "missed by [the] public for a long time": "The irony is how many of us enabled Tiger Woods to get away with the infidelities for as long as he did." Describing the control exerted over Woods's media image prior to the scandal, Keenan quotes Steven Ortiz, a sociologist and expert on "professional athletes' marriages." Among such athletes, Ortiz claims,

the adultery is so institutionalized, it becomes a culture of infidelity.
. . . They also display a certain level of narcissism. They think the world
revolves around them, which minimizes, in their minds, the consequences of serious issues like infidelity, violence or substance abuse like
performance-enhancing drugs. . . . What I found is a belief that they are
not accountable for inappropriate behaviors, off the field, off the ice, or
off the golf course.

In her concluding paragraph, Keenan extends the notion of a public
dimension to Woods's transgressions outward to the sense that the
public is in some sense to blame: "By not looking beyond the perfect
People cover shot of Tiger cradling his newborn's head in the palm of
his hand, we saw only what we wanted to see. The surprise that Tiger
Woods is not as decent a family man as well as the greatest golfer that
ever lived is partially our doing."[4] Of course, one might suggest that
Woods was *just* a golfer, and that his infidelities had no effect on his
game, let alone (as more plausibly in the cases of the politicians) on
the public trust. But that is clearly revealed as beside the point when
one notes how smoothly every element of Keenan's piece—the suggestion of a long-brewing crisis largely ignored, the resentment at a
powerful man who felt above standard codes of behavior, the sense
of public complicity through willful ignorance—also functions as a
description of the subprime mortgage crisis. In 2008 and 2009, what
we talked about when we talked about adultery was the crisis of capitalism that we couldn't talk about directly.

To begin to see what this has to do with the transformations of
literary realism under capitalism, and vice versa, we might note how
Kuttner's phrasing in particular recalls the origins of the English
novel as described by Nancy Armstrong. Armstrong argues, in her
classic 1987 study *Desire and Domestic Fiction*, that the English novel
and its characteristic narrative of "legitimate monogamy" serves to
body forth and naturalize the emergent middle-class subjectivity of
capitalism.[5] The novel models middle-class subjectivity insofar as it
foregrounds "a new female ideal" (9) based in private life in order to
replace "the intricate status system that had long dominated British
thinking" with a version of human worth centered on the individual's
"essential qualities of mind" (4). Hence Samuel Richardson's *Pamela*

(1740), with its story of a virtuous lower-class woman who avoids seduction and rape at the hands of her aristocratic employer only to ultimately win him over with her essential virtue, itself triumphed over *Robinson Crusoe* (1719) and other competitors to "inaugurate[ ] the tradition of the novel as we know it" (29).

Kuttner replays just this scene of seduction in his sentence-long story casting "speculative lenders" as Mr. B and investors in secondary mortgages as Pamela, although in this telling virtue does not win out. And indeed, Kuttner's larger story is one of decline caused by the deregulation that transformed the American (i.e., middle-class) dream of homeownership in place "since the era of the American Revolution" into a "secondary market in mortgage securities" exploited by predatory buyers and sellers.[6] Whereas the novel in Armstrong's account "translated the social contract into a sexual exchange" (38), Kuttner contends that the ideal of free and equal exchange undergirding the notion of contract is broken in a system where lack of government oversight enables some to prey upon others. But if Kuttner's explicit analysis takes a systemic tack, asserting that deregulation has transformed capitalism into a financialized system at odds with the yeoman dream of small property ownership, his sexual metaphor smuggles in the language of individual agency and its dereliction. Investors must be protected because they are "foolish"—not free and independent individuals of the sort that Pamela transforms herself into through her virtuous actions, but stereotypically flighty and feminine figures like Mr. B initially supposes Pamela to be. Eroticized financial desire, by providing a non-rational motive for individual actions, suggests that systemic explanations are always (at heart) individual ones, since the role of systemic intervention is to protect individuals from their own flaws. At the same time, by imagining not only a flawed victim but an exploitative villain, Kuttner also hints (as the Gothic novel did in an earlier era) at what gets suppressed when the mainstream novel stops imagining the world in terms of class differences and instead foregrounds a world of free exchanges between rational individuals. If, that is, the "two favorite gothic villains, the corrupt monk and the decadent and scheming lord of the mysterious castle" reminded early middle-class novel readers of the ancien régime they had not quite displaced,[7] Kuttner's predatory lending institutions hint at the way in which capitalism now reproduces the inflexible class hierarchies it once set itself against.

Here literary realism rubs up against the more vernacular sense of capitalist realism described by Richard Dienst in *The Bonds of Debt* (2011). To the question, What form of realism corresponds to the current state of capitalism? Dienst offers a deceptively simple answer: it is the realism of the popular injunction to be realistic, to accept the limitations of the given. We live now in a perpetual state of crisis, Dienst writes, mediated by a "market-media machine" whose

> expansion . . . creates its own apparatus of enforcement, whereby the mood swings and stubborn grudges of market discipline become the most decisive kind of reality. Heeding its mixed signals, the planners, bureaucrats, and managers set their watches and pretend to be in charge. Everybody else is supposed to keep working, obey the local authorities, enjoy the show, and wait patiently for a lucky break. Such is the historical role global capital wants to assign to the vast majority of the world's population, for now.[8]

The self-justifying regime of financial capitalism that Dienst describes goes far beyond the traditional function of ideology that classical literary realism both furthered and resisted. In "an atmosphere filled with endless chattering in praise of immense wealth" (3)—in which even the elite's "sense of history is calibrated by the split seconds of arbitrage, the volatile turnover of portfolios, the slipstreams of interest, the fitful jockeying over exchange rates, and the implacable arithmetic of the actuarial tables" (3)—capital becomes its own autochthonous justification, existing beyond the necessity of ideological justification. In this way it consumes not only the present but the past and the future as well: "By cornering the resources of memory and anticipation alike, the current order of things lays claim to all the time in the world, a world perpetually in debt to the power of what already exists" (5).

As Alison Shonkwiler has demonstrated, Don DeLillo's 2003 novel *Cosmopolis* wrestles with this historic transformation by engaging directly with the increasingly abstract ways in which we represent capital.[9] In order to begin sussing out a different (and arguably more widespread) novelistic response to the contemporary reconfiguration of capitalism, I would like to turn to Mohsin Hamid's 2007 *The Reluctant Fundamentalist*. Hamid's title is a complex joke that comments upon (and is rendered obscure by) his narrative, which takes the form of one side of a dialogue spoken by a repatriated Pakistani and erstwhile US financial sector employee to an American who may or may not be a CIA agent sent to capture or kill him for terrorist activities. The obvious referent for the title is Islamic fundamentalism, although Leerom Medovoi—in the course of a compelling reading of the book as an example of "world-system literature" that "cognitively, imaginatively, and affectively map[s] a world in which Pakistan orbits around the US in a larger global system of wealth, culture, and power"[10]— hints at its real resonance. Noting that the protagonist Changez, in his ultimately doomed infatuation with a New Yorker allegorically named Erica (America), at one point pretends to be the dead boyfriend Chris whose memory she cannot let go, Medovoi suggests that the title, "which the reader initially might assume refers to Changez's ultimate conversion to radical Muslim extremism, might well turn out instead to refer to his conversion to Christian fundamentalism, his embracing of the role of 'Chris' to satisfy his desire for a sickly Erica heading toward ruin" (656). Medovoi is on the right track, but, still caught up in the conventional association of fundamentalism with religion, he doesn't go far enough. The novel's one use of "fundamentalism" in the common sense—by Erica's well-off father—seems to suggest its function in deferring attention away from the global (rather than local) class interests that Changez's job for the "valuation firm" (5) Underwood Samson & Company abets: "I like Pakistanis. But the elite has raped that place well and good, right? And fundamentalism. You guys have got some serious problems with fundamentalism" (55). But when Changez himself describes the multiple constituencies protesting an appearance of the US ambassador to Pakistan, he refers to one group not as fundamentalists but as "religious literalists" (179). As Medovoi himself notes, moreover, Hamid for the most part uses variations of "fundamentalism" to refer not to religion, but to the work that Changez does for Underwood Sampson: "*Focus on the fundamentals.* This was Underwood Samson's guiding principle, drilled into us since our first day at work" (98); "That day [of an American raid into Afghanistan] I found it difficult to concentrate on the pursuit—at which I was normally so capable—of fundamentals" (100); "I suspect I was never better at the pursuit of fundamentals than I was at that time, analyzing data as though my life depended on it" (116). Changez becomes the novel's titular fundamentalist, that is, when he works for Underwood Samson analyzing precisely the sorts of quantitative information that Dienst describes, information which—as Changez's work increasingly takes the form of downsizing missions—comes into tension with both the human cost to workers and Changez's concern for his home country.

Yet even as it dramatizes the neoliberal projection of the fundamentalist menace as a way of eliding class politics, *The Reluctant Fundamentalist* somehow cannot provide a fully realist representation of the financial capitalism which in many ways it thematizes so acutely. The characters, as their names suggest, all tend toward allegory, and even more obviously the novel incorporates its moments of realism into an overarching narrative of the form that John McClure calls "late imperial romance"—a fact it quite self-consciously alludes to, among other places, when Changez notes that in Pakistan he has "felt rather like a Kurtz waiting for his Marlowe [*sic*]" (183).[11] It is almost as though the realist novel, so closely tied to a particular form of capitalism and the kinds of social mobility it enabled, must turn to genre fiction to represent forms outside of it, whether the residual feudal hierarchies that lingered into capitalism's heyday or the hierarchies of money that characterize an emergent post-capitalist capitalism.

The first principle for assessing the state of capitalist realism today might thus be that capitalism is no longer capitalistic, insofar as it increasingly reinforces economic and social hierarchies even as it celebrates idealized versions of its own opposition to such hierarchies. Of course we might note that this tension was always inherent in capitalism: thus Marx and Engels in *The Communist Manifesto* both admire (in the famous "All that is solid melts into air" section) capitalism's capacity to undermine "all fixed, fast-frozen relations" and insist that "the modern bourgeois society that has sprouted from the ruins of feudal society has not done away with class antagonisms. It has but established new classes, new conditions of oppression, new forms of struggle in place of the old ones."[12] But since 1981, as Ravi Batra, among others, has pointed out, very specific government policies have engendered a form of "crony" or "monopoly capitalism" at odds with the "free-market capitalism of small firms."[13] Under these conditions capitalism as it is practiced turns to the past not for melodramatic representations of the world it seeks to overturn but, on the contrary, for nostalgic fantasies of its own past incarnations. Indeed, the very distinction between "capitalism" and "corporatism" that in some circles registers the increasing concentration of corporate wealth and power can be turned toward a nostalgic defense of American "dynamism" versus European (via the fascist associations of "corporatism") rigidity and state control.[14] We live simultaneously in a real world of state-subsidized, increasingly neo-feudal capitalism and an Ayn Randian virtual capitalism embodied in such often invoked but seldom realized concepts as the free market, competition, risk, and—as my account of Kuttner has already foregrounded—contract.

As I have suggested, one place where this mismatch between actually existing and virtual capitalisms was experienced at the end of the aughts was around the subject of marriage, a state many people have experience of, and where contract, its violation, and the resulting fallout seem amenable (unlike in the world of finance) to depiction in straightforward and easily traceable ways. Given realism's constitutive investment in marriage as the site of middle-class subjectivity—as John Cawelti, anticipating Armstrong, notes, the opposite number of the corrupt monk and the scheming lord is the "chaste and marriageable young woman who often symbolized the cultural and social aspirations of the mobile middle classes" (101–102)—it is not surprising that the novel registers this crisis at the same time. This is not, of course, to argue that realist fiction suddenly discovers adultery a little less than a decade into the twenty-first century; one way to tell the history of realism as such, from the high-water mark of Eliot, Flaubert, and Tolstoy through the retrenched domesticity of minimalism, is as a history of stories about adultery. It is to suggest, however, that following the subprime mortgage crisis the novel—straining like the news media to think the crisis in the absence of a robust systemic critique of capitalism—figures the gulf between capitalist theory and capitalist reality as a crisis in realistic representation as such. I will now attempt to flesh out this contention with reference to two of the major novels of 2009: Jess Walter's *The Financial Lives of the Poets* and Lorrie Moore's *A Gate at the Stairs*.

* * *

Jess Walter's book just prior to *The Financial Lives of the Poets*, the 9/11 novel *The Zero*, published in 2006, is itself far from realistic. Continuing the transition Walter had begun in *Citizen Vince* (2005) from his Pacific Northwest–set crime fiction to a DeLillo-esque engagement with recent American history, *The Zero* incorporates the narrative device of having its protagonist Brian Remy—a police officer who was present at Ground Zero—experience frequent memory losses due to a self-inflicted gunshot wound, and also includes surrealistic touches such as Remy's work for the Office of Memory and Recovery, an agency tasked with gathering every piece of paper lost in the attacks and run by a sinister Rudolph Giuliani–manqué figure known only as The Boss. Compared to *The Zero*, with its formal experimentation and burlesque of post-9/11 politics, *The Financial Lives* seems like a further move into realism. It includes an early nod to *The Zero* (both its subject matter and its formal reworking of cognitive disability) via its narrator Matthew Prior's reminiscence about his dying mother's fear that "there will be another 7/11,"[15] and it features a version of the small-time criminals who populated Walter's early crime fiction: Prior is actually in a 7-Eleven after midnight, where some would-be gangbangers offer him drugs and initiate the subplot that will eventually lead to his visiting a pot farm that the owners are attempting to sell. But mostly Prior (despite taking his name from the late-seventeenth and early-eighteenth-century satirist and poet, a point to which I will return in a moment) inhabits far more banal terrain. A former business journalist who temporarily left his newspaper job to pursue his quixotic dream of starting a website that dispensed financial advice in verse, Prior has now been laid off from the job to which he returned after giving up his seniority. He cannot find another job in the bad economy, has lost the money he earned on initially thriving investments, and is about to lose his house because he cannot make the $30,000 payment on an ill-considered mortgage-refinancing scheme.

The Financial Lives registers the financial crisis of the late aughts via the home, in a double sense. First and most obviously, it does so by making Prior a participant in the questionable mortgage speculation that, abetted by high-risk loans and lax regulation, triggered the crisis in the first place:

> When the hole started opening two years ago, Lisa and I congratulated ourselves because at least we weren't in one of those La Brea Tar Pit adjustable-rate home loans. We had a normal thirty-year, with a normal fixed rate, and even though we'd unwisely cashed in equity for a couple of costly remodels, we were still okay. . . . But then my perfectly normal dream of starting my own business, the afore-derided *poetfolio.com*, turned out to take longer and be more costly than we thought, and we found ourselves taking another line of credit on the house, going deeper in debt. Then came Lisa's abnormal online shopping binge, and our credit cards rolled over on us a couple of times and the car payments lapsed and the ground began slipping away and the only thing that seemed rock steady was the house, so we took another chunk out of it, just to catch up, we said, to temporarily cover living expenses, and we refinanced at the peak value; like a snake eating its tail we borrowed against our house to pay the house payment of a house leveraged at forty percent more than the house was worth. When the dip came I scrambled back to the newspaper, but with the hole growing deeper and monthly interest charges eating us alive, we fell further behind, missed a few house payments and our helpful mortgage lender offered us an "agreement of forbearance," six months leeway (with interest!) to get on top of our payments, and we jumped at that lifeline, but then I lost my job and maybe we were distracted by that and by my father's collapse (we dragged him into the hole with us) because while we fretted and waffled and stalled, the stock market went out for milk, got stoned and lost forty percent of its value, depleting my 401(k), which, due to my stubborn love for financial and media stocks, had already begun to look like a 4(k). That's about the time I stopped showing Lisa the grim letters about the house, with their phony warm salutations ("Dear Homeowner . . ."). (28–29)

This passage neatly encapsulates the parallel between Prior's personal financial woes and the transformation of the US economy in general from a middle-class society grounded nominally in upward mobility through entrepreneurship (Prior's website) but actually in corporate employment (his newspaper job) into the financialized realm of George W. Bush's ownership society. In the ownership society individual participation in the stock market was, of course, supposed to supplant both entrepreneurship and steady employment, although in fact it engendered the conditions through which financialization assimilated and undermined the one piece of property most middle-class people still owned, transforming the "rock steady" home into yet another site of fictional speculation ("a house leveraged at forty percent more than the house was worth").

Yet Prior's reference to his father points to the other way in which *The Financial Lives* registers the financial crisis via the home, stressing—quite realistically, one is tempted to say—its deleterious effects on Prior's familial relationships. Prior is estranged from his wife (who is, he discovers, conducting a flirtation with an ex-boy-friend named Chuck), uneasy about his role as a father, and unable to cope with his own father's early-onset dementia. "It's all connect-ed," he notes at one point, "these crises—marriage, finances, weed dealing—they are interrelated, like the physical and mental decline of my dad, and my own decline, like the housing market and the stock market and the credit market" (212). While this is an inar-guable insight, and resonates quite directly with the realist project more generally (concerned as it is with investigating the correspon-dences between private and public), it marks Walter's participation in a certain longstanding fictional tendency to view economic problems in non-economic terms. The obviously symbolic nature of Prior's fa-ther's condition, no less than the fact that Chuck works at a lumber-yard (and thus retains a connection, however residual, to an old econ-omy of masculine labor with things), casts Prior's problems—and by extension those of the US economy—as a crisis of traditional mascu-linity. Here, as in Sam Lipsyte's *The Ask*—another novel, from early 2010, in which a man's loss of his office job proceeds parallel with his wife's affair—adultery is cast as a specifically gendered problem of men whom the economy renders insufficiently masculine to retain their role as *pater familias*.

Even setting its obvious gender politics aside, the problem with this characterization is that, as I have discussed elsewhere, the conflation of economic change with demasculinization is a longstanding tradition in US fiction that ignores the actual economy[16]—Prior's problems with his masculinity are the same problems that Bellow or Updike gave to characters they understood as too economically secure. Walter's nostalgia for an idealized version of the past American economy also shows up in his criminal subplot, which like the television series *Breaking Bad* portrays the drug economy as a last refuge of manly, competitive business but which also exhibits a Bellovian fascination with the petty criminal as the opposite of the pampered organization man. Prior is offered the chance to buy a hydroponic farm by the crooked lawyer Dave and his partner Monte, an autistic "genius" (163) who recapitulates the heroic history of the US middle class. A scientific farmer who uses shredded coconut to deter aphids (164), Monte has also concocted an ingenious system to disperse his power usage among neighboring businesses that in the process "keeps them [the other businesses] . . . alive"—making him, as another character notes, "like the last industry in town" (166). As if to make the point even more explicit, Dave and Monte are busted by a pair of federal agents who are disappointed because they would have preferred to keep the case—and their funding—going (273).

If this suggests a cynicism about the welfare state that we associate with proponents of the market, it is not entirely fair to tag Walter with this position: another episode, in which Prior recalls choosing private school for his son after intervening in a schoolyard beating that reminds him of a prison scene (53–54), reflects a certain wistfulness instead. But it is the general inability to imagine an alternative to the market that points to the biggest problem with Walter's equation of the economic and the familial: not that he uses the family to register the stresses of the economic, but that he can imagine the family as the only telos in a world in which such stresses exist. Prior rightly notes that privatization is the trajectory of his response to "Alcatraz Elementary"—"Parenthood makes such sweet hypocrites of us all" (54)—but his creator ends the novel with a literary version of such privatization. Prior, living alone in a small apartment and sharing custody of his sons while working at a low-paying start-up job, takes his wife and sons out:

> Sitting in a mall where I am gently trying to win back my beautiful wife, while our boys see a movie on the twenty bucks it has taken me three months to save, and Lisa and I fight over a single ice cream cone. I think we are supposed to somehow be better off now, out from under all of those middle-class weights and obligations and debts, all the lies that we stacked above our heads like teetering lumber. As Lisa said, we're trying. (290)

If "I think we are supposed to somehow be better off now" seems to criticize the ethos of voluntary poverty, the subsequent qualifying sentence reinstalls the problem in the personal realm: "But it's not easy, realizing how we fucked it all up" (290). The novel ends:

> No, we miss our things.
> But we have pockets.
> And Lisa and me—we're okay. (290)

Even at its very conclusion, I want to suggest, *The Financial Lives* vacillates from sentence to sentence between a sense that Prior and his family have lost something of value and the implication that their best response is to retreat to a chastened reconstitution of the family.

Or not quite from sentence to sentence, for in between lies a lyrical image that returns us to the significance of Prior's website, and of his name. One way of reading this name is as a reference to the earlier Matthew Prior's much-anthologized 1718 poem "A Better Answer," in which the speaker tells a lover offended at something he has written,

> What I speak, my fair Cloe, and what I write, shews
>   The Diff'rence there is betwixt Nature and Art:
> I court others in Verse; but I love Thee in Prose:
>   And They have my Whimsies; but Thou hast my Heart.[17]

Prior the poet here equates true love with a literal return to the prosaic, which is natural and serious in contrast to the artful and whimsical (and hence potentially faithless) realm of poetry. If this is indeed one resonance of Prior's name, then the ending of the novel subtly undercuts its domestic telos by suggesting the impossibility of giving up the poetic, even as it offers no adequate substitute. The novel's epigraph from Bellow makes much the same point: "Poets have to dream, and dreaming in America is no cinch." The achievement of Walter's novel, we might say, is to use Prior's website as a figure for relocating the American middle-class dream ("my perfectly normal dream of starting my own business") to the same realm of impossibility, and to figure both of them as what the novel itself (that is, the novel as a form) can no longer adequately represent.

The Financial Lives thus joins The Reluctant Fundamentalist in insisting upon the inadequacy of realism (indeed, in Walter's case, the inadequacy of prose fiction itself) to tell the truth about the contemporary world. Chapter 13 consists of a poem (presumably the narrator's) called "On the Spiritual Crises of Financial Experts," which begins: "This one admits to being a lifetime / proponent of deregulation / but now, on NPR, he doesn't know what to think—" (133). This poem lampoons the market fundamentalism of the titular expert, comparing him to "Mother Theresa, who at the end of her life / admitted she'd had a crisis and had / stopped hearing God's voice" (133). It thereby takes the financial crisis as a figure of salutary realism and insists, in a telling inversion of Dienst's account of the self-justifying financial system, that "the ultimate cause of this global crisis / in our financial system / is our financial system" (134). Yet the paradox that the novel can only declare this fact in poetry suggests, as does Hahmid's romance plot, the breakdown in the novel's historical capacity to translate fact into some sort of socially useful truth. Indeed, the poem ends by calling down God's vengeance on "this rich fat fuck / this expert who apparently slept through / history class, through every relationship / anyone was ever in, and through the entire / twentieth century, this sure dickhead who / has only now discovered that there is / a goddamned flaw in us all" (136). At the same time that it shifts agency into the theological realm, that is, the poem reduces both the public and private repertoires of realist fiction ("history class" and "every relationship anyone was ever in") to a declaration of essential human faultiness of the sort that, we might recall, underlies Kuttner's invocation of consenting adulthood. "There is a goddamned flaw in us all," and so, as at the end of *The Financial Lives,* we only feel bad that "we fucked it all up."

Walter's novel provides a marker of what has been lost even in the brief time since Kipnis's 1998 article "Adultery"—a time period that, if our public memory were even a little longer, we would remember as a series of economic downshifts that calls the very term "crisis" into question. Working against the "public face" of adultery (293) and "the unctuous strutting of public virtue" (319) that accompanied the Clinton-Lewinsky scandal, Kipnis seeks to describe adultery as a site—however inchoate and privatized—for imagining alternatives to marriage as a form of social labor organized around disciplined renunciation and thus "a training ground for resignation to the *a priori*" (294). "Under conditions of surplus monogamy," Kipnis writes, "adultery—a sphere of purposelessness, outside contracts, not colonized by the logic of productivity and the performance principle—becomes something beyond a structural possibility. It's a counterlogic to the prevailing system" (298). Kipnis locates adultery's proto-utopian potential in, among other places, its proliferation of unstructured desire over against the fulfillment of the marital contract: elsewhere in the essay, she describes surplus monogamy as the regime under which "desire is organized contractually, with accounts kept and fidelity extracted like labor from employees" (291), and she suggests that what is threatening about adultery is "the fear that it does indeed indicate that *all* vows, all contracts, are up for renegotiation" (311). Kipnis works, to be sure, with a Marxian notion of contract as a pretense of voluntary agreement that in fact masks the exploitation of labor by capital; and, moreover, the description of marriage as a contract suggests precisely the reductive transformation of an intimate relationship into work that she describes. But in stressing the disciplinary aspects of contract she fails to anticipate how it would subsequently become a site of nostalgia for a time when contract provided a restraint on capitalist power (a pension was a lifetime agreement that could not be revoked in the interests of cost savings) and, by extension, a metonym for the expanded version of the social contract associated with the welfare state. Adultery and the violation of the marriage contract that it constitutes has become the site for expressing otherwise inexpressible anger at the loss of these protections because, even more than in the nineties when Kipnis made the observation, "aspirations for collectivity have been downsized to about the size of a nuclear household" (307). As the loss of all forms of social commitment other than the family intensifies, it becomes even more difficult to criticize the family as itself a site of capitalist discipline. For Kipnis the problematic and valuable dimensions alike of adultery arise from the fact that "it resists narrative (favoring the lyric)" (324). Walter, as we have seen, concurs with this point, although he suggests that, in a world in which all forms of non-familial caring have become unnarratable in a different, more punishing way, one takes to the unlyrical family as the only lifeboat available.

* * *

Lorrie Moore's *A Gate at the Stairs* addresses this same complex of issues, and their relationship to realist form, from a slightly (but crucially) different angle. Moore's narrator Tassie Keltjin is not a member of a troubled marriage but a witness to one: the daughter of organic farmers from rural Wisconsin, Tassie, in her freshman year of college in the "university town of Troy, 'the Athens of the Midwest,'"[18] takes a job as babysitter for a couple, restauranteur Sarah and professor Edward, who are in the midst of adopting. The novel's investment in the family as a site of care and protection is announced by its titular object, "a plastic gate, suction-cupped to the wall" at the top of the stairs leading to the child's second-floor room (132), which Tassie encounters on her first actual babysitting session. Sarah, in her typical distracted way, tells Tassie, "You'll need to be watchful with that baby gate upstairs. I don't want her tumbling down. Or *you* tumbling up!" (130; Moore's emphasis). After a rumination on the post-1973 use of "gate" to signify scandal, and a mention that she'd used Tassie's father's trademark potatoes in her restaurant's minestrone the preceding evening, Sarah then tells Tassie, "Oh, before I forget . . . There's ipecac in the cupboard next to the sink. I'm not even sure how you use it," then concludes by saying, "If anything goes wrong, whatever the hell you do, don't phone *me*. I've left a number for emergencies. It's 911" (130; Moore's emphasis).

As both the form and content of Sarah's instructions suggest, *A Gate* is, properly speaking, a novel not about care but about carelessness, in all its literal and figurative meanings, a carelessness that encompasses but extends well beyond the family. Interviewing with a series of anxious mothers-to-be, Tassie recalls her own mother telling her, in the spirit of "indifferent reserve" she shares with her neighbors, "Dolly, . . . as long as the place was moderately fire resistant, I'd deposit you anywhere. . . . I wasn't going to worry and interfere with you" (8–9). Yet Sarah and her fellow Troy parents, beneath their veneer of hyper-vigilance, are no more focused on their children's well-being—a fact evidenced by the support group for interracial parents that Sarah hosts, and whose activities consist primarily of liberal one-upmanship and heavy drinking. Edward is a serial philanderer who hits on Tassie herself after the collapse of his marriage following the adoption's failure. This occurs because Sarah and Edward conceal an important detail about their past, although the novel suggests that the bureaucrats at the adoption agency are not exactly attentive themselves. More: Tassie's roommate carelessly eats a poisonous paste that Tassie stores unlabeled in their refrigerator for Sarah—"As with the wasabi at Christmas, I was careless with takeout" (251)—and Tassie is forced to drop a wine-tasting course that she has nearly completed after the university discovers a computer error that enabled her and nineteen other underage students to enroll (252). And in the novel's two key revelations, Sarah tells Tassie that she and Edward previously lived under different names back East, where they negligently caused the death of their birth son, Gabriel; and Tassie herself discovers, after her brother's death in Afghanistan, a long-unread e-mail in which he had asked her to talk him out of joining the army.

Elizabeth Anker characterizes *A Gate* as a 9/11 novel whose numerous "allegorical resonances" set up a meditation on liberal middle-class complicity with the nation's problematic response to the attacks.[19] But while Anker is quite right about Moore's critique of liberal "quietude and self-immersion" (479) and her merciless parody of PC rhetoric, stressing her characters' derelictions may miss a major dimension of the novel, which is to generate an almost unbearable sense of individual responsibility that has nowhere to go, either socially or—as the following meditation suggests—formally:

> Tragedies, I was coming to realize through my daily studies in the humanities both in and out of the classroom, were a luxury. They were constructions of an affluent society, full of sorrow and truth but without moral function. Stories of the vanquishing of the spirit expressed and underscored a certain societal spirit to spare. The weakening of the soul, the story of downfall and failed overcoming . . . this was awe-inspiring, wounding entertainment told uselessly and in comfort at tables full of love and money. Where life was meagerer, where the tables were only half full, the comic triumph of the poor was the usual demi-lie. Jokes were needed. *And then the baby fell down the stairs.* This could be funny! Especially in a time and place where worse things happened. It wasn't that suffering was a sweepstakes, but it certainly was relative. For understanding and for perspective, suffering required a butcher's weighing. And to ease the suffering of the listener, things had better be funny. Though they weren't always. And this is how, sometimes, stories failed us: Not that funny. Or worse, not funny in the least. (250–251)

Of course, one might argue that the realm of everyday life lying between aristocratic tragedy and lower-class comedy is precisely the realm of the realist novel, although what this passage struggles with is the inability to derive any larger structure of meaning from this realm. It positions such meaninglessness, moreover, alongside the context of economic decline that haunts the novel's fringes—appearing most directly in the scene where Tassie and Sarah travel to Green Bay to meet Bonnie, the birth mother of the child Sarah will adopt. Here Moore makes clear that the agency Sarah uses specializes in mothers who have economic reasons for giving up their babies: "These birth mothers wanted rich, rich, rich. They wanted to know their babies would have all the things they hadn't. And the babies would. They were cute; they would be fine. The person who most needed adopting, it seemed to me, was Bonnie" (93). In this passage Moore subtly departs from the sentimentalized language of children in need of protection[20] opened up by the Sarah and Edward subplot and suggests that adults too need care, although they, unlike cute babies, are unable to find it.

Tassie's brother Robert joins the army, we suspect, out of a similar desire for meaning and structure: seeing him off to "the ironically named Fort Bliss," Tassie thinks, "he was desperate for the knowledge and reasoning behind anything. I could see he felt shorthanded, underequipped, factually and otherwise" (268). His swift and literally unexplained death—"The letter said something different than the person on the phone" (293)—makes clear the irony of Robert's choice, as does a subsequent scene in which Tassie and her parents see his picture flash, along with that of other dead soldiers, on the news. It is not simply that the army as an institution provides no more care for its members than others do—"Each soldier's face stared out from the glass TV screen like a sweet, accusing child in the good-bye window of a terrible, terrible nursery school" (305)—but that it cannot, in the end, provide meaning either:

> Robert's, too, was the face of a baby with a hat jammed on. The hat was absurd, conferring nothing but a dark decoration as if to anchor the composition of the photo. His eyes were caught in the headlights of something—foreign policy? a bored remark of the cameraman? the portentous burst of the flash?—and he was not smiling. "Robert looks tired in that photo," my mother said finally. (305–306)

Robert, simply tired, has been failed by his story just like the imagined "suffering listener" in Tassie's rumination on tragedy and comedy. Note here the reference to a modernist ethos of the purely aesthetic—the dark shape anchoring the composition—as a mark of the absence of the social knowledge that should accompany the aesthetic in a fully functioning realism.

Like *The Financial Lives*, finally, *A Gate* too registers the absence of any institutional structure outside of capitalism as a failure of realism. Early on, the novel functions as a tour de force of keen social observation made possible in traditional realist terms by Tassie's social and geographic mobility, and emblematized by the way her half-Jewish family's celebration of Christmas denaturalizes and thereby makes visible multiple traditions (44–45). But after Tassie loses her job sitting for the child she has come to care for, and especially after Robert's death, the novel seems almost to unwind. Returning home for the summer after the adoption agency takes Sarah and Edward's child back, she works for her father by donning a handmade bird costume to chase mice and other animals before his thresher, but begins to wear the costume all the time. This eccentric and, importantly, aestheticized behavior anticipates the way in which Moore, like Walter, turns to poetry as a register of what the novel cannot comprehend: Tassie spends her free time on the farm's disused tennis court where she pins pages to a rope hung between the poles, in this way reading first Rumi, then Plath, and then finally recipes from old cookbooks: "They were the opposite of poetry, except if, like me, you seldom cooked, and then they were the same" (289).

Tassie cites as an advantage of this baroque reading apparatus the fact that "if I wanted to rearrange or reposition [the pages] in any way I could do so" (289). Here she directly figures poetry's difference from prose, the non-linearity that will come to seem explicitly desirable to her when she discovers Robert's e-mail and realizes that she failed to stop him from joining the army when she could have: "I wanted to go back in time. Just to send an email—was that too much to ask?" (307). In this later scene, though, she references not poetry but another narrative medium and, moreover, a work of non-realistic genre fiction within that medium, recalling the scene in Richard Donner's 1978 film *Superman* in which the hero flies around the earth backwards faster than the speed of light in order to travel back in time and prevent the death of Lois Lane.

If Tassie is realist enough to recognize this as an untenable fantasy—"The scientists and the comic book were in cahoots!" but "everyone else knew that things were simple and straight ahead" (308)—the novel elsewhere not only thematizes but briefly becomes genre fiction in a moment that we might see as oddly hopeful. In what is perhaps the climax of the book, Tassie lingers behind after her brother's funeral service and climbs into the coffin, "fitt[ing herself] inside to nestle next to him" (298) for the duration of the ride to the cemetery. Anker eloquently describes this scene as transcending empty patriotism and liberal rhetoric, an "imaginative immersion in the phenomenology of the dessicated body politic" through which Moore "demands that her readers, too, viscerally inhabit the claustrophobic space of American irresponsibility" (481). But at the level of novelistic form, we might note that this moment is made possible by the rejection of realism for what we can only describe as a high gothic scene (with a perhaps direct provenance in Poe's "Fall of the House of Usher").[21] This moment goes nowhere within the novel—at the cemetery, Sarah gets out, the pallbearers are surprised, her mother retrieves her, and the funeral goes on—but if Anker is correct that it operates in an important way on the reader, then it gestures toward a potential that the novel as a form has long possessed in addition to realism. Unlike *The Financial Life*, *A Gate* ends not with a gesture of acceptance of what is, but rather with the possibility of a different formal history as an analogue for the potential to change things more generally. Reached by Edward on the phone and invited to have dinner with him, Tassie concludes her narrative:

> Reader, I did not even have coffee with him.
> That much I learned in college. (322)

Returning to the novel that, by smoothing over Jane Eyre's illicit desires and presenting marriage as the proper denouement of realism, more than any other in the English tradition literally domesticates the gothic,[22] Moore suggests that a social institution did finally do something for her protagonist, even if it was only—extravagantly—to instill the germ of the impulse not to be realistic. This impulse means, crucially, not abandoning form altogether—a move that neoliberalism takes as its own form of coercive realism—but finding other, better forms in which to work.

NOTES

1   Robert Kuttner, "Debt Again," *Boston Globe* (19 August 2007), http://www.boston.com/news/globe/ideas/articles/2007/08/19/debt_again/.

2   Vikas Bajaj, "After Sure-Bet Investment Fails, a Bank Contends It Was Duped," *New York Times* (19 January 2009), http://www.nytimes.com/2009/01/20/business/20gem.html.

3   Laura Kipnis, "Adultery," *Critical Inquiry* 24.2 (Winter 1998): 294; hereafter cited parenthetically.

4   Marney Rich Keenan, "At Last, Tiger's Out of the Bag: Signs of Infideli-

ties Missed by Public for a Long Time," *Detroit News* (16 December 2009), http://www.detnews.com/article/20091216/OPINION03/912160348 /At-last—Tiger-s-out-of-the-bag.

5   Nancy Armstrong, *Desire and Domestic Fiction: A Political History of the Novel* (New York: Oxford, 1987), 29, passim; hereafter cited parenthetically.

6   Kuttner.

7   John G. Cawelti, *Adventure, Mystery, and Romance: Formula Stories as Art and Popular Culture* (Chicago: U of Chicago P, 1976), 101–102.

8   Richard Dienst, *The Bonds of Debt* (New York: Verso, 2011), 5; hereafter cited parenthetically.

9   Alison Shonkwiler, "Don DeLillo's Financial Sublime," *Contemporary Literature* 51.2 (Summer 2010): 246–282.

10   Leerom Medovoi, "'Terminal Crisis?' From the World of American Literature to World-System Literature," *American Literary History* 23.3 (Fall 2011): 645; hereafter cited parenthetically.

11   See John A. McClure, *Late Imperial Romance* (New York: Verso, 1994).

12   Karl Marx and Friedrich Engels, *The Communist Manifesto* (New York: Penguin, 2006), 7, 3–4.

13   Ravi Batra, "The Occupy Wall Street Movement and the Coming Demise of Crony Capitalism," *truthout* (11 October 2011), http://truth-out.org /news/item/3889:the-occupy-wall-street-movement-and-the-coming -demise-of-crony-capitalism.

14   See Edmund S. Phelps, "Capitalism vs. Corporatism," *Critical Review* 21.4 (2009): 401, 401–414 passim. Phelps himself notes only in his conclusion that "*actual* capitalism in a country such as the United States . . . departs from the well-functioning dynamic capitalism I have discussed. There are monopolies too big to break up, banks too connected to fail, undetected cartels, regulatory failures, and political corruption. Capitalism, in its innovations, may even plant the seeds of its own encrustation with entrenched power" (413).

15   Jess Walter, *The Financial Lives of the Poets: A Novel* (New York: Harper-Collins, 2009), 3; hereafter cited parenthetically.

16   Andrew Hoberek, *The Twilight of the Middle Class: Post–World War II American Fiction and White-Collar Work* (Princeton, NJ: Princeton UP, 2005).

17   Matthew Prior, "A Better Answer," *Poems on Several Occasions*, ed. A. R. Waller (Cambridge: Cambridge University Press, 1905), 77.

18   Lorrie Moore, *A Gate at the Stairs* (New York: Vintage, 2009), 4; hereafter cited parenthetically.

19   Elizabeth S. Anker, "Allegories of Falling and the 9/11 Novel," *American Literary History* 23.3 (Fall 2011): 478 ff.; hereafter cited parenthetically.

20   For the classic account of the centrality of this language to contemporary US political culture, see Lauren Berlant, *The Queen of America Goes to Washington City: Essays on Sex and Citizenship* (Durham, NC: Duke UP, 1997), 25–54.

21   I owe this key point to Rachel Greenwald Smith.

22   Cp. Armstrong 46–48.

Things Break Apart

James Kelman, Ali Smith, and the Neoliberal Novel

ALISSA G. KARL

> Who is society? There is no such thing! There are individual men and women. —Margaret Thatcher

This essay aims to pick up where the three texts referenced in its title leave off. For where Yeats and Achebe trouble the dis-integration of social collectivity in anti- and postcolonial moments, and where Scottish political theorist Tom Nairn argues in his 1977 treatise *The Break-Up of Britain* that the historically specific features of British political cohesion are now, well, history, how might we account for the current (many will say broken) status of social form?[1] I'll be suggesting that the falling- and breaking-apart of the social can be read as a feature of contemporary capitalist realism that accords with the status of collectivities and the individual laboring body alike under neoliberal capitalism. As I argue here, the status of the neoliberal nation-state is figured and interrogated by what I'm calling the neoliberal novel, in which textual, corporeal, and social forms undergo, yet never fully complete, the breaking-apart referenced above, and I'll detail how neoliberal novels generate national and social worlds in accordance with dominant economic formulations of laboring bodies.

Produced during and responding to the ascendancy of neoliberal economic doctrine in the UK during the late 1970s and 1980s and the so-called Scottish political devolution that began in the 1990s, the novels by Scottish-born authors James Kelman and Ali Smith that I examine here incorporate the counter-impulses of nation-making and the making obsolete of the political and economic borders of the nation-state. Against the oversimplified claim that the nation-state is obsolete under capitalism's contemporary neoliberal, transnational, and financial variants, I read Kelman's *How Late It Was, How Late* (1994) and Smith's *Hotel World* (2001) as examples of neoliberal form that is realized as the bodies in and of the texts break apart but also painfully cohere. In these arguably Scottish novels, the incongruities of the social and political forms implied by contemporary neoliberal capitalism are played out primarily through forms of embodiment that are metonymic and also metaphorical of social entities—both as literal, corporeal forms that are represented within the texts, and via the status of each text as an embodied object consisting of narration, space, and time. Kelman's and Smith's novels thus invoke and seem to deliberately dissolve Scotland and Scottishness as a function of their immersion in the formal and political contradictions of contemporary capitalism, according to which their textual bodies themselves break apart and also break apart the national, state, and social forms within them.

(Un)building the (Neo)liberal Body

As I use the term here, "neoliberal form" names the aesthetic modes that enact but also confront contemporary neoliberal capitalism's formulation of bodies and, by extension, social entities.[2] The theory underpinning neoliberalism draws from the traditions of classical liberalism and neoclassical economics and thus combines the former's assertion that the best society will be produced when individuals are allowed their liberty with the latter's view that markets are self-perpetuating and self-regulating because they consist of rational, profit-maximizing individuals and firms. The result is a combination of political and economic doctrine derived from the work of economists such as Friedrich von Hayek and later Milton Friedman, implemented in the policies of the Thatcher and Reagan administrations in the UK and US as well as in places such as Augusto Pinochet's regime in Chile and post–"Operation Iraqi Freedom" Iraq, and enforced by supra-statal institutions such as the World Bank and International Monetary Fund.[3] Postulating that markets are organized most effectively by private enterprise and that the private pursuit of accumulation will generate the most common good, neoliberalism in practice pursues the opening of international markets and financial networks and the downsizing of the welfare state and the public ownership of industry. Rather than distributing wealth or managing industry, the state's role (in theory) is to ensure that open markets and free enterprise can operate unimpeded, though the actual rise of neoliberalism has often seen the maintenance of heavy state security apparatuses.

David Harvey has called the idea of the state entailed by neoliberal thought "an unstable and contradictory political form."[4] For while neoliberal doctrine asserts that the state should not hinder trade or markets with regulation, the state is at the same time expected to foster a pro-business economic climate by restricting organized labor, encouraging foreign investment, and privatizing industries and services. The result, as Arjun Appadurai puts it, is a scenario in which states are "caught between the need to perform dramas of national sovereignty and simultaneous feats of openness calculated to invite the blessings of Western capital and the multilaterals."[5] Nationhood is similarly ambiguous under neoliberal doctrine. Though emphasized national collectivity might undermine neoliberal rhetorics of individuation, the nation can also serve as a conceptual structure that organizes nations as competitors on the world market.[6] Writing during the Thatcher years, for instance, Stuart Hall remarks upon the regime's merger of collectivist and individualist tropes: "Thatcherite populism," Hall claims, "combines the resonant themes of Toryism—nation, family, duty, authority, standards, traditionalism—with the aggressive themes of a revived neoliberalism—self-interest, competitive individualism, anti-statism."[7] Similarly, Tom Nairn argues that appeals to nationhood palliate the social atomization entailed by neoliberal policy; and of the Thatcher premiership, he writes that "exaggerated loyalism and hysteria over timelessness became a kind of compensation for the regime's self-conscious economic radicalism—as if only endorsement of . . . monarchic and other rituals, and of the state's untouchable unity, could prevent *everything* that was solid from melting into air."[8] In their collective span of the 1997 Scottish parliamentary referendum and the subsequent establishment of that parliament in 1999, Kelman's and Smith's novels draw attention to the uneven deployment and ambivalent status of nationhood in the post-Thatcher years and witness the devolution of the central authority of one multinational state (the UK) in favor of the consolidation of another, presumably mono-national one (Scotland).

Kelman's and Smith's novels both appeal to and recognize the irrelevance of "Scotland" as a political reality and a collective social imaginary—a struggle between forms of collectivity that I trace to a fundamental shift in the terms by which labor, autonomy, and the individual body are articulated under neoliberal capitalism versus its liberal and Keynesian predecessors. The novels do this via the embodiment of human forms within the texts, and as the figurative "bodies" of the texts themselves—their narrative and temporal structure and spatial imagination—register and resist the formal imperatives of neoliberal capitalism and governance. Through both of these modes, the texts enact not the organic social bodies of Enlightenment or liberal discourse or the enclosed technocratic systems of Keynesianism but what might be called a networked form of neoliberalism in which individual or corporate entities access tenuous economic apparatuses and national affiliations on an as-needed basis.

Of course, the analogy of the body with social formation has a long history that has been detailed by numerous scholars, and particularly richly in nineteenth-century literary and cultural studies. In his *Critique of Judgment*, Immanuel Kant establishes that what he calls "organized beings" operate on the basis of a fundamental reciprocity, where "every part not only exists *by means of* the other parts, but is thought of as existing *for the sake of* the others and the whole—that is, as an (organic) instrument."[9] Distinct from a mechanized instrument that is animated by external forces, an organized being "possesses in itself *formative* power of a self-propagating kind."[10] Kant applies this organic metaphor to the state (possibly to the new United States or to revolutionary France):

> In a recent complete transformation of a great people into a state the word *organization* . . . has often been fitly used. For in such a whole every member should surely be purpose as well as means, and, while all work together toward the possibility of the whole, each should be determined as regards place and function by means of the Idea of the whole.[11]

Like a living body, the state is organic because it is self-organizing and not subordinate to any cause or power outside itself and because it bears reciprocity between part and whole.[12]

In demonstrating how Adam Smith's theories of political economy are indebted to vitalist physiology of the later eighteenth century, Catherine Packham provides an analogous image of what we'd today call the economic system as "a body powered by internal forces and vital energies which steer it unconsciously and independently to well-being, ease and health."[13] And if the economic body, like the individual body, naturally seeks self-preservation and betterment, then so follow the dynamics of the body politic. Packham points out that "with its articulation of a system which is the sum of integrated and connected elements . . . the vitalist physiology enables Smith to offer an account of [the relationship between subject and nation, individual and part] as harmonious, integrated, and mutually beneficial."[14] Mary Poovey has shown how such a natural conception of the social body justifies liberal Victorian laissez-faire in social and economic matters (for if society is a self-regulating body, then it ought not to be interfered with) yet also prescribes intervention into the bodily lives of the poor, presumably to cure ailing parts for the well-being of the whole.[15] Catherine Gallagher has also detailed the persistence of organicism in nineteenth-century political economy, but has convincingly shown how the individual laboring body and the collective social body are placed under conceptual strain as they attempt to accommodate the contradictory impulses of industrial capitalism.[16] And Anson Rabinbach's convincing exposition of how, in the nineteenth century, the individual laboring body and its labor power form a crucial conceptual link between nature and advancing industrial capitalism, helps articulate the body as more than an index of dominant economic and industrial thinking.[17] The body doesn't merely reflect the status of economic society (though it certainly may do this); rather, its articulation is the means of reproducing economic paradigms. Thus we could read the theoretically self-contained economic nationhood of mid-twentieth-century Keynesianism—or what Harvey describes as a capitalist market "embedded" within the protective and regulatory functions of the state[18]—as picking up where liberalism leaves off by imagining the aggregate, national-economic body as in need of maintenance.[19] And if the body is both a conceptual and material basis for the enactment of economic orthodoxy, we could say that the mid-century welfare state, with which the coherent national body of Keynesianism coincides, "cares" for individual bodies with a similar aim of maintaining both demand and a fit laboring and consuming populace. I'd offer, then, that neoliberalism's extension of the contours of the market beyond the state entails a leaky, disjointed individual and national body with uncertain, malleable boundaries—one that accords in Kelman's and Smith's novels with ill and injured bodies, and with the difficulty of establishing the definite borders of Scottishness.

The hypothetically able, "healthy" body that is both metaphor and metonym of the liberal economy and state is thus a precursor to the porous social, corporeal, and textual forms that emerge in neoliberal novels. And though the conceptual history offered above is necessarily brief, it helps to specify the status of the body as both metonymic and representational of the social entities entailed by neoliberalism. Neoliberal novels name the body and national and state collectivities as broken at the same time that they expose the bases of the liberal, able body's formulation in the broken promise of social- and economic-systemic reciprocity under the wage labor system. For if, under industrial capitalism and classical political economy and to a certain extent under the managed economies of Keynesianism, the (hypothetical) autonomy and self-containment of the individual body inheres in its ability and choice to sell some of its capacities on the labor market at a price that the market will bear, and if each of these individual bodies is necessary to the aggregate social and economic body, since each does her own part based upon a reciprocity of worker and system (that is, the individual's self-interested sale of her labor constitutes her part of the whole), then neoliberalism's perpetual reconfiguration of the scope of the labor market undoes both the reciprocal pact of wage labor and, by extension, the basis for the liberal economic body and, as I'll address later, its eventual manifestation in the welfare state. This is the case because the ever-shifting boundaries and composition of the neoliberal labor market deem some body parts of the economy superfluous and can thus dispose of or replace them. As Manuel Castells puts it in his theory of economic networks, "everything, and everyone, which does not have value, according to what is valued in the networks, or ceases to have value, is switched off the networks, and ultimately discarded."[20] So where the liberal social body justifies measures to police and interfere with its sick and weak parts, neoliberal practice amputates unnecessary parts and replaces them with others deemed more relevant.

Furthermore, neoliberal capitalism's famed mobility renders the exchange of labor fundamentally non-reciprocal by undermining the autonomy of the individual body itself: labor doesn't freely sell itself at a price the market will bear, but rather the worker recognizes that another person elsewhere can probably do her job more cheaply, yet she often must accept the incongruities of the labor market lest her labor be cast aside. As Eva Cherniavsky explains it, "disposable labor obviates the need to manage and console for the laborer's diminished existence by dismantling the figure of the individual self-proprietor— the person who precedes (stands apart from or outside) capitalist so- cial relations and who withholds some part of himself or herself (an inalienable core) from the exchange."[21] In this second sense, then, the rational self-interest that purportedly animates a neoliberal econ- omy is undone when the laboring subject is recast as excess capacity, thereby attenuating the economic body of its self-generating parts. So if neoliberal capitalism breaks the hypothetical pact of wage labor by shifting the contours of the labor market and thus quite literally breaking apart the contained and autonomous body of the worker, then we realize two key things: first, that earlier forms of wage labor under industrial capitalism affirm the notion of the able, autonomous liberal body in the economic realm; and second, that the body is di- rectly indicative of social entities under economic conditions, given the latter's determination of corporeal status. As such, Kelman's and Smith's inheritance of the representational strategy of economy, na- tion, and state as body entails both metaphorical and metonymic ver- sions of this conceptual relationship. The metaphorical figuration of the social body via ill, injured, and wasting bodies (as we see in Kel- man and especially in Smith) renders a system that does violence to individual bodies and demonstrates the deterioration of older tropes of social cohesion, including that of the liberal body. And Kelman's, and to a certain extent Smith's, literal metonym whereby porous bodies and disposable, amputated body parts are the pieces into which the pact of social cohesion has fallen under neoliberal doctrine directly indexes laboring capacities to regimes of economic organization. Ultimately, then, the ambivalent assertions of Scottishness that we see in both novels amount to more than periodically resurgent nostalgia. I'd argue that they contest the attenuation of individual and collective sovereignty, even if they must unwittingly appeal to the myth of a complete, able liberal body in order to do so.

"Ye wake in a corner and stay there hoping yer body will disappear"

The opening words of Kelman's Booker Prize–winning 1994 novel *How Late It Was, How Late*[22] that invoke the body even as it is willed to "disappear" prefigure the text's neoliberal problematics at a number of levels. The injured, vulnerable body of Kelman's protagonist Sammy Samuels has received a good deal of critical attention, and it is perhaps Sammy's grotesqueness that has made *How Late* Kelman's most famous (and infamous) novel to date. Beaten in police custody and subsequently losing his eyesight, ex-con Sammy's bruised, presumably foul-smelling body (despite all intentions, he never does manage to complete a bath in the approximate week that the text spans) is the novel's central physical presence even though it is never described in visual terms in the narrative. Although or perhaps because we can't "see" Sammy's body, its status is a fixation of the text: his injured back and ribs are remarked upon throughout the novel, as are the nipping at his toes caused by a pair of ill-fitting trainers, his overall "clatty" odor, and his self-admonitions to get back to doing his exercises. That this body's status is indicative of that of the state is referenced in the text's thematic preoccupation with how Sammy's body is registered in public (he endeavors throughout the novel to change his job-seeking and unemployment status, be seen by a doctor, and have his injuries photographed for a potential suit against the police department), thus linking the care of the body with its subjection to state and economic discipline and Sammy with social form at large. And the novel's final words, which place Sammy in a taxicab moving "out of sight" (374), emphasize how the apprehension of his literal body is key to the matters of class, power, agency, and Scottishness that permeate the text.

But this body upon which readers focus is also decidedly porous and leaky. Sammy has trouble making sense of his profuse secretions of blood, tears, pus, saliva, snot, and earwax: "his chin was soaking wet and all around the sides of his mouth and like snotters from his nose, fucking blood maybe" (7). Indeed, Sammy is by turns curious about and repulsed by his body's discharges, and his corporeality is emphasized at the same time that it seems out of his control. Kelman often writes of Sammy's delayed recognition of his body's secretions, such as when Sammy throws himself onto his jail cell bed in a fit of anger, only to acknowledge a few moments later that "he was greeting" (262). Even as the text fixates upon Sammy's body against a world that remains unseen and is perilously navigated (an issue I will return to below), that very body is in the process of seeping away.

Sammy's corporeal status has been convincingly linked to matters of political agency, class, and masculinity.[23] I'd assert, moreover, that the simultaneous intractability and insecurity of the body in *How Late* is metonymic of the social and economic conditions under which Sammy's body is permeable and insecure yet also scrutinized. Such conditions entail an ambivalent view of the social as both ruptured and emphasized. Having undermined the self-contained and seamless body from the outset, the novel conceives instead of an imperfectly networked social totality that is a function of the neoliberal economic climate that it narrates. Sammy's disjointed body makes temporary, prosthetic, and faulty connections with a similarly fragmented world around him, such as with his improvised walking stick that still doesn't prevent him from getting lost outside his own flat (127–129), or when his hearing, which becomes acute in the absence of sight, still proves uncertain (127, 131). Such physical isolation is coupled with an abiding paranoia of surveillance, such as when he is alone in an elevator and worries that "it was probably fucking bugged man know what I'm talking about, or else a VCR, probably there was a VCR. And that security cunt was sitting watching him right at this very minute. . . . Aye fuck you, he said and moved his head around, Fuck you" (91). Sammy's admonition to the perhaps-imaginary viewer certainly achieves a comic effect, but his later arrest by the police confirms some of its merit. In thinking himself to be alone (both in that moment and in a more general sense) while recognizing the claims made upon him by state-sponsored authority (here, he's in a medical building), Sammy affirms the novel's sense of neoliberal collectivity as a fraught network in which bodies and subjects link up periodically with other atomized subjects and administrative units—and not always effectively (as in the case of Sammy's disastrous confrontation with the doctor [223–226]) or when needed or desired (as in his detention by the police).

Indeed, *How Late* homes in upon the subject's alienation from the state as a primary feature of social disjuncture. Ally's "repping" for Sammy in his complaint against the police is a case in point; and while Ally's advice that Sammy refrain from cursing (306) and that he strategize carefully his interactions with authority (239) speaks to the novel's larger dramatization of the politics of language, nationalism, and literary representation, it also indicates the discontinuity between the state and individual subjects.[24] Rather than functioning as a reciprocal piece of the whole, Sammy imagines that state's punitive authority and approaches it via the trope of consumption. He dreams of going to the seaside in England, where "every cunt was rich so . . . they would give him his own fucking DSS office" as well as a bacon-and-egg breakfast and a guide dog (256). England's distinction from Scotland, then, consists in its relative affluence. Not a cultural oppressor but a kind of rich uncle from whom he is entitled his due, England's (and for that matter, Scotland's) national particularity is effaced in Sammy's consumerist orientation—here, a blend of antagonism, alienation, and entitlement—toward the welfare state that attenuates it into pieces (a giro payment here, a guide dog there). It has been argued that the welfare state masks and therefore promotes the systemic inequalities of a capitalist economy,[25] and I'd add that it can be read as forming and protecting the national body in the interests of maintaining a populace equipped to facilitate the requirements of capital. Sammy's attitude toward the DSS is an example of the way in which *How Late* links the welfare state with police, corporate, and consumer institutions by failing to distinguish their functions and thus sketches a neoliberal version of state caring that enforces social atomization.

Kelman further debunks the myth of the able, liberal body and the welfare state that maintains it when Sammy imaginatively exaggerates his blindness to ponder what it would be like were he "a torso, an upper trunk just" advocating for himself along with the rest of the "almost totally dysfunctional":

> [Y]ez would all meet at yer meeting place, getting yer living conditions improved, yer quality of life, start yer petitions to parliament and the town council and sending yer man to Brussels although ye would have to post the cunt if it was a torso, except if ye couldnay talk and ye couldnay see then ye would be fuckt, even having yer wee discussion with the members, yez would all be fuckt, yez wouldnay even know ye were there, except listening for sounds; sounds of scuffling and breathing and sniffing and muttering, sneezes and coughs, which ye couldnay hear if ye were deaf, ye would need folk to listen for ye and to translate, to represent ye, yer interests, except ye couldnay tell them what yer interests were so they would just have to guess, what it was ye wanted, if ye wanted something, they would have to guess it. (316–317)

Sammy's bizarre imagination of a torso going to the European parliament literalizes the fraught status of collectivity under neoliberal capitalism and the uncertain scope of the state. Kelman places a body *part* among the historical institutions of the body politic (town council, British parliament, and European parliament), and as the scale of political representation increases, Sammy's account of what it takes to make a collective body becomes increasingly absurd—from a meeting of the "totally dysfunctional" to discuss their conditions to sniffing and coughing in the chambers of parliament. Kelman's literalization of such a dilemma dismantles the body's hypothetical laboring sovereignty, such that Sammy's torso is a "totally dysfunctional" body extraneous to the machinations of politics (and, we'd think, to economic life), not a constituent part of the whole. As a metaphor for the political subject, Kelman's mute torso references the older trope of the able liberal and national body to effectively point out how that form has been lost. At the same time, the torso's metonymic status exposes the basis upon which corporeal autonomy and, by extension, collective reciprocity are impossible in a neoliberal climate: an unemployed consumer of welfare state services, Sammy can no longer inhere in a system of reciprocity but is rather dismantled by the atomizing institutions that meet the demands of mobile capital and an ever-shifting labor market and economic system. As such, Kelman relies upon the notion of the able liberal body at the same time that he retroactively exposes the economic priorities by which it is composed.

So where critics such as Carole Jones and Scott Hames have convincingly read Sammy as representative of his gender, class, region, and nation, Kelman's literal disassembly of social and political collectivity invites us to read Sammy's body as metonymic for the social body at large and in general under neoliberalism. And though Ally insists to Sammy that the money he's seeking from the state as compensation for his injuries "isnay their[s] . . . it's ours" (297), the model of social form enacted by the novel is far from cohesive or self-contained. The constituent pieces of class and national solidarities have broken apart, leaving an atomized, disposable labor force and consumer market whose enforced docility is doubly emphasized by Kelman's corporeal metonym and the conflation of the state's policing and caring functions. Thus, despite How Late's emergence during a wave of Scottish nationalist politics, the novel posits Scotland as a temporary base for capital. For instance, Glasgow is cast as a neoliberal rather than a post-industrial city, though the former designation does not altogether preclude the latter. Sammy's thoughts on visitors to the city are consistent with such a conception when he speculates that a group of people on the street are "gentleman foreigners" being encouraged by the city council to "invest their hardwon fortunes" in Glasgow (2). Kelman thus begins with a view of Glasgow as open to foreign capital investment and positions Sammy as marginalized excess (in this scene, he's down an alley, having just come to after his lost drunken weekend). The "foreigners" turn out to be plainclothes police officers by whom Sammy is soon arrested; Sammy's mistaking police for foreign businessmen is thus telling of the indeterminacy between neoliberal state and corporate management. I'd suggest that in neoliberal Glasgow, Scottish particularity persists in Sammy's focalized, pained body insofar as the novel's ambivalent regional- and nationalism is akin to its implied appeal to the whole, able body as a protest against the diminished agency and integrity of laboring bodies by neoliberal governance.

How Late's narrative is itself structured by the temporality of alienating state entities and labor mobility such that the novel's form inheres in the very manner of Sammy's body. The present tense of the novel begins when Sammy wakes from a lost drunken weekend and isn't sure what day it is, and continues its ramble through just over one week. In particular, when the novel ruminates on Sammy's battered body, a definite sense of clock and calendar time is lost:

> [His ribs were] still sore . . . So he needed to rest. Except it was so
> fucking
>   it was just
>   he needed to be doing things he really fucking needed to be fucking
> doing things he couldnay hang about he couldnay afford to. What the hell
> time was it man ye couldnay even tell the fucking time! (72)

Sammy's fractured body thus correlates with the breaking-off of external clock time, even as the external time of state bureaucracy threatens to impose its "timebar" (68): "Delay a day and [the DSS] would fuck ye forever" (72). So while the internal time of the novel is as uncertain as Sammy's corporeal state, the external temporality of the novel is organized by discrete encounters with the welfare state and the police: though Sammy's blindness renders the first few days in jail temporally indistinct, upon his release the meandering narrative is delineated by the arrival of his giro payment and an initial trip to the DSS on Friday; a preliminary visit to the Health and Welfare office on Saturday morning; his second arrest by the police on Saturday night; and his release on Monday in order to make his doctor's appointment at 10:45 a.m. The police even deliver Sammy to his Monday morning appointment, thus further aligning the policing of the social body with its supposed protection and care.

The past is likewise indexed to Sammy's two stints in prison of four and seven years, respectively, and memories of working construction in England—not only the site of welfare state consumerism discussed above, but also a destination for mobile, anonymous labor: "He remembered this test, a long time ago, it was in London, it was for a job . . . him and another ten thousand and 96 guys, all stuck in a long corridor" (14). The timing of the English work stints isn't calendrically precise, but it forms a general outline of the past along with the prison sentences. The security state and mobile capital are thus interchangeable within and essential to the novel's temporal structure such that the novel enacts a formal (dis)order that is "realist" as it accords with the temporalities of contemporary capitalism. So where the liberal economic body promises to incorporate wage labor as a constituent of the social and economic whole, I'd suggest that *How Late*'s temporal circuit (which takes Sammy from prison to remote labor to unemployment and back to prison again) indicates how the laboring body and by extension the working class is criminalized when it exceeds the requirements of mobile capital.

Where the novel's temporal form is that of overlapping state, social, and economic institutions that, like the literal and figurative bodies of the text, are in the process of rupture even as they imperfectly cohere, its spatial and regional scope is similarly poised. I've noted above how Sammy sees Glasgow as a temporary home for mobile capital; writing the city in the wake of Thatcherism, the novel's acclaimed hyper-regionalism bears the marks of the ascendancy of neoliberal policy during which municipal budgets were slashed (first and perhaps most shockingly in 1979) and organized labor weakened, most famously in the wake of the National Union of Miners strike between 1984 and 1985. On the one hand, the novel invokes geographic specificity through its sole reliance on Sammy's Glaswegian dialect in its narration; on the other, that language is peppered throughout with the bureaucratic jargon of the "Community Work Provision," "sightloss dysfunction," and "Disability Benefit claim" which simultaneously render the remnants of the welfare state foreign to the dialect's regional particularity but also pervasive—a welfare state whose status, as I noted earlier, is no longer a large-scale institutionalization of the body-state metaphor and metonym but is dispersed and indistinguishable from corporate and police power. *How Late*'s imagination of Glasgow is thus akin to Sammy's physical body. Tenuously held together by temporary, sometimes faulty and arbitrary tropes and forms, Glasgow is intensely regional at the same time that it is fragmented into a collection of heard street corners, claustrophobic council flats, state services offices, jail cells, and pubs. The connective tissue between these sites consists in Sammy's uncertain and partially narrated movements among them, sometimes with the aid of his stick, sometimes without. The novel's form thus coheres in the networked style of Glasgow's topography: where Nicola Pitchford rightly points out that Kelman's narration highlights its own holes and gaps even while provoking the reader's desire for complete disclosure,[26] I'd argue that this lack of narrative totality that has been such a critical preoccupation is a function of the novel's economic form. This form invokes totalization (of Sammy's body and his narrative, of Glasgow, of contemporary Scotland) yet plays upon the gaps, seams, contradictions, and uncertainties by which those totalities are supposedly formed: the indeterminacy of national boundaries and state authority in mobile labor and consumer markets; the imperfect networking of individuals, state entities, and corporate authority; the messy cohabitation of welfare state temporality and neoliberal fluidity; and the undermined corporeal autonomy of the laboring subject among all of these.

"All over the world"

Against the emphasized regional markers of Kelman's novel, Scottish-born author Ali Smith's *Hotel World* (2001) is centered around an outpost of the Global Hotel chain in an unnamed British city. The namesake setting emblematizes the interchangeability and homogenization that are features of contemporary economic life, and Smith simply describes the city in which the novel is set as a "rough rainy northern town."[27] But Smith also suggests Scotland when one character, a homeless woman named Else, mentions Robert Owen's New Lanark experiment (44) and references the commodification of history thus: "The historic city she's sitting on the pavement of, full of its medieval buildings and its modern developments teetering on top of medieval sewers, is all that's left of history now; somewhere for tourists to bring traveller's [sic] cheques to in the summer" (45). Smith thus takes care to leave the novel's location uncertain to underscore the sameness imposed by transnational corporations like the Global Hotel, but also to reference the distinctive regional and national histories that are transformed but still persistent (quite literally) under corporate auspices. And for all of·Hotel World's preoccupation with material bodies, illness, and pain, which I'll discuss shortly, in the final pages of the text the narrator reminds us of the mobility of contemporary capitalism by pointing out that this novel could have taken place in "any town" (229).

The branch of the Global Hotel in the novel has been reproduced "all over the world" in accordance with Global International PLC's philosophy, which "believes that site duplication within still-individual architectural structures reinforces attitudes of psychological security, nostalgia, and preserves a climate of repeated return in worldwide Global clientele" (111). Like the unique buildings that the corporation standardizes, the regional particularities where the Global is sited are "clipped into a style." Else thus describes the accent of the hotel's receptionist, Lise, when she hears the latter talking on the phone: "Something is clipping at her words as they come out of her mouth" (69). And indeed, throughout the novel language itself—accents, words, and vowels—is under threat of standardization and eradication but, like the physical bodies in and of the text, persists even as it erodes. The novel thus renders physical the language of the text (the words that typographically constitute the body of the novel) by emphasizing links between its characters' language and their bodies.

Within and against the anonymous global city of the text are a series of ill, injured, and literally decomposing bodies that struggle to generate coherent language and narrative either under or outside the auspices of the corporation and the neoliberal corporatist state. The novel begins with the narrative of the "ghost" of Sara Wilby, a dead nineteen-year-old chambermaid who was quite literally swallowed alive by the Global Hotel when she crawled into a dumbwaiter and crashed to her death in the basement. Sara's disembodied narrative voice is distinctly separate from Sara's decomposing body, which the voice visits in the grave and decides to inhabit for a time (14–15), and which details the actual breaking-apart of her former body in the dumbwaiter accident: "My back broke, my neck broke, my face broke, my head broke. The cage round my heart broke open and my heart came out" (6). The dismantling of Sara's body corresponds to her loss of singular autonomy, since she splits into two when her ghost separates from her. And as goes Sara Wilby's material body, so goes her ghost's capacity for language. At the same time that she misses "having a heart" (7) and "want[s] . . . to have a stone in [her] shoe" (3), she loses words, especially those for body parts (for instance, eyes become "the things she saw with" [15]) and then drops words altogether: "I mean the way of the . Dead to the . Out of this . Word" (30). Smith's word-play is thus also world-play: words and the worlds into which they materialize parallel one another, as when she transposes letters to constantly modify short sentences in the refrain that is repeated throughout the novel to analogize linguistic and physical decomposition: "Remember you must live. Remember you most love. Remainder you mist leaf" (30). In the case of Sara's ghost, she moves from a desire to re-live the experiences of her physical self ("Remember you must live"), to recalling distinct but fleeting bodily sensations ("Remember [that which] you most love"), to quite literally witnessing her decomposing body disperse "all over the world" at a cellular level ("Remainder you mist leaf"). The novel further emphasizes the process of physical decomposition as Sara's sixteen-year-old sister Clare collects tiny remnants of Sara's body by picking dust from their bedroom carpet that she imagines contains cells and flakes of skin (191–192).

Like the deceased Sara, homeless woman Else drops the letters in her words, repeating "Spr sm chn?" throughout the portion of the narrative that is focused upon her (35–78). Else also "imagines leaving the pavement littered with the letters that fall out of the half-words she uses (she doesn't need the whole words)" (47). This, as Else contemplates "the idea of being a fucking nobody, just a space where a body might be" (35) in light of her social invisibility and as her name Else, shortened from Elspeth and subject to numerous plays on words in the text, continually defers her personhood. At the same time that Else's language literally erodes, however, her physical body coheres through its illness, by a "wall holding her upright [that is] made of phlegm" (40). So even as Else's body and language diminish in accordance with her irrelevance in capitalist labor and consumer markets, her body persists in and through its illness and the social and economic marginalization that is its purported cause.

Against bodies that are imperiled as they are instrumentalized by or, like Kelman's Sammy, excessive to the neoliberal economy, Global Hotel receptionist Lise must quite literally fit her body into the languages of corporate homogeny and the welfare state. We've seen already how she "clips" her language at work, and she also struggles to document an undiagnosed illness within the forms of the health bureaucracy. A large portion of a section of the narrative that focuses on Lise shows her in bed, attempting to articulate the pain in her body in terms of the "Incapacity For Work Questionnaire" (86). When the form instructs her to "tell us about yourself" (81), Lise variously thinks, "I am a nice person"; "I am a sick person" (81); and "I am a ( ) person" (85). Smith's use of empty space to designate language that is unavailable recalls the dilemmas of the dead chambermaid and ill homeless woman who quite literally lose self-representation when they are extraneous to capital's norms, but likewise suggests how living within the parameters of the contemporary neoliberal economy and state entails a painful manipulation of one's body and language. For, after a pages-long free indirect discourse on Lise's view of herself and the world, the narrator reminds us that "she was wondering how to say all this on the form" (89). No longer an autonomous body that organically complements a larger whole, the individual is either extraneous to or "clipped" to fit capitalist relations rather than existing prior to them.

Smith positions such corporeal and linguistic dilemmas against the corporate language created by Penny, a journalist sent to stay in the Global Hotel and review it. Checking her bedsheets for bloodspots and hairs (179), Penny exemplifies the impulse to regulate and contain actual bodies within the neoliberal corporate sphere even as she seeks out clichéd pornography on the Global's Pay-Per-View. The PR piece that Penny eventually writes promises the bland, disembodied pleasures of neoliberal consumerism in the "lush, plush settings" of the hotel (180). Penny is in fact unable to recognize the status of bodies outside of the predictable language of the corporate media. Encountering the teenaged Clare in the hallway outside her hotel room, Penny can't register the girl's distress (she is visiting the spot of her sister's death) but imagines her modeling "something northern-urban-wintry" (135) in the Lifestyle section of the newspaper. Likewise, Penny takes the homeless woman Else, who has secretly been given a room for the night by receptionist Lise, for "some kind of druggy eccentric guest or maybe even a minor rock-star" (139) and eventually follows Else out of the hotel to roam around the city's suburbs under the assumption that the latter is hunting for real estate.

The novel's temporal organization along the lines of shift work bolsters the stultifying effects of corporate and bureaucratic languages but also counters the corporeal and linguistic decomposition detailed above. The disparate narratives of the text converge during one particular evening shift, when Lise gives a hotel room to Else, Penny tags along on a nighttime expedition with Else, and Clare sneaks into the hotel in search of the dumbwaiter. Sara Wilby's deadly accident also took place during such a shift a few months prior. Thus, the diffusion of language and physical bodies in the novel is partly checked by the centripetal temporal form of shift work. The novel narrates in mundane detail a four-minute stretch of Lise's shift at reception that evening, where she watches the minutes tick by on the clock on her computer (101–103) as if to emphasize the temporal regimentation to which workers like herself are subject. Following this section, however, Smith quite literally breaks Lise's shift apart by parsing out individual sentences from the previous description. Smith places the initial text in bold italics, and follows it with commentary, forecasting, or elaboration, as in this example:

> **Drums her fingers on the desk:** In a rhythm approximating the opening lines of the first verse of Neil Sedaka's 1962 UK chart hit 'Breaking Up Is Hard To Do'. See above, **Instrumental version of 'Breaking' etc.**

The fabric of her lapel: Global Hotel uniforms are 78 per cent polyester, 22 per cent rexe. They induce perspiration.

Waste bin: Lined with plastic, this waste bin contains only an empty Advil blister-pack (Lise's) and a plastic container labeled St Michael Pasta and Spinach Salad With Tomato Basil Chicken, now empty except for the used white plastic fork. (116)

In a novel already consisting of multiple individual stories narrated in vastly different styles, from Penny's PR-speak to Clare's stream-of-consciousness interior monologue, this section suggests that any portion of the novel might splinter away into yet another narrative strand. So while, on the one hand, the novel coalesces around the capitalist temporality of the evening shift, on the other hand, Smith takes pains to refute the absolute enclosure of the textual body itself.

But at the same time that the narrative is breaking apart and multiplying, individual language is, as we have seen, slipping away. In the textual and historical logic of *Hotel World*, multiplication implies a loss of self-determination, autonomy, and discrete personhood afforded by bodily singularity. Such a process of multiplication comments upon and emerges from the neoliberal fracture of older social forms such as national identification and class alliances at the same time that it suggests that no single form of capitalist homogeny (temporal, spatial, linguistic, etc.) can ever entirely prevail. Smith's novel thus enacts a struggle between individual bodies and their regional languages, and neoliberal capitalism and states; even as those bodies and their language disintegrate, they maintain ambivalent links with "the world" through the temporal and rhetorical forms of contemporary capitalism and its state variants and are poised to break apart those dominant forms themselves. So while the ill and decomposing bodies of the novel might reference a prior "fit and able" paradigm, Smith's neoliberal bodies nonetheless exercise agency in their broken states.

Smith in fact situates her textual dynamics precisely within British politics of the late 1990s. Penny imagines a story she could do for the paper based upon her late-night trek through the suburbs with Else: "The Garden of England. Blair's Britain at the Dawn of the New Millennium kind of thing. . . . Thought-provoking, kitsch-value, old-fashioned class value as well as social value" (177). While the irony that this idea emerged from a walk with a homeless woman looking into houses from the cold outside may be lost on Penny, it is of course clear to the reader that "Blair's Britain" is based upon a series of social ruptures (of subjects marginalized from the "healthy" national economic body; of households atomized from a larger social collectivity) and conflations (of England for Britain; of "kitsch" for social value) that are held together by the force of its rhetoric. *How Late's* appeals to regional Glaswegian and Scottish national particularity in light of Sammy's and the novel's ongoing fragmentation can be read as similarly ironic, for why ought Scotland to hold together when all else is breaking apart?

Indeed, Appadurai has claimed that our contemporary moment is witnessing a challenge to the dominant corporeal, or what he calls "vertebrate," model by "cellular" systems of social formation. Citing the modern nation-state as a prime example of the former and our current "'post-Fordist,' 'disorganized,' 'flexible,' and 'post-industrial'" economic society as well as non-state networks such as the Taliban as the latter, Appadurai identifies a "mutual dependence and antagonism" between these two modes of political formation that he argues animates contemporary geopolitics.[28] Recently a writer for the *Guardian* got at this struggle from perhaps a more practical angle when he pointed out in the paper's series on devolution and national identity (titled "Disunited Kingdom") that "there is something perverse about founding ever-smaller countries increasingly at the mercy of globalized capitalism."[29] Kelman's and Smith's novels undoubtedly invoke this dilemma, though the analysis above suggests that the breaking-and falling-apart of the neoliberal novel not only extends some of the anxiety of its literary predecessors named at the beginning of this essay; neoliberal form also bears the conditions—and erosion—of laboring sovereignty and social cohesion in the contemporary phase of capitalism. While the illness, leakage, and rupture in and of Kelman's and Smith's neoliberal novels certainly announce the disintegration of so-called vertebrate or liberal corporeal form, their partial appeal to these paradigms nonetheless exposes the terms upon which the "whole" social-economic body (however large or small) is predicated—terms that the broken bodies in and of the novels announce as both obsolete and persistent.

NOTES

I am indebted to Megan Obourn, whose thoughtful comments helped me develop this essay.

1   Chinua Achebe, *Things Fall Apart* (1958; New York: Penguin, 2007). Tom Nairn, *The Break-Up of Britain: Crisis and Neo-Nationalism* (London: NLB, 1977). William Butler Yeats, "The Second Coming," *The Collected Poems of W. B. Yeats*, rev. 2nd ed., ed. Richard J. Finneran (New York: Scribner, 1989), 187.

2   Walter Benn Michaels has recently used the term "neoliberal novel" in reference to texts that he claims prioritize identity categories over the exposition of economic inequalities. While I agree with Michaels on the broader point that economic paradigms are reproduced and also challenged by literary form, this essay takes an alternate approach to the literary manifestation of neoliberalism by tracking the ways in which it formulates individual bodies and social entities. See Michaels, "Model Minorities and the Minority Model–the Neoliberal Novel," *The Cambridge History of the American Novel*, ed. Leonard Cassuto (Cambridge: Cambridge University Press, 2011), 1016–1030.

3   For a detailed account of the forced implementation of neoliberal policy in Chile and Iraq, see parts 2 and 6 of Naomi Klein, *The Shock Doctrine: The Rise of Disaster Capitalism* (New York: Picador, 2007).

4   David Harvey, *A Brief History of Neoliberalism* (Oxford: Oxford University Press, 2005), 64.

5   Arjun Appadurai, *Fear of Small Numbers: An Essay on the Geography of Anger* (Durham, NC: Duke University Press, 2006), 22.

6   Harvey 85.

7   Stuart Hall, *Hard Road to Renewal: Thatcherism and the Crisis of the Left* (London: Verso, 1988), 48.

8   Tom Nairn, *After Britain: New Labour and the Return of Scotland* (London: Granta Books, 2000), 48.

9   Immanuel Kant, *Critique of Judgment*, trans. J. H. Bernard (1790; New York: Hafner, 1972), 200. Emphasis in original.

10   Kant 221. Emphasis in original.

11   Kant 221n. Emphasis in original.

12   See Pheng Cheah, *Spectral Nationality: Passages of Freedom from Kant*

to *Postcolonial Literatures of Freedom* (New York: Columbia University Press, 2003). As Cheah explains, "reciprocal causality implies equality amongst citizens. That the parts and whole produce each other and the whole at the same time that the whole produces the parts implies the liberty of the citizens vis-à-vis the polity" (91). Cheah has attributed the popularity of the organic-corporeal metaphor in the late eighteenth and early nineteenth centuries in part to the fears of mechanization bred by encroaching industrial capitalism (58–59) and links prominent theories of the novel (primarily those of Georg Lukács and Benedict Anderson) directly to the organicist conception of the nation-state, since both offer a "symbolic resolution" of the alienated modern subject (243).

13 Catherine Packham, "The Physiology of Political Economy: Vitalism and Adam Smith's *Wealth of Nations*," *Journal of the History of Ideas* 63.3 (2003): 469.

14 Packham 477.

15 Mary Poovey, *Making a Social Body: British Cultural Formation 1830–1864* (Chicago: University of Chicago Press, 1995), 32.

16 A case in point is Catherine Gallagher's discussion of the early Malthus, who, Gallagher argues, emphasizes how the laborer's body is imperiled by classical political economy's "misrepresent[ation] of the [food] resources available to laborers" because it "encouraged people to believe that the nation's wealth equals its *exchangeable* value"—thus encouraging the worker to reproduce her- or himself, when in fact the domestic production of food could not keep up with a steady increase in population. See Gallagher, *The Body Economic: Life, Death and Sensation in Political Economy and the Victorian Novel* (Princeton, NJ: Princeton University Press, 2006), 45.

   Similarly, Timothy Alborn has traced the contested notion of circulation in Victorian political economy and social thought, showing how it refers to competing and sometimes overlapping mechanized and natural-corporeal conceptions of economic society. See Alborn, "Economic Man, Economic Machine: Images of Circulation in the Victorian Money Market," *Natural Images in Economic Thought*, ed. Philip Mirowski (Cambridge: Cambridge University Press, 1994), 173–196.

17 Anson Rabinbach, *The Human Motor: Energy, Fatigue and the Origins of Modernity* (New York: Basic Books, 1990), 3.

18 Harvey 11.

19 For instance, where Keynesianism prescribes government intervention to engineer a balance of production and consumption, employment and investment, the national economy is construed, as Timothy Mitchell puts it, as "a self-contained structure." See Mitchell, "Fixing the Economy," *Cultural Studies* 12.1 (1998): 93. Elsewhere I have elaborated on the

implied national form of Keynesianism as one that imagines an economic body consisting of balanced producerist and consumerist components and in orderly conduct with other, similarly appointed national-economic entities. See Alissa Karl, "Rhys, Keynes and the Modern[ist] Economic Nation," *Novel: A Forum on Fiction* 43.3 (2010): 424–442. Jed Esty also reads Keynesianism as an example of the inward, "anthropological turn" of national discourse in Britain's late imperial years. See Esty, *A Shrinking Island: Modernism and National Culture in England* (Princeton, NJ: Princeton University Press, 2004), 166–182.

20 Manuel Castells, *The Rise of the Network Society*, 2nd ed. (Oxford: Blackwell, 1996), 134.

21 Eva Cherniavsky, *Incorporations: Race, Nation and the Body Politics of Capital* (Minneapolis: University of Minnesota Press, 2006), 40–41.

22 James Kelman, *How Late It Was, How Late* (1994; New York: Norton, 2005), 1. Subsequent page references will be noted parenthetically in the text.

23 Scott Hames, for instance, claims that Kelman's "'leakier' narrative subjects exercise less control over their own boundaries" than do more traditional male subjects. See Hames, "Dogged Masculinities: Male Subjectivity and Socialist Despair in Kelman and McIlvanney," *Scottish Studies Review* 8.1 (2007): 85. Carole Jones builds upon Hames's analysis to suggest that Kelman's persistent "interruption" of the body enacts the perilous status of male autonomy and stability ("Masculinity" 114–115) and ultimately "protests the representational pact that has forced working-class men into visibility in contemporary Scottish narratives to assume the burden of representing the nation" ("Illiterate Savage" 283). See Jones, "'Acting the Part of an Illiterate Savage': James Kelman and the Question of Postcolonial Masculinity," *Journal of Postcolonial Writing* 45.3 (2009): 275–284. See also Jones, "Kelman and Masculinity," *The Edinburgh Companion to James Kelman*, ed. Scott Hames (Edinburgh: Edinburgh University Press, 2010), 111–120.

24 The awarding of the 1994 Booker Prize to *How Late* caused a great deal of controversy, which centered mainly upon the novel's sole use of working-class Glaswegian dialect, as well as its prolific deployment of four-letter words. Nicola Pitchford points out that this controversy exposed the fraught status of "English" literature as a category as well as its troubled alignment with "British" and "Scottish" culture alike. And writing of Kelman criticism more generally, Mary McGlynn claims that while the uses of language and treatment of working-class Scotland in *How Late* "interrogate nationalism and, more importantly, idealization of the working class, both types of essentialism have sometimes been wistfully reinscribed by [Kelman's] critics" (51). See Pitchford, "How Late It Was

for England: James Kelman's Scottish Booker Prize," *Contemporary Literature* 41.4 (2000): 693–725. See also McGlynn, "'Middle-Class Wankers'
and Working-Class Texts: The Critics and James Kelman," *Contemporary
Literature* 43.1 (2002): 50–84.

25 As Bruce Robbins puts it, the welfare state "is the institution that bribes
us with minor restitutions and supplements so as to divert us from deep
and systematic injustice." Robbins, *Upward Mobility and the Common
Good: Toward a Literary History of the Welfare State* (Princeton, NJ: Princeton University Press, 2007), 206.

26 Pitchford 706.

27 Ali Smith, *Hotel World* (New York: Anchor Books, 2001), 134. Subsequent
page references will be noted parenthetically in the text.

28 Appadurai 27, 29.

29 Owen Jones, "Britain Could Be a Model Unhappy Family," *Guardian Online*, 11 Oct. 2011, 12 Oct. 2011, http://www.theguardian.com/
commentisfree/2011/oct/11/britain-model-unhappy-family.

Things as They Were or Are

On Russell Banks's Global Realisms

When in the summer of 2009 I first read *Rule of the Bone: A Novel* (1995), written by Russell Banks, one of the most important radical American novelists working today, a small scene relatively late in the action stood out for me. *Rule of the Bone* offers a brilliant updating for our era of globalization of Mark Twain's *Adventures of Huckleberry Finn.*[1] The novel relates the story of a shiftless fourteen-year-old, Chapman "Chappie" Dorset, and his struggles to make his way among the broken lives and "throwaway" populations inhabiting the vicinity of his home in the small town of Au Sable Forks, New York, located in the northeastern section of the state's six-million-acre "Forever Wild" Adirondack Park.[2] In the scene of interest here, Chappie, now renamed Bone, and his adult companion I-Man—an illegal immigrant whom Bone first encounters in Plattsburgh squatting in the wreckage of a school bus that plays a prominent role in Banks's previous novel, *The Sweet Hereafter* (1991)—attempt to board a flight bound for I-Man's home of Jamaica. (While in Jamaica, Bone encounters his estranged father, and I-Man is ultimately killed.) At the ticket counter an unexpected complication arises:

> She scooped up the money and counted out the bills and gave I-Man the change and started punching a bunch of keys on her computer. Let me see your passports please, she said and me and I-Man looked at each other and both of us raised our eyebrows the same way. Like, Passports? He was an illegal alien and I was a homeless youngster missing and presumed dead, practically a milk carton kid and it suddenly looked like the truth was about to come out.[3]

While I-Man does produce a passport (although Bone observes it would "show he'd only been allowed in for picking apples in New York and cutting cane in Florida and couldn't go home until the company said so"), Bone notes that he possesses no more than a "phony ID I'd once bought off a kid at the mall that said I was eighteen but except for Art the tattoo guy no one believed whenever I tried to use it" (248).

However, at that moment the ticket agent's attention is drawn to "I-Man's Jah-stick," which, she tartly informs him, will not be allowed to accompany him on the aircraft. As she reaches for it, Bone warns her, "The stick's *alive*, man. Nobody can touch it but him" (249). Sure enough, when she grabs it, she is "bitten" and yells out in pain. (With this, Banks does not shift registers into magical realism, as we soon learn that I-Man has inserted an all-but-invisible needle in the stick that he flicks when anyone touches it.) As she reacts in surprise and confusion, the scene comes to a close: "I-Man took his Jah-stick then and his passport and his bag and boom box and I grabbed up my pack and ID and our tickets and boarding passes and we split from there without another word. We found our gate and went through the x-ray machine and sat down to wait for the boarding announcements" (249–250).

What struck me on my initial reading of this scene was a palpable sense of its unreality, of the unlikeliness of this simple subterfuge being sufficient for the pair, and especially this pair, to con their way onto an international flight. To be more precise, the scene became for me what Aristotle identifies in his *Poetics* as an *improbable possibility*, an event that may in some extraordinary circumstances occur in our world, but whose presence in a work of fiction strains the limits of a reader's credibility. Aristotle first introduces this concept in the penultimate paragraph of section 24—"Accordingly, the poet should prefer probable impossibilities to improbable possibilities"—and develops his claims in more detail in the subsequent section.[4]

Aristotle opens section 25 by noting, "The poet being an imitator like a painter or any other artist, must of necessity imitate one of three objects—things as they were or are, things as they are said or thought to be, or things as they ought to be."[5] The Chicago School Aristotelian Richard McKeon points out that for Aristotle and indeed "as late as the eighteenth century imitation was the mark and differentia of the arts. . . . Imitation, being peculiar to the processes of art, is not found in the processes of nature or of knowledge."[6] Aristotle is interested here in distinguishing between two kinds of errors that occur in these particular aesthetic mimetic activities, those "inherent in the poetry" and those "not essential" to it. While he counsels that "every kind of error should, if possible, be avoided," there are times when representations of the impossible are permissible: for example, if the goal is an ethical one, presenting things as "they ought to be" in order to educate the desire of readers; or if the representation in question meets the dictates of communal consensus ("This applies to tales about the gods," Aristotle notes); or finally, if the end result is a product of an effective marshalling of the poetic or figural resources of language. Aristotle thus concludes, "In general, the impossible must be justified by reference to artistic requirements, or to the higher reality, or to received opinion. With respect to the requirements of art, a probable impossibility is to be preferred to a thing improbable yet possible."[7] Interestingly, while the former category takes us into the realm of the fantastic, it is the one sanctioned by Aristotle—as one recent online commentary notes, "The suggestion seems to be that if a poet can successful[ly] establish a fabulous or uncanny series of events, we as readers will be more willing to suspend our disbelief than if the poet represented ordinary actions in a strained, unconvincing manner."[8] However, even within these terms there is a hierarchy implicitly at work, one that prefigures the much-debated distinction between the "high" popular form of science fiction and the "low" one of fantasy.[9]

There are two further comments that need to be made at this juncture. First, the four terms that Aristotle sets into play here generate two further possible combinations, those of *probable possibility* and *improbable impossibility*. While the former names the field of which Aristotle's two categories identify the antinomic limits, the latter serves as the placeholder for that which would seem to break with this field altogether. We can represent the relationship between these four terms through the semiotic square developed by A. J. Greimas and further refined by Fredric Jameson, which in two recent essays I take up in conjunction with the three orders of Jacques Lacan.[10] The resulting schema of relationships among these terms would appear as shown in Figure 1. What this presentation makes evident is that the category occupying the place of Greimas's neutral, the double negation of the *improbable impossibility*, would function for Aristotle in a way similar to the mathematical concept of ∞ (infinity), "a special type of thing that exists potentially but not actually,"[11] and hence can be bracketed from consideration—as does Aristotle in his *Poetics*.

Second, Aristotle emphasizes the deep historicity of these categories, the aim being a representation adequate to either "things as they were or are." In other words, what is very much possible and probable in one historical situation becomes improbable if not impossible in another. My initial response to the scene in *Rule of the Bone* described above thus tells us less about Banks's art than it does about the immense changes that occurred in the little less than a decade

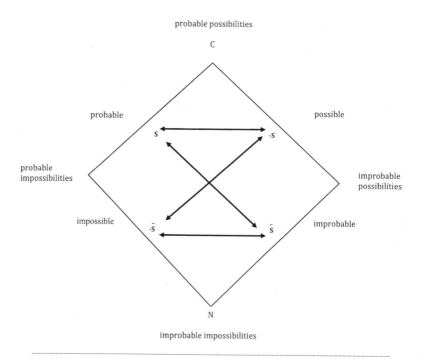

Things as they were or are.

and a half that passed between the novel's publication and my initial encounter with it.

It is precisely these transformations that are also, perhaps unexpectedly, the subject of Bank's first novel of the twenty-first century, *The Darling* (2004). Indeed, as the novel's protagonist and narrator, the protean Hannah Musgrave—the privileged child of a Northeastern intellectual turned Weathermen radical turned white American wife of a Liberian bureaucrat turned Adirondack organic chicken farmer—observes in the book's final paragraph, the US is, in the first decade of the twenty-first century, "a nation whose entire history was being rapidly rewritten" in ways far more dramatic than what had occurred in the previous fifty years.[12] In the following pages, I explore the contours of the changing situations of both our national and geopolitical present as narrated by this highly original novel, changes that have made the strategies of realism deployed in Banks's earlier work, and especially that published in the period of the 1990s, less and less viable.

There are a number of significant connections between *The Darling* and the novels that Banks published both before and after it. First, *The Darling*, along with *The Sweet Hereafter, Rule of the Bone*, and *The Darling*'s immediate predecessor, *Cloudsplitter* (1998), deploy unreliable first-person narrators. Through this device, Banks is able to explore the ways a variety of characters, in different times and situations, attempt what Fredric Jameson describes as "cognitive mapping," the struggle to position oneself in a world undergoing rapid and dramatic social, cultural, and political changes. Such efforts entail coordinating the existential and phenomenological experience of one's everyday life and the abstract global economic, political, and social realities each of us always already inhabits, efforts that are necessary before we can act effectively in these realities.[13]

Second, *The Darling* is the second of three historical novels authored by Banks, following *Cloudsplitter* and preceding *The Reserve* (2008). *Cloudsplitter* focuses on events in the antebellum nineteenth century, culminating in John Brown's October 1859 raid on the federal arsenal located in Harpers Ferry, Virginia. *The Darling* explores a much more recent history, ranging, with a few excursions further afield, from the mid-1970s through the opening years of the new millennium, while *The Reserve* again moves the action further back in time, to the Great Depression 1930s. In all three novels, Banks experiments with conventions of the historical novel form, blurring the distinctions between what Catherine Gallagher identifies as the three types of characters found in these fictions, the historical, fictional, and counterfactual.[14] For example, in *Cloudsplitter*, Banks presents one historical personage, Lyman Epps, Sr., a freed black farmer and Adirondack neighbor and ally of John Brown, as suffering a very different fate in the world of the novel than he did in ours: in the novel, Epps is accidentally shot and killed by the narrator and Brown's son, Owen, in the months leading up to the infamous 1850s events in Kansas, whereas in our historical world he outlives John Brown by nearly four decades.[15] Moreover, not only do historical figures interact with fictional characters; Banks draws freely upon the biographies of significant historical personages in the creation of prominent fictional characters in both *The Darling* and *The Reserve*—respectively, the famed pediatrician and anti-war activist Dr. Benjamin Spock and the radical painter and illustrator and longtime Adirondack resident Rockwell Kent (whose Asgaard Farm is located on the outskirts of Bone's hometown of Au Sable Forks). Even more significantly, Banks paradoxically suggests, especially in the pair of *Cloudsplitter* and *The Darling* that I will discuss in more detail below, that while the upheavals of the antebellum period are very near to the 1990s present of the novel's publication, the more recent historical past in focus in *The Darling* is separated from its present by an immense gulf.

Finally, all five of the novels Banks published in this sixteen-year span are set at least in significant part in the High Peaks area of the northern Adirondacks.[16] This locale, where Banks himself has lived for a number of years now, functions in his fiction in way similar to William Faulkner's "apocryphal county" of Yoknapatawpha, "patterned upon Faulkner's actual home in Lafayette County, Mississippi."[17] However, while Faulkner's Yoknapatawpha is a fictional landscape based upon an actual one, Banks's High Peaks is an actual place, where not only historical, fictional, and counterfactual characters intermingle but where actual places (Au Sable Forks, North Elba, Keene Valley) exist side by side with fictional ones (e.g., Sam Dent, the hometown of the children killed in the terrible bus crash at the center of *The Sweet Hereafter*). Banks's High Peaks differs from Faulkner's Yoknapatawpha in another significant way: whereas throughout his fiction Faulkner maps the often fraught relationship between the uneven modernities of the Southern *region* and the emerging modernist *nation-state*, Banks situates the High Peaks region in a decidedly postmodern *global* spatial and political economy.[18] In this way, Banks's work gives further substance to Jameson's axiom concerning the "geopolitical unconscious" at work in a range of contemporary representations: "All thinking today, is *also*, whatever else it is, an attempt to think the world system as such. All the more true will this be for narrative figurations."[19]

One of the most striking ways in which these kinds of narrative figurations unfold in Banks's High Peaks fictions is through the presentation of major characters in circulation within and across older national borders. This is not only the case for Banks's earlier works set in the present day—where even the service workers and post-industrial throwaways of *The Sweet Hereafter* and *Rule of the Bone* move between northern New York State and the Caribbean—but for the historical fiction as well. John Brown and his family are shown to be continually on the move, relocating their base of operations from Ohio to Massachusetts to North Elba, New York, to Kansas; and at one point, John and Owen Brown retrace the third leg of the golden triangle, traveling to Great Britain and the European continent. Moreover, the very fact that the novel focuses on the radical abolitionist Brown signals Banks's interest in these kinds of transnational flows of people, commodities, and ideas: Brown is, as W. E. B. Du Bois persuasively argues, as deeply influenced by the events of the Haitian uprising as was Hegel decades earlier.[20]

Nowhere is this transnational mobility more central to the action than in *The Darling*. In fact, in this novel, the High Peaks setting serves as a frame for an action that ranges across the eastern US and West Africa. The novel opens with Hannah Musgrave recounting events that took place in the recent past. The opening lines suggest the deep interconnections in a global political economy between these diverse locales:

> After many years of believing that I never dream of anything, I dreamed of Africa. It happened on a late-August night here at the farm in Keene Valley, about as far from Africa as I have been able to situate myself. I couldn't recall the dream's story, although I knew that it was Africa, the country of Liberia, and my home in Monrovia, . . . and found myself overflowing with the knowledge that I would soon return there. (3)

After narrating for a few pages daily life on her Shadowbrook Farm, land that she purchased in 1991 (right at the beginning of a 1990s regional land boom), the scene abruptly shifts: "Ten days later, I rode overland in the dark traveling northwest from Côte d'Ivoire into Liberia" (10). Hannah then recounts some of the details of her voyage into the civil war–ravaged country, before moving back to the events of the late August day she decided to return to Africa, and then even further back in time to the last weeks before her 1991 flight from Liberia. She then turns the narrative clock to 1975, as she tells the story of how she ended up in Africa in the first place.

This nonlinear intercutting *sujet* (plot) continues throughout the novel, only returning in the final pages to Hannah's farm and the narrative present. In this fashion, Hannah's life story gradually emerges while the various times and places through which she circulates are interwoven into a complex network. The daughter of a "world-famous pediatrician" (109), Hannah enrolls at Brandeis University in the early 1960s and becomes involved in the civil rights and antiwar movements, first traveling into the southern US and then inhabiting a variety of locales in the Northeast. As her revolutionary commitments deepen, Hannah joins the Weathermen, constructing explosive devices (though she notes she "was never trusted to place and set the bomb itself, a job reserved for only the more charismatic comrades" [172]) and forging IDs, the latter skill serving her especially well in later years when she is slipping across state and international borders. In the early 1970s, a federal warrant is issued for her arrest, and she goes underground, where she remains until an untrustworthy fellow Weatherman, Zachary Procter (implied to be a scion of the Procter family of Cincinnati), convinces her to accompany him to West Africa. After a few months in Accra, Ghana, she moves to Monrovia, the capital of Liberia, to take up a position in a US-funded primate research facility. There she discovers the horrific and abusive conditions in which the chimpanzees are housed. At this time, Hannah also meets Woodrow Sundiata, the assistant minister of public health in the governments of William Tolbert and Samuel Doe. After a brief courtship, which includes a fraught voyage inland to Sundiata's ancestral homeland, Hannah marries him and in the next few years gives birth to three sons, Dillon and twins William and Paul. Except for a period of exile in the US in the mid-1980s, where she helps future rebel leader and president of Liberia Charles Taylor escape from prison, Hannah remains in Liberia until the fall of 1990, when her husband is murdered by supporters of Doe, and then Doe, who came to power in an April 1980 military coup, is in turn brutally executed by a group of rebels—a group that, Hannah discovers to her great horror, includes her three sons. In all these ways, Hannah becomes a direct witness and even contributor to the explosive political upheavals that take place in this small African nation.

Hannah's narrative thus serves, like the classic noir detective novel, as a way of enabling readers to enter into worlds to which they would not normally have access, including radical political subcultures in the US and the periphery of the Cold War world system.[21] However, if the movements of the noir detective produce for the reader cognitive mappings of the networks of power circulating through and binding together the modern urban environment and the nation-state, Hannah's narrative brings into focus the often obscure political and economic flows constituting US global power in the Cold War period.[22] In Liberia, Hannah experiences firsthand the corrosive and destructive effects of US Cold War political machinations on small nations such as Liberia. Early on, in describing the elites that have long ruled the nation, Hannah gives concrete expression to exactly these influences and the ways they seed the tragic conflicts that will soon follow:

> Consequently, to the delight of U.S. politicians and State Department officials, when the Cold War arrived, the Americos [Liberians who traced their ancestry to former African American slaves who founded the nation in the nineteenth century] turned out to be as anti-Communist as Barry

Goldwater, making the Cold War years, for the Americo ruling class, boom years. Foreign aid fluttered down from the skies like manna onto the wide verandahs and lawns along Broad Street from Mamba Point to Tubman Boulevard, missing altogether the rest of the country, where millions of increasingly disgruntled savages lived in near-starvation in mud-hut jungle villages. (90)

Indeed, Hannah learns that this influence even shaped her own actions, indirectly aiding her efforts to help Taylor escape from prison: the US "cultural attaché" Sam Clement later informs her, "Back then, the last place we wanted Charles Taylor was in a cell in Massachusetts. We wanted him in Liberia. Our man in Africa" (376). Of course, re-enacting a tragic plot that occurs again and again throughout the Cold War peripheries, Clement also acknowledges that these interventions unleash forces that very quickly escape "our" control: "We just didn't get what we wanted in the form we'd imagined or planned. But that's history" (377). It will be this Cold War "history" that will, not long after, have devastating and equally unanticipated "blowback" consequences for life in the US as well.

This theme of global interconnectivity is treated in another profound way in the novel. Early on in her narrative, Hannah informs the reader that a good portion of her time in Liberia is spent caring for the chimpanzees, whom she names "dreamers." The uncanny fascination of these figures for Hannah arises from their profound kinship with us: "they share nearly ninety-nine percent of our genes and more closely resemble humans than a bluebird from the East Coast of the United States resembles a bluebird from the West" (20). Yet precisely because of this closeness, the border between chimpanzees and humans is one that is rigorously policed. Exploring the etymology of the word "chimpanzee," Hannah discovers that "it's a bantu word from the Congo, meaning 'mock-man'—a name derived, not from the creature's own nature, but from its relation to us, to humans, as if its essential nature were a lesser version or a negation of ours. It's the only species named in such a purposefully distancing way. It's the not-human. The not-us. The un-man" (21). She later notes that this dialectic of nearness and farness makes these fellow inhabitants of our planet especially imperiled: "All species are in danger of being killed by humans, even the human species, but only a few are as endangered as the one that most resembles us. . . . They are not our distant ancestors; they are our close cousins" (333–334).

This thread in the novel offers ample material not only for consideration by the growing body of scholarship on human and animal relationships, as well as the more general ethical turn in cultural theory of which these labors are a significant part, but also for a meditation on the proximity of otherness in a fully urbanized global capitalism.[23] Indeed, the same dialectic of nearness and farness recurs in relationship to the various "human" groups Hannah encounters. For example, when she first returns to the US after nearly a decade-long absence, Hannah reflects, "The whites didn't look quite human to me. . . . They looked dangerous, so self-assured and knowing, so intent and entitled" (251). Similarly, after she arrives back in Liberia, she notes the growing distance she experiences between herself and her family: "The bamboo wall that separated me from Woodrow's family and village was cultural and linguistic, not racial or even economic, and I should have been able to scale it and join them on the other side, but I was unwilling, perhaps unable, to do fieldwork on my own family" (339). Later still, she points out that her age, authority, and most significantly, her resources—"I am the one with the money. Let us not forget that"—create a deep gulf between her and the younger women who work for her on the farm; she even notes that "the girls and I are as different as two separate species" (382–383). The negotiation of these often-fraught zones of contact is, the novel so pointedly reminds us, one of the central dilemmas of an emergent integrated global order.[24]

Yet for all this, the novel also locates the events and places it recounts decidedly *in the past*. Early on Hannah observes, "At a certain point one's personal history, one's *story*, simply stops unfolding. Change just ends, and one's history is not completed, not ended, but stilled—for a moment, for a month, maybe even for a year. And then it reverses direction and begins spooling backward" (32). However, in its surprising closing pages, Hannah makes it clear that the story she has to tell has indeed come to an end. Bringing the reader up to the moment of her return to the garden of her former Liberian home where her husband is reportedly buried, Hannah abruptly breaks off and locates her story in a precise historical moment: "There is not much more to tell. It was September 10, 2001, and one dark era was about to end and another, darker era to begin, one in which my story could never have happened, my life not possibly been lived" (391).

This dramatic and unexpected act of periodization brings to a close both Hannah's personal narrative and the Cold War reality to which it gives such a powerful figuration. Even more significantly, the novel stresses that it is the terrible events of September 11, 2001, that have made Hannah's story and the moments that compose it improbable possibilities. Indeed, earlier, the novel seems to refer back to the scene in *Rule of the Bone* that I discussed in the opening of this essay, indicating precisely how the events of 9/11 render these episodes and others like them hereafter improbable:

> Also inside the jacket pocket was a U.S. passport in the name of Charles Davis. The photo was of a round-faced black man who resembled Charles only slightly, but close enough that a white man would think it was an exact likeness. This took place some fifteen years ago, remember, when it was safe to assume that Charles's face and passport photo would not be examined by a black man in uniform until he got to Egypt. Also, back then, before Americans started seeing anyone whose skin wasn't pink as a potential suicide bomber, security was light and the technology of surveillance was slow and unreliable. (299)

And yet, the novel suggests that something even more significant has changed in the aftermath of the historical rupture that is 9/11. One way to bring into clearer focus the profound nature of these changes is to glance back at Banks's pre-9/11 novel *Cloudsplitter*. Both *The Darling* and *Cloudsplitter* are fundamentally concerned with the question of revolutionary political commitment at crucial moments in American history. And in this, both also serve as meditations on the contemporary legacy of the 1960s. In a 2001 essay in which he outlines his reasons for turning his attention to John Brown, Brown's family, and their historical context, Banks observes:

> I was, like many of my contemporaries, a political activist in the 1960s, a founder of the SDS chapter at my university, an antiwar and civil rights protester. Thus, certain questions raised by the figure of John

Brown—such as: When does an obsession with a cause, no matter how just, become fanaticism? and When, if ever, is a violent course of action against a democratically elected government justified?—were questions whose answers, or lack of answers, impinged upon my own life. I took them personally. They weren't merely theoretical. They weren't academic. The questions mattered to me, to the meaning of my life so far, and they continued to matter and grow increasingly difficult to answer as the years passed, even as I gained distance on those turbulent years and so few of the bright and shining promises of the 1960s were realized and I grew sadder and, presumably, wiser. Should we have been more violent or less? Should we have been more committed to our causes or less? Was our idealism tainted at the source by our naïveté, or by our hedonism? Or was it all hopeless from the start? Nearly 150 years after his death, the question of whether I could truthfully imagine John Brown as a heroic visionary or as a well-intended fanatic, or both, had meaning for me personally.[25]

However, what makes *Cloudsplitter* a work of art and not merely a disguised private autobiographical reflection is that these are all questions that take on a new urgency—and not only for other members of Banks's generation—in the period that I describe in *Life between Two Deaths, 1989–2001* as the "long nineties": a situation in which the unexpected end of the Cold War made concerns apparently long since settled newly pressing and the topic of much debate, and even more significantly, in which at the decade's end new forms of radical political action would come to prominence on the global stage. In this moment, Banks and others take up the task of exploring for the present the lessons to be had from both Brown's radicalism and that of the 1960s.

Cloudsplitter's narrator and central protagonist is not in fact John Brown but rather Brown's third-eldest son, Owen. There is a good deal of similarity between Hannah and Owen. Both are at once participants in and witnesses to an extraordinary history. Early on Owen notes, "I have been unfortunately blessed by having been placed in my life so as to witness firsthand most of the tragic and painful events that have afflicted my family, and thus have been too often obliged to carry the sad news to the others."[26] These others include the intended audience for these pages—Katherine Mayo, a research assistant to Oswald Garrison Villard, the author of one of the first major biographers of John Brown, to whom Owen writes nearly a half century after his father's execution, together with the readers of Banks's novel.[27] This multiple framing, moreover, suggests a kinship between Banks's first-person narrators and Charles Marlow, the great participant narrator of Joseph Conrad's major fictions: all three are burdened with conveying the truth to an audience, Conrad's "privileged men," who may not want to receive it.[28]

Throughout his recounting of these episodes, Owen repeatedly expresses his own ambivalence about his father's and family's activities on behalf of the cause to bring to an end the institution of slavery, a cause whose universal dimensions his father makes clear when he asserts, "Slavery, however, was 'the sum of all villainies,' and its abolition was therefore the first essential work of all modern reformers. He was perfectly convinced that if the American people did not end it speedily, human freedom and republican liberty would pass forever from this nation and possibly from all mankind" (643). Of these activities, Owen will go so far as at one point to claim, "But that did not mean that I did not know the truth about Father and why he did the great, good things and the bad, and why so much of what he did was, at bottom, horrendous, shocking, was wholly evil" (446).

One thing about which Owen remains resolutely clear is that his family's actions do transform history in a significant way—crucially though, Owen has in mind not so much their more celebrated and failed intervention at Harpers Ferry as their earlier actions in the "bloody Kansas" border war. In learning of the sack by pro-slavery forces of the Free State settlement at Lawrence, Owen falls into a momentary despair, crying out, "Our cause, is lost, Father! Lost without even a whimper from those cowards in Lawrence, and now the whole territory, it looks like, is ruled by Franklin Pierce's soldiers" (602). John Brown, however, refuses to accept this seeming inevitability, or what Aristotle would call a probable possibility: "We might yet upset this neat arrangement. Something must be done, though. Something dramatic and terrible" (602). The dramatic and terrible course he decides on is for them to brutally execute five pro-slavery men settled in the vicinity of Pottawatomie, Kansas, a singularly outrageous act that launches a full-out war in the region and ultimately sets the stage for the US Civil War.

Later, meditating on the consequences of their actions, Owen dramatically switches generic registers from historical memoir to the counterfactual or the science fiction alternate history:

> Simply, I showed them at the time and afterwards that if we did not slay those five pro-slave settlers and did not do it in such a brutal fashion, the war in Kansas would have been over. Finished. In a matter of weeks, Kansas would have been admitted to the Union as a slave-state, and there would have been nothing for it then but the quick secession of all the Northern states, starting with New England, and the wholesale abandonment of three million Negro Americans to live and die in slavery, along with their children and grandchildren and however many generations it would take before slavery in the South was finally, if ever, overthrown. There would have been no raid on Harpers Ferry, certainly, and no Civil War, for the South would not have objected in the slightest to the breakup of the Union. Let them go. We will happily keep our slaves.[29]

Crucially, Owen concludes, "When we went down to Pottawatomie, I believed all that. I believe it still. . . . I truly thought that we were shaping history, that we were affecting the course of future events, making one set of events nearly impossible and another very likely" (607).

In this way, the actions at Pottawatomie become in Banks's presentation an example of the absent fourth category in Aristotle's *Poetics*, the improbable impossibility—or more precisely, what the contemporary philosopher Alain Badiou calls an *event*. Badiou defines the event as something that happens "that cannot be reduced to its ordinary inscription in 'what there is.'"[30] Explicating Badiou, Peter Hallward further notes that the event "takes place in a situation but is not of that situation"; hence, the event is the "void of the situation, that aspect of the situation that has absolutely no interest in preserving the status quo as such."[31] Crucially, from the perspective of that status quo the event is impossible and unimaginable, and yet for all that, it is nevertheless true.

The great achievement of *Cloudsplitter* is thus to give literary expression to that which in effect is unrepresentable (for the truth of the event cannot be "communicated," Badiou emphasizes, but only "encountered"[32]): the deep, lived, and I would say realist sense of the proximity of the event, not only characteristic of the 1850s, but also of the 1960s and again of the 1990s. This is, of course, a realism in the very different sense that the great philosopher of Utopia, Ernst Bloch, defines it, a representation or imitation of a reality that is shot through with the potentiality of the new: "Where the prospective horizon is omitted, reality only appears as become, as dead, and it is the dead, namely, naturalists and empiricists, who are burying their dead here. Where the prospective horizon is continuously included in the reckoning, the real appears as what it is in concreto: as the path-network of dialectical processes which occur in an unfinished world, in a world which would not be in the least changeable without the enormous future: real possibility in that world."[33]

This also casts in a new light Owen's claim that his father's and indeed his own actions were "wholly evil"—for while this is the case, they are so in the sense of Kant's *radical Evil*, which Slavoj Žižek defines in the following manner: "The possible space for Good is opened up by the original choice of radical Evil which disrupts the pattern of the organic substantial whole. . . . Although the motivations . . . were undoubtedly 'good,' *the very formal structure of his act was 'radically evil'*: his was an act of radical defiance which disregarded the Good of community."[34] Only this kind of radical defiance enables real substantial change, or change in the real, to occur.

Badiou furthermore maintains that "the essence of the event is to be undecidable with regard to its belonging to the situation," and hence requires a "decision with respect to its belonging to the situation," a decision—or what Owen describes as the "belief" that one can make one reality "nearly impossible and another very likely"— that is at the basis of any intervention in the world.[35] For Badiou, this decision and the actions that follow from it transform the individual into an authentic *subject*. Moreover, such a subject remains in effect only as long as the fidelity to the potential of the event continues. The subject is, as Owen effectively puts it, "an ordinary man in a plain brown suit who happened to possess the truth"; or as Ralph Waldo Emerson states in his essay "Heroism," as paraphrased by Owen, "The characteristic of heroism is its persistency" (313).

And yet, it is the terrible burden of being a subject from which Owen expresses an all too human individual desire to escape: "Don't you wish our life were different? Don't you wish we could live normally someplace, like other people, in a town or even on a farm close to other farms?" (193). Owen seems finally to achieve this release following his flight to California after Harpers Ferry (which the real-world Owen did as well—in fact, the cover of *Cloudsplitter* has a photo of an aged Owen at his cabin outside of Pasadena): "But I was alone. Alone, and free. The entire continent lay out there. I was a man, a white man, and could go to any place on it where no one knew me, and I could become new. I could become an American without a history and with no story to tell. I believed that then and for many years to come" (757). However, in the end, Owen realizes that once the story has been told it will not disappear and that their interventions have a lasting impact on the world. The real struggle becomes over how that story will be re-told, and it is here that Owen's final battle lies.

In *The Darling* a similar sense of the imminence of an event indelibly marks Hannah's early life: "For years, since adolescence, I'd lived with the sense that soon, very soon, something life changing, maybe world changing was going to happen, that a political Second Coming was locked into the calendar, into my personal calendar. That belief had made my life seem exciting to me and purposeful" (53). Hannah here makes explicit Badiou's fundamental insight that fidelity to an event and its potentiality sustains and even defines any subject. Moreover, it is precisely this being-in-the-world as subject that Hannah feels she squanders in her later years:

> *The years I had spent being other people*, had displaced, erased, obliterated the girl I had been in my early twenties. The idealistic girl who was passionate about justice, especially for people of color, the girl who was convinced that in the fight for justice her life and sacrifice would count for something. The girl who, in the interests of justice and equality for all people everywhere, was perfectly willing to break as many laws as seemed necessary. The girl who found moral clarity in the phrase *by any means necessary*. (396)

While she acknowledges that this is because "the dream of a truly democratic socialist revolution in America or anywhere else in the so-called developed world had died shortly after 1969," she becomes a subject once again following on the heels of her conversations with the imprisoned Charles Taylor:

> But as Charles continued to describe his vision of a Liberia that was free and democratic and economically self-sufficient, a small country quietly going about its own business of providing its own food and shelter and health care and education, trading agricultural products with the rest of the world for the technology and manufactured goods it would require and no more than what it required—no luxury goods, he said, no Mercedes limos or Rolex watches, no private jets, nothing imported that did not advance the people as a whole—I began to believe that it could be done. It could happen, and very possibly Charles Taylor was the man who could make it happen. (294–295)

It is this renewed fidelity, Hannah also maintains, that makes her different from so many others in her generation: "The very idea of revolution, which in the late sixties and early seventies had seemed ready for immanence [sic], had been turned into a comic metaphor for self-indulgent self-delusion. Not for me, however" (334). She notes shortly thereafter that her meeting with Taylor had re-kindled "a certain long-held dream of violence against people and institutions and governments that exploited the poor and the weak—a dream that over the years had faded and nearly been forgotten, but that had been called back vividly into service by Charles Taylor" (340).

This vision gives Hannah upon her return to Liberia focus and a sense of purpose, and she quickly persuades Samuel Doe to allow her to create an international primate sanctuary. Her work with the chimpanzees also leads her to a new insight concerning what she describes as

> the built-in limitations of empathy. . . . We who have more power in the world, like men with good intentions, try to empathize with those who have less. We try to experience racism as if I who am white were black, to see the world as if I who am sighted were blind, and to reason and communicate as if I who am human were non-human. . . .
>
> I'm talking here about the difference between *empathy* and *sympathy*, between feeling *for* the other and feeling *with* the other. The distinction came to matter to me. It still does. When you abandon and betray those with whom you empathize, you're not abandoning or betraying anyone

or anything that's as real as yourself. Taken to its extreme, perhaps even pathological, form, empathy is narcissism.[36]

Here, Hannah offers the vision of a new foundation not only for political action but for communities forged across different interests and needs.

At first glance, then, it would seem that events in Liberia that occur shortly after the "first death" of the Cold War period (the 1989 fall of the Berlin Wall and the subsequent demise of the Soviet-dominated second world) have finally extinguished Hannah's fidelity, as she subsequently asserts, "I did not know what Charles Taylor would become and what he and the thousands of men and boys who followed him would do to the people of Liberia and to my family and to my dreamers. I could not have imagined it" (341). In a grotesque parody of the authentic event, it is the genocide in modern Liberia and West Africa, as in the former territories of Yugoslavia or later in Darfur, that serves as the actualized improbable impossibility of the post–Cold War world. However, as the last sentences of the novel make clear, and where the significance of the title is also finally revealed, it is in fact only the "second death" of 9/11 that brings both Hannah's personal story and the larger cultural and political possibilities of which she was a part to their definitive conclusion:

> And that is how I got to Abidjan, where I boarded a Ghana Airways flight to New York and made my way home to a nation terrorized and grieving on a scale that no American had imagined before, a nation whose entire history was being rapidly rewritten. In the months that followed, I saw that the story of my life could have no significance in the larger world. In the new history of America, mine was merely the story of an American darling, and had been from the beginning.[37]

In rendering this final damning judgment upon her life, Hannah invokes Anton Chekov's fin-de-siècle tale "The Darling" (1899), identifying herself with the story's protagonist, Olga Semyonovna. Olga is singularly without subjectivity, her views and behaviors mimicking those of the various men with whom she becomes connected: "Her husband's ideas were hers. If he thought the room was too hot, or that business was slack, she thought the same. Her husband did not care for entertainments, and on holidays he stayed at home. She did likewise."[38] Hannah now likewise judges herself to have been similarly always already without any real subjective being. Earlier on, Hannah resisted efforts by others to hollow out her selfhood: "And everyone wanted me to stay exactly where I was. *You're beautiful, Hannah darling, don't ever change. Stay in your box*" (188). What these others could not accomplish, however, the events of 9/11 will finally and definitively achieve.

Here lies *The Darling'*s assessment of the deeper tragedy of September 11, 2001: not only has the renewed sense of the potential for radical change in the world, of an event or an improbable impossibility, that was characteristic of the 1990s been once more extinguished, its very real presence in the past is occluded as well, and a baleful new sense of capitalist realism and its own set of improbabilities and impossibilities put into place.[39] Of course, as Banks's work also notes, this too is a process with an agency, the reigning powers actively rewriting and revising both the American past and present.

In such a situation, the labor of the critical realist novelist is again transformed: another among the company of Walter Benjamin's historical materialists, such a writer struggles "to hold fast that image of the past which unexpectedly appears to the historical subject in a moment of danger." Benjamin then concludes in a way that effectively grasps the continued urgency of *The Darling*, and indeed of all of Banks's work: "The only historian capable of fanning the spark of hope in the past is the one who is firmly convinced that *even the dead* will not be safe from the enemy if he is victorious. And this enemy has never ceased to be victorious."[40]

NOTES

1   For a useful comparison of *Rule of the Bone* with *Adventures of Huckleberry Finn*, see Kenneth Millard, *Coming of Age in Contemporary American Fiction* (Edinburgh: Edinburgh University Press, 2007), 16–31.

2   I take the concept of the throwaway from Evan Watkins's brilliant diagnosis of an emergent global service economy, *Throwaways: Work Culture and Consumer Education* (Stanford, CA: Stanford University Press, 1993). I discuss Watkins's book in more detail in *Life between Two Deaths, 1989–2001:*

U.S. Culture in the Long Nineties (Durham, NC: Duke University Press, 2009), 111–116.

3   Russell Banks, *Rule of the Bone: A Novel* (New York: HarperCollins, 1995), 248. Hereafter cited parenthetically in text.

4   Aristotle, *Poetics*, in *Critical Theory since Plato*, ed. Hazard Adams (San Diego, CA: Harcourt Brace Jovanovich, 1971), 63.

5   Ibid., 64.

6   Richard McKeon, "Literary Criticism and the Concept of Imitation in Antiquity," *Modern Philology* 34, no. 1 (1936): 1, 18.

7   Aristotle, *Poetics*, 65.

8   *Critical Link. Guide to Aristotle: Poetics. Guide to Book XXIV;* http://www .english.hawaii.edu/criticalink/aristotle/gloss/gloss24.html.

9   For a discussion of the distinction between science fiction and fantasy and the often-implicit evaluative criteria at work in it (but not in terms of his own dialectical treatment), see Fredric Jameson, *Archaeologies of the Future: The Desire Called Utopia and Other Science Fictions* (New York: Verso, 2005), 57–71.

10   Phillip E. Wegner, "Greimas avec Lacan; or, From the Symbolic to the Real in Dialectical Criticism," *Criticism* 51, no. 2 (2009): 211–245; and "Lacan avec Greimas: Formalization, Theory, and the 'Other Side' of the Study of Culture," *Minnesota Review* 77 (2011): 62–86. A revised and expanded version of the first essay is the centerpiece of my book *Periodizing Jameson: Dialectics, the University, and the Desire for Narrative* (Evanston, IL: Northwestern University Press, 2014).

11   David Foster Wallace, *Everything and More: A Compact History of Infinity* (New York: Norton, 2010), 65.

12   Russell Banks, *The Darling* (New York: HarperCollins, 2004), 392. Hereafter cited parenthetically in text.

13   I discuss the development and importance of cognitive mapping in Jameson's work from the 1980s onward in *Periodizing Jameson.*

14   Catherine Gallagher, "What Would Napoleon Do? Historical, Fictional, and Counterfactual Characters," *New Literary History* 42 (2011): 315–336.

15   See Epps's *New York Times* obituary published March 27, 1897, online at http://query.nytimes.com/gst/abstract.html?res=F10613FF3F5913738D DDAE0A94DB405B8785F0D3. Banks briefly touches on his fictionalization of Epps's life in Mel Gussow, "John Brown Lives Anew as a Writer's Inspiration," *New York Times* (April 27, 1998); available online at http:// www.nytimes.com/1998/04/27/books/john-brown-lives-anew-as-a -writer-s-inspiration.html?pagewanted=all&src=pm. Finally, for a fascinating exchange between the historian James M. McPherson and Banks on the historical accuracy of *Cloudsplitter,* see Mark C. Carnes, ed., *Novel*

History: Historians and Novelists Confront America's Past (and Each Other) (New York: Simon and Schuster, 2001), 61–76.

16   Banks's most recent novel, *Lost Memory of Skin* (2011), returns for its setting to the Florida that, along with New Hampshire, had been a major setting of his earlier fictions. However, even in this work, Banks makes an explicit connection to his Adirondacks novels: appearing late in the action is the bus driver, Dolores Driscoll, from *The Sweet Hereafter*. See Russell Banks, *Lost Memory of Skin* (New York: HarperCollins, 2011), 325–328.

17   "Yoknapatawpha County," in *People, Places, and Events: A Faulkner Glossary*, http://www.mcsr.olemiss.edu/~egjbp/faulkner/glossary.html.

18   For a significant discussion of modernist regionalisms, see Susan Hegeman, *Patterns for America: Modernism and the Concept of Culture* (Princeton, NJ: Princeton University Press, 1999), especially 19–27, 126–157.

19   Fredric Jameson, *The Geopolitical Aesthetic: Cinema and Space in the World System* (Bloomington: Indiana University Press, 1992), 3–4.

20   For a reading of John Brown's life and work that places it squarely within the context of the Haitian and other slave revolts of the early nineteenth century, see W. E. B. Du Bois, *John Brown* (New York: Modern Library, 2001); for the influence of the Haitian Revolution on Hegel, see Susan Buck-Morss, *Hegel, Haiti, and Universal History* (Pittsburgh: University of Pittsburgh Press, 2009). I discuss both Du Bois's and Buck-Morss's arguments in "W. E. B. Du Bois's Universal History: Crisis and Generic Innovation in *John Brown* (1909)" (unpublished essay).

21   For a now-classic analysis of the labor of the noir detective, see Fredric Jameson, "On Raymond Chandler," *Southern Review* 6, no. 3 (1970): 624–650. I also use this model in my discussion of John D. MacDonald's *The Executioners*, the 1959 novel that was the basis of the two *Cape Fear* films (1962 and 1991), in *Life between Two Deaths*, 88–95.

22   Jameson discusses the ontological limits mapped in the noir fictions of Raymond Chandler in "The Synoptic Chandler," in *Shades of Noir: A Reader*, ed. Joan Copjec (New York: Verso, 1993), 33–56.

23   For a sampling of work in this emerging field, see Cary Wolfe, *Animal Rites: American Culture, the Discourse of Species, and Posthumanist Theory* (Chicago: University of Chicago Press, 2003); Leonard Lawlor, *This Is Not Sufficient: An Essay on Animality and Human Nature in Derrida* (New York: Columbia University Press, 2007); Jacques Derrida, *The Animal That Therefore I Am*, trans. David Wills (New York: Fordham University Press, 2008); Ron Broglio, *Surface Encounters: Thinking with Animals and Art* (Minneapolis: University of Minnesota Press, 2011); and Glenn Willmott, *Modern Animalism: Habitats of Scarcity and Wealth in Comics and Literature* (Toronto: University of Toronto Press, 2012). For a useful overview of the ethical turn in literary studies, see Dorothy J. Hale, "Aesthetics

and the New Ethics: Theorizing the Novel in the Twenty-First Century," *PMLA* 124, no. 3 (May 2009): 896–905; and the engagement with Hale's claims in John J. Su, *Imagination and the Contemporary Novel* (Cambridge: Cambridge University Press, 2011), 155–156.

24 Watkins similarly notes that, already in an early-1990s service economy, "destabilization brings together, in the same social spaces, people who occupy those spaces across multiple and often conflicting interests, values, and behaviors. And it thereby creates conditions that can lead to intense antagonisms, which are only heightened by the breakdown of categories that no longer supply the norms of behavior in the situation. Even the simplest, most routine everyday behavior can become a 'problem' requiring negotiation." *Throwaways*, 45.

25 Banks, "In Response to James McPherson's Reading of *Cloudsplitter*," in *Novel History*, 71.

26 Russell Banks, *Cloudsplitter* (New York: HarperCollins, 1998), 107. Hereafter cited parenthetically in text.

27 Interest in Villard's biography has waned as more readers have turned to a book published immediately before it and at the time savaged by Villard and his supporters, W. E. B. Du Bois's *John Brown* (1909). For a useful overview of the relationship between Villard and Du Bois, see David Roediger, Introduction to *John Brown* by W. E. B. Du Bois, xi–xxii.

28 Joseph Conrad, *Lord Jim* (New York: Penguin, 1989), 292.

29 Ibid., 606–607. I discuss the alternate history in "The Last Bomb: Historicizing History in Terry Bisson's *Fire on the Mountain* and Gibson and Sterling's *The Difference Engine*," *The Comparatist* 23 (1999): 141–151; and "Learning to Live in History: Alternate Historicities and the 1990s in *The Years of Rice and Salt*," in *Kim Stanley Robinson Maps the Unimaginable: Critical Essays*, ed. William J. Burling (Jefferson, NC: MacFarland, 2009), 98–112. Bisson's novel is of particular interest as it is about what could have happened if the raid at Harpers Ferry succeeded.

30 Alain Badiou, *Ethics: An Essay on the Understanding of Radical Evil*, trans. Peter Hallward (New York: Verso, 2001), 41.

31 Peter Hallward, *Badiou: A Subject to Truth* (Minneapolis: University of Minnesota Press, 2003), xxv, 114.

32 Badiou, *Ethics*, 51.

33 Ernst Bloch, The *Principle of Hope*, trans. Neville Plaice, Stephen Plaice, and Paul Knight (Oxford: Basil Blackwell, 1986), 223.

34 Slavoj Žižek, *Tarrying with the Negative: Kant, Hegel, and the Critique of Ideology* (Durham, NC: Duke University Press, 1993), 96–97.

35 Alain Badiou, *Being and Event*, trans. Oliver Feltham (New York: Continuum, 2005), 193, 202–203.

36 Ibid., 326–327. For a more detailed discussion of this passage and the

theme of narcissism in the novel, see Aliki Varvogli, "Radical Mother-hood: Narcissism and Empathy in Russell Banks's *The Darling* and Dana Spiotta's *Eat the Document*," *Journal of American Studies* 44, no. 4 (2010): 657–673.

37　Varvogli, "Radical Motherhood," 392. I develop the concept of 9/11 as a "second death" in more detail in *Life between Two Deaths*.

38　Anton Chekov, "The Darling," http://www.eastoftheweb.com/short -stories/UBooks/Darl.shtml. Mary Gordon also connects the novel to Chekov's story in her review, "'The Darling': Among the Dreamers," *New York Times* (October 24, 2004), http://www.nytimes.com/2004/10/24/ books/review/24GORDONL.html; and Russell Banks suggests the link between Hannah and Olga, as well as with Emma Bovary, in Valentin Lo-coge, "An Interview with Russell Banks," *Cercles: Revue Pluridisciplinaire du Monde Anglophone* (2005), http://www.cercles.com/interviews/banks .html.

39　The renewal of radical possibility in the 1990s is a central concern of *Life between Two Deaths*; see especially chapters 1, 7, and 8.

40　Walter Benjamin, "On the Concept of History," in *Selected Writings, Volume 4, 1938–1940* (Cambridge, MA: Harvard University Press, 2003), 391.

PART II *Genres of Mediation*

Capitalist Realism and Serial Form

The Fifth Season of *The Wire*

LEIGH CLAIRE LA BERGE

> Work it like a real case and it will feel like a real case. And, more importantly, it will read like a real case. —Detective Lester Freamon, *The Wire*

When speaking about *The Wire*, the HBO series he co-created with Ed Burns, David Simon frequently compares the show to a nineteenth-century realist novel and suggests that any particular episode might be read as an individual chapter. Indeed, some critics, following Simon himself, have used the term *visual novel* to mark *The Wire*'s radical break with standard televisual aesthetics.[1] Simon, of course, is not the first to compare television to nineteenth-century realism. In his 1954 "How to Look at Television," Theodor Adorno unfavorably compared mystery shows to nineteenth-century French novels and concluded:

> The meandering and endless plots and subplots [in the novels] hardly allowed the readers . . . to be continuously aware of the moral. Readers could expect anything to happen. This no longer holds true. Every spectator of a television mystery knows with absolute certainty how it is going to end. Tension is but superficially maintained and is unlikely to have a serious effect anymore. . . . The spectator feels on safe ground all the time.[2]

Of course, nothing within the formal constraints of television necessitates its lack of realism any more than the printing press assures the production of dime novels.[3] Nonetheless, only a handful of television programs in some fifty years have used the medium of television, with its combination of film's visuality and print culture's seriality, to raise the medium to, as Adorno famously defined art elsewhere, the level of "negative knowledge of the actual world."[4] That Simon explains its structure in terms of the nineteenth-century realist novel is unsurprising, then. Simon strives for the aesthetic and mimetic credibility of literary realism precisely because critics such as Adorno made it critical common sense to think that television could not accomplish more. And if, since Adorno, television has been derided as a conveyer of a commercialized, vernacular culture, then the realist novel has been hailed since Georg Lukács as the only generic medium that can glimpse the historical truth of social totality.[5]

This essay first explores *The Wire*'s televisual realism and then examines that realism through the show's fifth season, the one judged by critics to be *nonrealist*.[6] I argue that the fifth season adds a new element to the realist series as the production of representation itself is brought into view through an examination of Baltimore's *Sun* and other news-media outlets. In season 5, realism is transformed from a mode into an object as Simon and Burns turn their attention to the production of realism itself in its serial form. Season 5 does for serial realism what the other seasons did for the unions, the schools, and the criminal justice system: it allows us to watch the production of an institution with all its internal compromises and failures. I locate this self-reflexivity chiefly in the actions of Detectives Jimmy McNulty and Lester Freamon, who replace Marlo Stanfield, the series' most ruthless killer, with a fictitious serial killer in order to divert money from other city agencies to their now-underfunded police department. The Baltimore police "couldn't catch a real serial killer, well, maybe they need the make-believe" (5.3[7]), McNulty explains, as the violence of a white media economy is narratively substituted for that of a black drug economy. This narrative substitution, together with the bifurcation of the representation of real and fictitious racialized violence, become the season's central narrative tension and provide, among other things, a form of self-critique that had been absent. Thus, the fifth season departs from the previous four, whose defining aesthetic feature was their realism as measured against a black underclass and the violence of its illicit economies. By substituting the melodrama of newsroom-serial violence for the structural violence of urban poverty as the main narrative thread, season 5 invites us to critique the relationships among race, violence, economy, and seriality in the construction of realism.

The Wire in its entirety demonstrates how realism is always economic realism, what I will refer to as *capitalist realism*, a term from the visual arts that I think deserves broader translation into cultural studies.[8] The entire series is an investigation into how the realistic representation of an urban nexus of race and economy reveals forms of social violence—structural and interpersonal—as a kind of metonymic totality. Season 5 continues to engage this problematic, but at the metaformal level. It invites us to examine the racialized trope of seriality itself, particularly racialized serial violence as it undergirds the television series. The representation of black economic violence produces one form of seriality—that is, the series' realism. Conversely, white fictitious killing, the form of seriality that emerges in season 5, offers a critique of the series' previous realism and its reception. *Black serial killing* is read transparently as economic: it is treated as real within the narrative frame, and it is read as realist by the viewer; *white serial killing* is treated as psychological within the narrative frame and therefore read as not realist by the viewer.[9]

It is the representation of money itself through which these tensions among race, realism, and serial form are mediated, distributed, and narrated. The representation of black economic violence produces the series' realism by fetishizing illicit economic activity and giving us a model with which to proceed: follow the money. But in season 5, this proposition is reversed: following the money trail no longer produces the series' realism; rather, the series' realism begins to be sold for money, as McNulty and the fraudulent *Sun* reporter, Scott Templeton, inadvertently collude to fabricate a serial killer, and this transposition is structured through the representation of a kind of white, psychological violence that seems, at the level of content, to disavow the economic. This essay develops along similar lines: I follow the representation of money until it cannot be followed any further, and I argue that, at the end of the money trail in season 5, we find a transformed representation of realism itself. Capitalist realism, then, addresses itself to the realistic representation of the commodification of realism; it renders dynamic the tension so ably located in a text such as Walter Benn Michaels's *The Gold Standard and the Logic of Naturalism* (1988) but nonetheless presented there as static—namely, the tension between the representation of capitalist circuitry and a vantage point from which to evaluate it.

Predictably, then, *The Wire*'s fifth season must endure the charge that it has abandoned the very realism that so many critics and viewers cherished. In the popular press—really, the only one that has yet engaged the fifth season—the level of critical anticipation that greeted that season was matched only by the immediate disappointment that followed it.[10] The fifth season *is* the series' most didactic. From the season's first episode, whose epigraph is a quote by laconic Detective "William 'Bunk' Moreland"—"The bigger the lie, the more they believe"—to Detective Norris's response that "Americans are a stupid people by and large. We pretty much believe whatever we're told," the editorializing is heavy-handed, if not condescending (5.1). Those who actually are in the business of editorializing, the staff at the newspaper, are presented as remarkably uncomplicated and divided between the neat ethical and characterological dichotomies of good and bad, ambitious and restrained, and narcissistic and intersubjective—all mutually exclusive divisions which intimate a kind of melodramatic tone throughout the season.[11]

Meanwhile, the viewer is aware that all discussions within the narrative frame about the production of news are simultaneously discussions of *The Wire*'s own narrative choices: "We don't want some amorphous series detailing society's ills," one of the managing editors quips during an editorial board meeting (5.1). But we would be wrong to agree with the *Sun*'s own review of the show, which claims that "the most disappointing aspect of [season 5] is that Simon offers such a simplistic critique of media and their effects on mass consciousness" or to agree with Simon's own claim that season 5 is about "perception versus reality."[12] When a series noted for its realism changes its narrative frame from realist, economically driven violence to sensationalist serial killing, the first response of the critic needs to be to the problem of seriality itself. Most literally, an examination of the fictitious serial killer is an examination of the narrative device that kills the series (if nothing else), and in representing what kills the series this device provides a site to understand what had enlivened it, structured it, and in a word, made it real.

Capitalist Realism

The Wire has correctly been labeled as unique to the televisual medium for its use of a realist mode. It tends to eschew melodrama, sentimentality, romance, and excessive individualism, and it minimizes their associated techniques of nondiegetic sound, flashback, voice-over, dream sequence, and dialogue-dependent jump cuts. In their place, the show uses long tracking shots, wide-framed environmental shots, and many exterior settings, as well as incorporating forms of surveillance into the viewer's point "perspective" through photograph-like freeze-frame shots. The viewer is repeatedly reminded of the techniques of viewing and spectatorship through this last device, a reminder that serves to highlight that the show's realism is produced through the voyeuristic viewing of black, informal, and illicit economic formations. Conversely, the revelatory pleasure of viewing illicit economic activity stands in for the desired moment of viewing the economic per se. If something as derided, secretive, and illicit as the drug trade may be represented, then what economic activity may not be represented? All of these might be considered *The Wire*'s techniques of the real, under which we could also group the old Soviet theater technique of having real-life individuals play themselves. Here, Baltimore police, news reporters, politicians, and dealers (including former Baltimore mayor Kurt Schmoke) appear as themselves on the show; former *Sun* reporter David Simon himself makes an appearance in season 5. And certainly *The Wire*'s expansive, plotting, methodological realism is made possible by its serial, as opposed to episodic, form. There is little sense of narrative progress; instead, progress and narrative are disentangled as each season follows a novel-like spatialization of Baltimore. Simon suggests that *The Wire* "sprawl[s] a story over a city," and indeed narrativization and spatialization go hand in hand to reveal the mechanics of a deindustrialized city, from its addicts to its union members, from its politicians to its developers, and, of course, from its police force to its drug dealers. And, finally, in its trenchant socioeconomic study of Baltimore as both specific and typical, *The Wire* implicates the late capitalist urban sphere as such.

There are many potential sites from which to examine *The Wire's* realism. Raymond Williams has said that the realist novel needs "a genuine community: a community of persons linked not merely by one kind of relationship—work or friendship or family—but by many, interlocking kinds."[13] Realist television requires something similar, and *The Wire* meets that requirement through demarcating the circulation of what actually does link us all: money.[14] The ostensible object of the Major Crimes Unit is the drug trade and the violence necessary to sustain it, but, as Lester argues in the first season, "if you follow the drugs, you get drug dealers and drug addicts, but if you follow the money, you don't know where it will take you" (1.8). Indeed, by the series' end, Lester's claim that, if we "follow the money" we realize that "we're all vested, [that] every one of us [is] complicit," has been understood to be the simultaneous foundation and destination of the show. Lester's claim also emphasizes that the difference between a specific commodity, in this case heroin, and its abstract incarnation as money will be treated as a narrative problem in the series.

In this section, I analyze how *The Wire's* representation of money structures its capitalist realist aesthetic but also how, as with all money forms, a tension emerges between money's dual roles as a medium of exchange and as a store of value.[15] In the first four seasons, the tension is managed through tracing money as it is exchanged, representing otherwise obscure connections as they come into contact. Money is the narrative device that places the socially legitimate characters in the same contemporaneous time/space as the mostly black, criminally illegitimate ones; money is also the narrative device that places the viewer in that same time/space. Everyone has an interest in money, after all; money also, quite literally, has an interest in everyone. In the fifth season, however, there is a structural reversal between money being exchanged, in order to enable representation, and representation being *sold* as though it were simply another commodity, a store of value that may now circulate as freely as any other. It is the narrative maintenance and exfoliation of this contradiction—between money as medium and as store of value—as a narrative problem that renders *The Wire* what I am calling a kind of *capitalist realism*. This is a term that literary and cultural studies is just beginning to incorporate, although Patrick Brantlinger's claim that realistic fiction "is always in some sense about money" certainly establishes a foundation for such a move; it also shows how necessary it is to specify the operations of money that will become realism's objects.[16]

My claim is that each of these aspects of money—medium of exchange and store of value—is marked by a distinctive symbolic and iconographic vocabulary through *The Wire*'s representations of racialized, serialized violence. When money is represented in the service of exchange, the viewer sees an illicit economy of mostly black entrepreneurs whose representation seems to disallow symbolic abstraction or self-critique; violence is seen as interpersonal and purposefully economic. This connection between race, violence, and economy in the service of realism is represented most dramatically by Marlo, a serial killer whose race and economic acumen prevent him from appearing as one. But it is also present in the representations of money that obtain through various characters' conceptions of it. If those characters of the street have more varied, interesting, and contradictory philosophies of money, it is because in *The Wire* money itself is being marked as a racialized form, and money has its own narrative limits and possibilities when it operates in an illicit context. Variations on money are a key preoccupation of the series, since they offer a site for the maximum exploration of the formal properties of money as money in the maintenance of an even, disinterested, and realistic representation of the act of exchange. Throughout the first four seasons, and particularly in the context of the drug trade, a respectful distance is observed: money can buy everything except the truth, because the truth is, as Marlo himself claims, that "money is money." This tautology is both adhered to and critiqued throughout the series; it tracks a structural transformation that is deeply implicated in the relationship between money and realism. If capitalist realism is the realistic representation of the commodification of realism, then it must also identify the difference between money that represents money and money that represents realism.

Many characters on the show possess a distinctive philosophy of money, and these philosophies are in frequent contact and tension. Lester is a Georg Simmel–like philosopher of money whose dedication to tracing and thus narrating its circulation, to "routing it all over town," is the verbalization of Simon's sprawling city. When State Senator Clay "Cash and Carry" Davis tries to buy him off, Lester responds, "I don't get paid like that. I get paid when I come back with questions and you, sir, have answers" (5.9). Clay Davis is, in fact, a veritable mediating institution between formal and informal economies. With the arrival of a subpoena, he exclaims, "Money laundering? They gonna talk to me about money laundering in West Baltimore? Where do they think I'm gonna raise money? . . . I'll take any motherfucker's money if he's giving it away." Proposition Joe simply states that the only worthwhile business ethos is "buy for a dollar, sell for two" (4.2). Each of these philosophies is distinct but also commensurable, and that is a result of the money form itself. On *The Wire*, characterization is almost always action based, and characters repeatedly narrate, act out, and represent their own philosophies of money.

Omar's approach to money befits his own occupation as a stickup boy: "Money ain't got no owners, only spenders." When McNulty searches Stringer Bell's apartment after his murder, he finds a copy of *The Wealth of Nations*. But minor character Slim Charles is the true Smithian economist. When he learns that other drug crews' expansions are threatening certain profitable corners in East Baltimore, he complains, "All this theorizing about how it's all product and not territory; you can't talk that shit if a nigga's snatching all of your territory and won't take none of your product" (4.4). Slim Charles thus presents the classic dilemma of any political economy: how to balance the relationship between control of space and the rate of profit, a problem complicated by the fact that money does not necessarily buy real estate within the drug trade.[17] When Avon Barksdale declares, "Since when do we buy corners? We take corners," he is making a claim that delineates the limits of money in the drug trade. But just as forcefully Stringer Bell responds, "You're gonna buy one way or another. . . . [You buy with] time in the joint that's behind us or ahead of us. You gonna get some shit in this game but it ain't shit for free" (3.6). Marx describes money as a "general equivalent" for its ability to bring disparate spheres of social life together and to "level all distinction."[18] It is Stringer, more than anyone else, who maintains the hope that money *can* be a general equivalent, that all time and space can be monetized and circulated. For Stringer, of course, this philosophy of money turns out to be a utopian promise; he is gunned down by Omar and Brother Mouzone at his nascent downtown condominium site but not before being told, "You still don't get it, do you, huh? This ain't about your money" (3.11).

It is Marlo, however, whose approach to money rivals Lester's in determining the series' denouement. Marlo, the only character to succeed in getting himself with his money out of the ghetto, cannot (or will not) think metaphorically about it. When Andre, one of his dealers, is robbed by Omar, Marlo tells him that he still expects to be paid. Andre then enters into an elaborate discussion about risk and insurance, about the need to be exempt from debt in extraordinary circumstances. He then proffers a metaphor: "You know what he's [Omar] like?" he asks Marlo. Omar is "like a terrorist" and he himself is "like Delta Airlines"; when there is a terrorist attack, the government supports legitimate institutions because the chief object of a terrorist attack is legitimacy itself. Marlo responds with his characteristic intense gaze, both empty and evocative at the same time: "Omar ain't no terrorist. He's just another nigga with a gun. And you ain't no Delta Airlines. You just another nigga who got his shit took" (4.4).

In this instance, a lack of metaphorical approach toward money showcases Marlo's power; in season 5, however, the same lack seems as if it might limit his ability to transact outside the illicit economy. When he attempts to circumvent Proposition Joe and deal directly with the wholesaler and chief heroin supplier, Spiros Vondopolous, he brings a briefcase full of cash, which is summarily refused on the grounds that the money is "dirty." Confused, Marlo replies—and this is perhaps the key narrative tension of the entire series—"Money is money. What's the difference who bring it to you?" (5.4). Vondopolous responds that he was "talking in symbols," but Marlo, of course, doesn't traffic in symbols, a characteristic on display again when he flies to the French Antilles and asks to "see my money," after it has been laundered and deposited there. Just as Marlo does not engage with money's symbolic qualities, *The Wire* does not engage with Marlo symbolically; his economic violence represents economic violence, and he lacks any interiority.

These philosophies of money, each with its own idiosyncrasies, are related through exchange; in turn, the representation of exchange creates connections, just as it also creates an extended present within the story frame. The traveling shot—repeatedly used on the street, and particularly in scenes with Joe and Marlo—is one formal mechanism for representing how monetary circulation connects temporal development with a spatial situatedness. In one such shot from season 4, we see Joe and Marlo sitting on a hilltop bench while discussing which agency might be conducting surveillance of Marlo. The shot opens from the left of the screen, and we see a line of row houses behind the characters as their bodyguards stand in the immediate background. As the conversation progresses, however, the camera begins traveling toward the right so that the background opens up and reveals an expansive cityscape. This single take continues for upward of fifty seconds, and during its course Joe and Marlo travel from the far right to the far left of the mise-en-scène while the depth of the shot remains constant (4.7.16 minutes). This shot, which is almost circular but never completes the full pan, is repeated in many scenes in which an illicit transaction transpires. In a remarkably similar scene, Joe calls the police department from a phone booth and pretends to be a lawyer. The camera travels around him upward of thirty seconds, providing a 270-degree panorama (4.8.29 minutes). Indeed, such transactions demand the outdoor setting and panoramic vision it provides, while the circularity reveals movement without progress and a momentary equality through exchange that, we know, will soon be fractured, only to be immediately reestablished elsewhere. In both scenes, the camera movement recapitulates the narrative movement as it "follows the money."

The *different* economies that result from the circulation of a *general* equivalent ground the show's realism at several levels. Realism must always be economic realism in that capital itself is what is most obfuscated. Capital itself, then, becomes a kind of apotheosis of the potential of realist representation; and the only narrative of realism must be to follow the money, as *the money* is the original condition for the realism itself.[19] Poverty has long been a site of realist fixation because it is what is most economically necessary and simultaneously what is most ideologically disavowed within capitalism.

The representation of money produces a realism that hopes to render not a metonymic totality, in which a temporal part stands in for the historical whole, but rather to render all equivalent, to show that any one point in space may be exchanged for or through any other. This spatial logic is, of course, central to *The Wire*'s focus on the economic spaces hidden behind regulatory and juridical structures. The narrative does not provide totality by representing "the other half" of what usually remains unseen; rather, it shows how what remains unseen produces the conditions for sight itself. In a similar manner, the war on drugs is not futile (although it is futile so far as ending the drug trade). The war on drugs is *productive*, and through the regulation of vice, capital creates a new channel for itself to circulate ever more freely as more and more material becomes available for monetization.[20]

But if all is rendered equivalent, then at some point representation itself must meet a similar fate: representation, too, enters a circuit of exchange. And this, I think, should be the mark of a narrative form of capitalist realism. Season 5's final confrontation between McNulty and the state attorney, Rhonda "Ronnie" Pearlman, concerns identifying "who lost the money trail": those who refused to follow it (i.e., the state) or those who followed it illegally (i.e., McNulty and Lester). Ronnie argues to McNulty and Lester that "you lost the money trail when you decided to start coloring outside the lines." Within the police department's own administration, the accusation is different. Police Deputy of Operations William Rawls criticizes McNulty by asking, "This was all for money? You couldn't live without the OT [overtime]?" McNulty answers, "It wasn't about the money," but he can hardly disagree with Rawls's retort that "you got paid." With the collapse of the Marlo Stanfield case, the fact that there will be "no assets investigation" is essentially the coda that ends the series. Even *The Wire* cannot follow the money as far as it goes. And this is a dichotomy that the series cannot rise above—its own medium of narrative exchange (money equals realism) is also its own store of value (realism requires money)—but rather must find a way to incorporate within its own content/form dichotomy. If these problems cannot be structurally overcome, then they can be made manifest. Following the exchange of money produces realism, but at a certain point, what is valued—that is, realistic representation of exchange—is traded *for* money. Season 5 does this by deviating, however briefly, from the money trail only to reveal how it is constituted at multiple levels, and this process allows for an emergence of the series' own interpretive system.

Serial Killers and Serial Realism

Each season of *The Wire* offers a critique of selected institutions as money circulates through them, and the differential aspects of these representations of money form what is perceived as the show's realism. The two institutions that ground the series—the police department and the drug trade—will be present in all seasons, while each individual season will have a mediating institution such as the port union, the schools, the city's democratic political machine, and so on. The specificity of these institutions provides a technical language, work ethic, and ethos for each particular season. The narrative of the show is to follow the money, but ultimately, of course, it is possible to follow the money only to the extent that everything is for sale, including, as revealed in season 5, representation itself. Now, with this understanding of what constitutes *The Wire*'s realism, I want to consider the continuities and discontinuities of the realist mode in season 5, and how season 5 both critiques and ultimately, I think, completes the series' realism.

Of course, there are also structural differences to consider in an analysis of the fifth season: there is the necessary limitation that it is the last, so there will be a certain amount of abruptness to new

characters and institutions; there is more of a focus on individual action and its effects, and therefore more of a theme of causality, which
is pitted against description in a manner that previous seasons had
avoided; and finally, one of the selected institutions represented in
season 5, homelessness, remains a kind of empty signifier inasmuch
as we are never given a sympathetic portrayal. Consequently, one
of the show's chief reality effects—the transposition of local sites of
work and knowledge into an immanent critique—is missing in its
homeless narrative thread, which serves only to confirm its fraudu-
lence in the story line. That said, many of the aforementioned formal
features remain consistent, and many of the criticisms of season 5 are
directed at the level of plot—that this type of fraud could not "really"
happen—or at the level of character—that the staff at the newspaper
is underdeveloped.[21]

I claimed earlier that the series' realism is structured through the
representation of money as it is exchanged in illicit spaces between
black, male bodies: the context of these exchanges is social and interpersonal violence. In season 5, this structure is abstracted, as it
were: the groundedness of economic violence is transformed into
the psychological violence of the serial killer. This psychological,
serial violence both critiques and undercuts the series' realism by
self-consciously moving the narrative from following the exchange of
money to create representation to now following the sale of representation for money. This meta-exchange produces the series' first sustained moments of self-referentiality and self-critique. Indeed, Simon
himself suggests that realism should avoid such tendencies. "Less is
more," he argues. "Explaining everything to the slowest or laziest
member of the audience destroys verisimilitude and reveals the movie itself, rather than the reality that the movie is trying to convey."[22]
For Simon, then, a focus on form is enough to compromise a realist
mode, yet this is precisely the turn that season 5 makes. Indeed, the
key institution of season 5 isn't so much "the media" or the *Sun* as it
is realism itself, and particularly realism in its serial form.

There are in fact four serial forms that structure season 5: (1) The
Sun's initial *series* on the failing Baltimore schools, which will be sus-
pended in favor of reportage on the fictitious serial killer and which

also had been the subject of the fourth season—thus this strain manifestly gestures toward the problem of self-reflexivity and critique; (2) Marlo Stanfield, the drug dealer/*serial* killer from previous seasons whose ruthless managerial style placed twenty-two murdered corpses in various abandoned houses throughout Baltimore; (3) the fictitious *serial* killer, invented by McNulty and Freamon, whose well-publicized terror causes the city to fund the police department again; and (4) *The Wire* itself, a realist television *series* that investigates the co-construction of race, violence, and money itself in the representation of urban space, moving seamlessly between the tropes of regulation and accumulation. If we accept, as I'm arguing, that serial realism is the key institution, then we have to restructure our perception that the institutional doubling that occurs in all seasons is between the police department and the *Baltimore Sun*; rather, it is now between serial violence and serial realism.[23] Under what conditions does the first constitute the second, and under what conditions does the second constitute the first?

Serial realism, is, of course, a very different institution from courts, ports, unions, or schools. But it does retain one feature common to all institutions on *The Wire*: its manifest representation reveals that it is failing. The *Sun* is the gateway to this critique: "This is not a good time for newspapers," one of the editors explains by way of introduction.[24] But by this point in the series, we know that *this* is not a good time for anything: not dealing, not policing, not unionizing, not teaching, and not reporting. Indeed, as we move through the series, we might be tempted to believe that the one institution that isn't failing is precisely the realist television series. The fourth season, the series' best, offered finally only an affective truth of indiscriminate suffering amidst structural poverty and racism, and the more punishing the characters' lives and livelihoods became, the more adept the series seemed to be at representing this truth. But the affective truths of "James-like authenticity" are seemingly jettisoned in season 5 with the arrival of the serial killer, who has the ironic effect of killing the realism in the series and nothing else.[25]

Can the language of seriality contribute to the show's own immanent critique in a manner similar to that in which the language of

industrial labor did in season 2? The term *serial killer* was coined in
the 1970s by the cofounder of the FBI's behavioral science unit, who
recalled that he had two things on his mind: first, the British designation "crime in series," and second, "the serial adventures we used
to see on Saturdays at the movies."[26] Thus, the term is the result of
detectives watching narrative violence, not fictional producers mimicking the language of detectivity. The structure of serial violence is
itself already a narrative form. Now, just as an accurate representation of the economy of drug dealing was used to ground the series'
realism, an economy of sensational, violent narrative will take its
place and critique that realism. Season 5 presents this problem as a
kind of challenge to its own realist mode: Can *The Wire* represent serial killing without itself succumbing to the discursive sensationalism
that defines the serial killer? Can the realist series escape the serial
killer?

One of the challenges of the fifth season, then, is to manage another genre, to collect its expectations in an almost novel-like manner
and synthesize these extrageneric elements into its form. Indeed, the
focus on the number of corpses left by Marlo, as well as the fact that
the Major Crimes Unit had had a betting pool on the number of bodies at the end of the fourth season (4.13), already intimate a certain
idea of seriality in its fixation with numerical representation. Preston
"Bodie" Broadus offers a characterization of Marlo that seems to in-
dict him as a serial killer: "This nigga kill motherfuckers just 'cause
he can, not 'cause they're snitching, not 'cause it's business, but 'cause
this shit just come natural to him" (4.13). But, of course, Marlo is not
a serial killer; his context forbids such a definition, and it is the differential racial, economic context that grounds the series' realism.
Indeed, the realist serial killer would seem to be an impossibly mixed
generic construction.

Throughout the fifth season, we are given a window into how the
substitution of serial (white, psychological) violence in place of interpersonal (black, economic) violence reflects the construction of an
aesthetic. "Work it like a real case, and it will feel like a real case.
More importantly, it will read like a real case," advises Lester as he
and McNulty wander through a homeless encampment. Lester's claim

is true enough: after all, the police always in some sense invent their object, and it is the working of it as though it were real that has guided the series' realism thus far. In response to his direction, McNulty asks Lester, "What do you want me to do?" "What detectives do, detective," Lester replies. Each phrase contains an ironic doubling of the keywords: real, real; do, do; detective, detective. As they search for their fictitious killer so that their case may appear real, they actually create a serial killer. McNulty hands a card to the man who will enact the killings that he and Templeton have been fictitiously describing and thus provide narrative closure to the season. Here, description produces the conditions it itself describes, a problematic that is a continual preoccupation of the fifth season and, in many ways, a deconstruction of a realist aesthetic. Thus, the doubling here is between serial violence and the form the serial takes. As McNulty walks among the homeless, he is bewildered. None of the photography, freeze-frames, or formal evidence of viewing are present; the viewer is not reminded of the viewing. Instead, the viewer recognizes a now-homeless stevedore from the second season—McNulty does not—which further highlights the self-referential motif within the show's own narrative frame.

We can locate a similar dynamic when McNulty confronts Templeton after the fictitious attempted abduction of a homeless man near the *Sun's* headquarters. When McNulty asks for a physical description of the serial killer, Templeton offers the following: "White guy, not heavy, not skinny either, six foot, nondescript." "Nondescript?" asks McNulty, as this conversation transpires between two of the few characters on the show who actually fit this description (5.10.23 minutes). "Yeah, nondescript," Templeton confirms. Like the previous dialogue between Lester and McNulty, this dialogue again contains an ironic doubling. *The Wire's* serial killer is, above all, an effect of the descriptions of McNulty and Templeton. This conversation is yet another instance of this production process, but it here transpires through a repetition of the term *nondescript*.

To this analysis we can add the fact that a serial killer *can* be nondescript. Serial killing is a genre unto itself—"Give people what they want from a serial killer," Lester encourages McNulty. Thus, together they decide to add bite marks to their corpses and consequently their fictitious case files. The serial killer offers the pleasure of genre, but so does the serial television program *The Wire* itself.[27] The viewers of *The Wire*, however, do not want a serial killer, but an economic killer. The joke, then, is to flatter the viewers and give them the pleasure of generic differentiation and identification. But this joke is also an insult: What do the viewers have invested in the economic killer, and, at the level of form, what is the difference between preferring one generic pleasure to the other? *The Wire*'s attempt simultaneously to manage two genres provides a site for a critique of genre and for an understanding of its own generic construction. Once put in place, the serial killer will circulate discursively. Indeed, discursivity is his place. This is not because, as *Sun* metro section editor Gus claims in classic newsroom phraseology, "if it bleeds it leads"—indeed, the entire series has been dedicated to showing just how contingent that claim is; rather, it is because if it bleeds and is noneconomic and nonstructural, then it leads.

But we could also rephrase this in the following way: violence committed in the commission of accumulation produces realism, whereas violence committed in the commission of gratification produces melodrama. The viewer of *The Wire* again is in an odd place; for her it is the violence committed in the commission of accumulation that produces gratification. On a structural level, the crucial difference between the serial killer and *The Wire* as a television series is that the serial killer disavows economy in the construction of his personal melodrama, whereas *The Wire* uses the representation of economy to ground its realism and disavow personal melodrama. Psychology disavows economy; economy disavows interiority. The narrative force, and challenge, of the fifth season is to bring these two together and attempt to hold them in tension. We know that Lester is "proud to be chasing Mr. Marlo Stanfield," and that "stupid criminals make stupid cops," but what effect do fictitious, fantastic criminals have on cops?

At one level, the fictitious serial killer kills the series by destroying for the viewer the fantasy of this, or perhaps of any, realism. The structural irony of the fifth season, of course, is that by fabricating noneconomic, de facto white, psychological violence, McNulty and

Freamon hope to produce a return to the economic scene. Indeed, it is only through the production of a fictitious serial killer that Marlo is killed and his crew is finally decimated, with some killed and others imprisoned. Obviously, this makes no difference at the level of drug distribution or saturation, but it certainly does make a difference at the level of narrative form and, specifically, how the series' content shapes and is shaped by its divergent narrative structures. When the fabrication of the serial killer is revealed, again we are returned to a critique of serial form. "The cases are not connected in any way," Lieutenant Cedric Daniels explains to "Councilman Tommy Carcetti." The claim is the converse of the show's most important narrative insistence, that if we follow the money, we realize that we are all connected in many ways. Obviously, the fact remains that the homeless are being murdered and are dying, but, without a sufficient and sensationalist narrative thread, that fact is uninteresting. And, of course, this is the point of the whole *series*. A narrative thread is needed to render the violence, but what the fifth season implies is that only certain narratives can render certain violence: realistic violence is only rendered interpersonally and requires the presence of an illicit black economy; there is no abstract, symbolic violence. We are given the shadowy, ambiguous figure of "the Greek" who is not Greek as a segue into the global economy, but this figure is really more of a hint at what remains *not* narrated and not represented in the show. Indeed, the serial killer is the first representation of a kind of abstract violence, and it is unable to be contained by the realistic narrative.

We might see this, however, as an effect of the type of capitalist realism that *The Wire* pursues. The old adage that "it takes money to make money" is here transformed into something like "it takes money to follow money." To obtain funds means, on some level, to relinquish the money trail narratively with the hope of returning to it again at some future point in time. The economic narrative, then, has been seemingly misplaced: the serial killer produces a structurally different narrative whose purpose is not to represent money, and to show how money is not represented. At some level, the serial killer kills the series by exposing the structural limits of the realist mode; at another level, the serial killer reconstructs the series by rendering visible its own conditions of production, circulation, and reception. The series asks its viewer to consider that realism dwells now in a new historical moment; it remains agnostic on the relationship between capitalist realism and older realisms of yore. And, of course, the serial killer plotline mocks the fact that *The Wire* itself has never garnered the kind of prize that the *Sun* does through its fraudulent reporting and shameful self-promotion.[28]

It falls to Lester to summarize, finally, the condition of possibility and limitation of the serial itself. Not only is representation being systemically sold off by Templeton and McNulty, but the hoped-for end of Lester's money trail, the information that leads to a grand jury indictment, is also revealed to have been for sale all along with the realization that city prosecutor Gary DiPasquale's gambling addiction has led him to sell sealed grand-jury information to criminal defense attorneys. Still, Lester is indefatigable: "If we can turn Levy and some of these other drug lawyers, we can route the money all over town. Sad business I know, but at least we know the truth now." For Lester, money produces information when it is *not* sold; but, for the political establishment, the journalistic establishment, all establishments, money is valued in itself, they want more of it, and that accumulation is realized through selling a certain kind of information. *The Wire* is not above this metabolism. It, too, begins to offer its viewer the kind of sensational, individualistic, melodramatic violence that it had spent the previous four seasons rejecting.

The Wire ultimately offers two alternative suggestions for representation at the end of the money trail: the first at the level of form, here realized as genre (from cop procedural to melodrama), and the second at the level of content. I claimed that "the money" can be followed only to the extent to which the perceptual world of representation is itself for sale. One reading of season 5's self-critique would posit that its own turn to sensationalism is a representation of the show "selling itself." But this is not the same as "selling out," since *The Wire* maintains a critical posture. Furthermore, this self-reflexivity contains an important formal lesson: When you follow the money, the one position that you are assured of reaching is an understanding of the vantage point that enabled you to get there. Because you realize that perception/representation is ultimately for sale, you now understand why it was so important to have followed the money in the first place. The generic transformation of season 5 indicates how such a claim may be made at the level of form.

The second suggestion is located in one of the few stories of individual redemption in the series: Bubbles overcomes his heroin addiction and the trauma of his accidental killing of his protégé, Sherrod. The point of this narrative thread in the series is not exactly individual redemption or personal development per se, but rather that Bubbles's transformation is coincident with his standing on a street corner and selling his own story in the *Sun*. His journey has been painfully but accurately represented. Not until he has a *Sun* reporter following him and willing to transform his suffering into a commodified narrative does he finally find the strength to narrate his own life at his Narcotics Anonymous meeting.

Both suggestions, however, insist that all narrative constructs—the first of realism and the second of real life—will, at some point, be sold. This conclusion—of my essay and of the series—should not be read as cynical. Indeed, it is actually more utopian and critical than the regressive fantasy that lurks throughout every season of *The Wire*: namely, the fantasy of a better capitalism, of a return to the Keynesian days of yore when community policing reigned, newspapers were robust sources of information, unions were powerful, schools taught children to read, and the CIA had not yet facilitated the importation of heroin into the United States from Southeast Asia.[29] One of the narratives that neoliberal capitalism generates is a haunting social nostalgia that "things were better then." But the logic of capital requires something different: things were better then on the condition that they are worse now. It is not until the realist mode, what *The Wire* distinguished itself in—indeed, what *The Wire* redefined in the world of television—is put up for sale in season 5 that the finality of this claim is realized: there is no going back. There is only going forward into new forms, new genres, and new epistemologies; *The Wire* as a whole exemplifies precisely such a movement.

NOTES

This essay is republished from *Criticism: A Quarterly for Literature and the Arts*, vol. 52, no. 3&4, copyright (c) 2010 by Wayne State University Press, reprinted here by permission of Wayne State University Press. A version of the essay was first presented as "Race, Realism and Serial Form" at the Heart of the City: Black Urban Life on *The Wire* conference at the University of Michigan, Ann Arbor, 29–30 January 2009.

1   Jason Mittell: "For many critics, bloggers, fans, and even creator David Simon himself, *The Wire* is best understood not as a television series, but as a *visual novel*. As a television scholar, this cross-media metaphor bristles—not because I don't like novels, but because I love television. And I believe that television at its best shouldn't be understood simply as emulating another older and more culturally valued medium. *The Wire* is a masterpiece of television, not a novel that happens to be televised, and thus should be understood, analyzed, and celebrated on its own medium's terms" ("All in the Game: *The Wire*, Serial Storytelling and Procedural Logic," JustTV, http://justtv.wordpress.com/scholarly-writings).

2   Theodor W. Adorno, "How to Look at Television," *Quarterly of Film Radio and Television* 8, no. 3 (1954): 213–235, quotation on 215.

3   The irony that *The Wire* and its claims to a new realism have circulated alongside the rise and expansion of reality television should not be missed (and probably should be explored further).

4   For the Adorno quote, see Theodor Adorno, Georg Lukács, Bertolt Brecht, Walter Benjamin, and Ernst Bloch, *Aesthetics and Politics: The Key Texts of the Classic Debate within German Marxism*, ed. and trans. Ronald Taylor, Radical Thinking Classics series (London: Verso, 1977), 160. For *The Wire* as the aesthetic apotheosis of the televisual medium, see, for example, J. M. Tyree's "*The Wire*: The Complete Fourth Season," *Film Quarterly* 61, no. 3 (2008): 32–38.

5   See, for example, Georg Lukács, "Narrate or Describe," in *"Writer & Critic," and Other Essays*, ed. and trans. Arthur D. Kahn (New York: Grosset and Dunlap, 1971), 110–148.

6   See, for example, the *Sun*'s own review of the fifth season: David Zurawik, "'The Wire' Loses Spark in Newsroom Storyline," *Baltimore Sun*, 30 December 2008, http://www.baltimoresun.com/entertainment/bal-al .wire30dec30,0,266826.story.

7   References to *The Wire* will be by season and episode number.

8   All realism could, in some sense, be said to be capitalist realism, with the exception of socialist realism, which, by definition, separates itself from capitalist realism. I am going to rely here on the best social contextualization of realism that I know, that of Fredric Jameson, who describes *real-*

ism as "that processing operation variously called narrative mimesis or realistic representation [which] has as its historic function the systematic undermining and demystification . . . of preexisting inherited traditional or sacred narrative paradigms which are its initial givens. In this sense, the [realist] novel plays a significant role in what can be called a properly bourgeois cultural revolution—that immense process of transformation . . . [in which populations] are effectively reprogrammed for life and work in the new world of market capitalism" ("Realism and Desire: Balzac and the Problem of the Subject," in *The Political Unconscious: Narrative as a Socially Symbolic Act* [Ithaca, NY: Cornell University Press, 1981], 141–175, quotation on 152). See note 19 below for a more complete genealogy of capitalism and realism. What strikes me as the biggest difference between older realisms and newer realisms is that totality as a category is arguably given over to exchange, a possibility of worldly equivalence. Other structural hallmarks of realism, particularly operations of typicality, of characters standing in for a social world larger than their immediate present, are still operative here.

9   As Mark Seltzer notes, serial killing is generically racialized as white even though, relative to population, serial killers are no more likely to be white than to be black or Latino; they are, obviously, more likely to be male (*Serial Killers: Death and Life in America's Wound Culture* [London: Routledge, 1998]).

10   In addition to the *Sun*'s review, see the *Washington City Paper* review: Mark Athitakis, "What Happened to Our Show? For Four Seasons *The Wire* Reinvented the Crime Drama: Now the Viewer's the Victim," *Washington City Paper*, 1 February 2008, http://www.washingtoncitypaper .com/articles/34511/what-happened-to-our-show.

11   I am thinking of melodrama as Linda Williams has conceived of it in "Melodrama Revised," in *Reconfiguring American Film Genres: Theory and History*, ed. Nick Browne (Berkeley: University of California Press, 1998), 42–88. Using Williams's reformulation, Martha P. Nochimson has a wonderful reading of *The Sopranos* (1999–2007) and focuses, in particular, on Tony Soprano's relationship to his own body as a site for the staging of innocence. *The Wire* certainly does not approach this level of melodrama, but season 5's literal concerns with innocence and guilt do intimate a kind of melodramatic tone not seen in the earlier seasons ("Waddaya Lookin' At? Re-Reading the Gangster Genre through 'The Sopranos,'" *Film Quarterly* 56, no. 2 [2002–2003]: 2–13).

12   See Zurawik, "'The Wire' Loses Spark." Margaret Talbot claims, "This final season of the show, Simon told me, will be about 'perception versus reality'—in particular, what kind of reality newspapers can capture and what they can't. Newspapers across the country are shrinking, laying off

beat reporters who understood their turf. More important, Simon believes, newspapers are fundamentally not equipped to convey certain kinds of complex truths. Instead, they focus on scandals—stories that have a clean moral. 'It's like, find the eight-hundred-dollar toilet seat, find the contractor who's double-billing,' Simon said at one point. 'That's their bread and butter. Systemic societal failure that has multiple problems—newspapers are not designed to understand it.'" See Margaret Talbot's profile of David Simon in "Stealing Life," Profiles, *The New Yorker*, 22 October 2007, http://www.newyorker.com/reporting/2007/10/22/071022fa_fact_talbot.

13   Raymond Williams, *The Long Revolution* (New York: Broadview, 2001), 286.

14   Raymond Williams: "'Let's be realistic' probably more often means 'let us accept the limits of this situation' (*limits* meaning 'hard facts,' often of power or money in their existing and established forms) than 'let us look at the whole truth of this situation' (which can allow that an existing reality is changeable or is changing)" (*Keywords: A Vocabulary of Culture and Society* [London: Oxford University Press, 1985], 259).

15   Money has a formal specificity different from the commodity or from finance; it has a different critical resonance, as well. It was of course a central economic heuristic used in displacing the commodity form in literary criticism during the 1980s New Historicist moment. Fredric Jameson summarizes this problem well by explaining that in such literary and cultural criticism, "money enters the picture here insofar as only exchange" ("Culture and Finance Capital," in *Cultural Turn: Selected Writings on the Postmodern 1983–1998* [New York: Verso, 1998], 136–161, quotation on 145). See also Marc Shell, *Money, Language, Thought: Literary and Philosophic Economies from the Medieval to the Modern Era* (Berkeley: University of California Press, 1982), for an examination of what Jameson refers to as *exchange*, a construct that dominates New Historical approaches and the inheritors of this tradition. But money is not simply about equal exchange; rather, it is also about the forms that value takes and the tension that results from these seemingly contradictory positions. See, for example, Karl Marx, "Part 2: The Transformation of Money into Capital," in *Capital*, vol. 1 (New York: Penguin, 1973), 247–280.

16   See Patrick Brantlinger, "Debt, Fetishism, and Empire: A Postmodern Preamble," in *Fictions of State: Culture and Credit in Britain, 1694–1994* (Ithaca, NY: Cornell University Press, 1996), 1–47, quotation on 14. In a recent publication, Richard Godden has also used the term *capitalist realism* ("Money and Things: Capitalist Realism, Anxiety, and Social Critique in Works by Hemingway, Wharton, and Fitzgerald," in *A Companion to the Modern American Novel, 1900–1950*, ed. John T. Matthews [London: Blackwell, 2009], 181–201).

17 For a new, "Smithian Marxism" that considers the interplay of time and
    space, territory, and capital, see Giovanni Arrighi, *The Long Twentieth
    Century* (London: Verso, 1994), and, more recently, his *Adam Smith in
    Beijing: Lineages of the Twenty-First Century* (London: Verso, 2007).

18 See Marx, "Part 2: The Transformation of Money," 282.

19 There are different genealogies of realism that could produce such a
    claim. For example, there is the Lukacsian imperative to demonstrate a
    kind of totality, in that this demonstration is what is most challenging;
    Barthes's insistence on representation of the quotidian as what produces
    a reality effect; and the Jamesonian narrative of basic fault, a reification,
    where senses and sensibilities are enclosed and elongated so that reifica-
    tion at the perceptual level mirrors a fracturing at the historical level.
    Perhaps the most apt study of *The Wire*, however, is Raymond Williams's
    narrative of secularization, social extension, and contemporaneity in his
    "A Lecture on Realism," *Screen* 18, no. 1 (1977): 61–74.

20 See R. T. Naylor, "Treasure Island: Offshore Havens, Bank Secrecy, and
    Money Laundering" (in *The Wages of Crime: Black Markets, Illegal Finance,
    and the Underworld Economy* [Ithaca, NY: Cornell University Press, 2002],
    133–195, quotation on 136–137), although this whole book is of great
    interest for thinking through narrative constructions of capitalism. Rosa
    Luxembourg (*The Accumulation of Capital*, 1913) claims that capital must
    have a geographical outside to expand, while for David Harvey (*The Lim-
    its to Capital*, 1984) that structurally similar outside is a temporal one.

21 See Zurawik, "'The Wire' Loses Spark"; and Athitakis, "What Happened to
    Our Show?"

22 Simon, quoted in Mittell, "All in the Game," 7.

23 Each season is structured through a kind of institutional doubling, a
    process by which the narrative truth of any season is negotiated between
    opposing institutions. There is no causality per se; indeed, causality is
    repeatedly displaced by the constructions of coincidence and proximity.
    For example, with the so-called killing of the state's witness in season 4,
    a productive tension, as well as a productive truth, emerges between the
    police department and the city's democratic political machine. In season
    5, this technique is most evident in episode 7, in which both the police
    department and the *Sun* radically increase the resources they will devote
    to the investigation of the serial killer and its reportage, respectively.

24 Indeed, those who promote realism, from Georg Lukács to Simon to
    even someone like Tom Wolfe, have a complicated relationship with
    newspapers. On the one hand, realism traffics in information, and this
    is precisely what a newspaper provides. On the other hand, newspapers
    transform fact into information, whereas realism transforms information
    into worldview and reveals how information is always immanent to its

own time and place, to its own local codes and relations. In Margaret Talbot's interview ("Stealing Life"), David Simon uncannily echoes Lukács, who, some seventy years ago, was already explaining how newspapers obstruct, rather than reveal, the essence of a certain goal of realism: that is, totality itself. For Simon, however, this is the result of a decline of ethics and standards in the newspaper business, whereas for Lukács it is endemic to the form of the news itself.

25 The "James-like" reference is from Tyree, "The Wire."

26 Seltzer, Serial Killers, 16.

27 Lauren Berlant defines genre as "an aesthetic structure of affective expectation, an institution of formation that absorbs all kinds of small variations or modifications while promising that the persons transacting with it will experience the pleasure of encountering what they expected." For Berlant, pleasure does not connote a positive or negative value judgment; rather, it implies the return to an "affective scene" ("Introduction: Intimacy, Publicity, and Femininity," in The Female Complaint: The Unfinished Business of Sentimentality in American Culture [Durham, NC: Duke University Press, 2008], 1–32, quotation on 4).

28 Apparently this kind of overt racism in the television industry (i.e., that minority-dominated casts aren't prizeworthy) has become a kind of badge of ironic pride among the cast: what critics repeatedly deem the best show in the history of television cannot garner an industry award (Tyree, "The Wire").

29 See Alfred W. McCoy, The Politics of Heroin: CIA Complicity in the Global Drug Trade (Chicago: Lawrence Hill Books, 2003), for this fascinating history. It sounds almost too conspiratorial, but, as Dehlia Hannah frequently reminds me, with a system like this, you don't need a conspiracy.

Like Some Dummy Corporation You Just Move around the Board

Contemporary Hollywood Production in Virtual Time and Space

J. D. CONNOR

I.

Early in Oliver Stone's *JFK* (Warner Bros., 1991), Jim Garrison is conducting his infamous "walking tour" through "the heart of the United States government's intelligence community in New Orleans" and explaining how it is that ex-FBI man and staunch anticommunist Guy Banister is mixed up with ostensible communist Lee Harvey Oswald. As Garrison tells the tale of a magical building with two addresses, one belonging to Banister's office, one that appears on Oswald's pro-Castro leaflets, we are treated to a high-contrast black-and-white pseudo-flashback to a very particular moment, where we can see, if we are paying careful attention, Oswald catch sight of Clay Shaw, aka Clay Bertrand, aka Tommy Lee Jones, walking down the street. Stone is remaking some television footage that was shot on August 16, 1963.[1] The furtive eyeline match is the barest hint of what is to come in *JFK*, a bizarre homosexual plot to destroy King Kennedy, a Freudian slaughter by the primal horde that Michael Rogin has so incisively unpacked.[2]

These are the rewards of something like audience paranoia, but when Stone's manic editing met up with the intense and protracted home viewing that DVD made possible, it turned out that there was a second figure off in the distance, a fluttering banner reading "Tax Free." Like most such pieces of free-floating signification in contemporary cinema, it was duly enrolled in the IMDb, under the heading "goofs."[3]

The rationale for its enlistment is simple: in 1963, there was no program to rebate taxes to international visitors to New Orleans. The banner is part of a program promoting tax-free shopping in Louisiana begun in 1987; it is thoroughly anachronistic. And yet, as Jerome Christensen has argued, Stone's film is a remarkably intense allegory of TimeWarner's corporate agonies circa 1991.[4] At its heart is the conspiracy of the folks from Warner against those from Time. The Time, Inc.'ers thought they were purchasing Warner Communications; in reality, they were being subverted at every step. In addition to the evidence he marshals, it turns out that Kennedy's real assassins are from ACME, that the Garrison children watch the WB cartoon "Dripalong Daffy," that the agreed-upon alibi for David Ferrie's trip to Texas is that he is going "duck hunting," that Kennedy was killed in a "turkey shoot," etc., etc. Seen in this light, the sign is not a goof at all, but part of what Christensen calls Warner's "humiliation" of Time. Coming on the heels of the grand, hotly litigated but ultimately tax-free merger, the banner is a corporate badge of honor.

Yet there is even more to it than that. As Eugene Schreiber, then the chairman of Louisiana Tax Free Shopping and the managing director of the New Orleans World Trade Center, explained, "The idea

JFK's Clay Shaw, head of the International Trade Mart (*JFK*, Oliver Stone; Warner Bros., 1991).

Louisiana Tax Free Shopping.

for Tax Free Shopping in Louisiana arose at a meeting of the World Trade Center's International Business Committee in early 1987 as an additional way to promote both tourism and retail trade throughout the state, as was done in many countries in Europe. We felt that being the first state in the United States to offer it would create significant attention and publicity."[5] The World Trade Center was formed in 1985 through the merger of two longstanding New Orleans organizations, the International House and the International Trade Mart, and in the 1950s the director of the International Trade Mart was Clay Shaw, the man we see walking down the street in *JFK*. Indeed, Oswald chose to hand out his leaflets in front of the Mart ostensibly because the Trade Mart and its leadership were major funders of New Orleans anti-Castro organizations.[6]

JFK makes this link clear, repeatedly: When Garrison's investigator first learns, to his astonishment, that Clay Bertrand is Clay Shaw, he puts it this way: "Clay Bertrand is Clay Shaw, the guy who used to run the International Trade Mart?" Midway through this sentence, a figure from the danse macabre leaps into the shot, cackling maniacally, drawing further attention to Shaw's occupation. When the investigator relays this information to the rest of the team, he is positively gleeful. "Grab your socks and hose and pull. Clay Bertrand is Clay Shaw." The immediate response? "Director of the Trade Mart?" "Former director." Finally, and in keeping with the Hollywood rule of three, when Shaw is at last being questioned, he defends himself by incriminating himself: "I'm an international businessman. The Trade Mart I founded is America's commercial pipeline to Latin America. I trade everywhere. Like all businessmen, I am accused of all things." All of which makes the banner less a goof or an anachronism than a prophecy: through the Trade Mart, Shaw has begun to assemble a global, tax-free trading system centering on Latin America.[7]

In the film, the avatar of this free-trade system is, naturally enough, Oswald himself. In the days leading up to the shooting, he is spotted in Dallas, in New Orleans, in Miami, and in Mexico, where he is looking to get into Cuba and from there to Russia.[8] Garrison's investigators think this is "positively spooky," but the DA understands that the processes of political conspiracy and free market economics are the same. "God damn," he declares, "they put Oswald together from day one, like some dummy corporation from the Bahamas you just move around the board."

II.

If every screenplay is a business plan, then every production is a dummy corporation, a virtual corporation that gives rise to and reflects the actual corporation that it is. In *Production Culture*, John Thornton Caldwell puts it like this: "Because film and television are so capital intensive, a script also functions as a financial prospectus, a detailed investment opportunity, and a corporate proposal." "A fictional scenario is always tied to and considered alongside an economic one."[9] This dummy corporation can be "moved around the board" as necessary in order to find an ideal combination of location, labor, financing, and distribution. "The board" here is the matrix of possible combinations of time, space, labor, and capital. (In more contemporary movies, such as the *Bourne* series, it is called "the grid.") Is a star available? Is a location "fresh"? Should this movie be marketed for Christmas release? Does it have a guaranteed cable slot? How will it play across the windows of distribution? These are a film's virtual times and spaces, and as they become actual, they may also, and by that very same maneuver, be retained in their virtuality, as images and sounds, as self-allegorizations.

Surprisingly, perhaps, Gilles Deleuze makes a similar point in *Cinema 2: The Time-Image*:

> The cinema as art itself lives in a direct relation with a permanent plot [*complot*], an international conspiracy which conditions it from within, as the most intimate and most indispensible enemy. This conspiracy is that of money; what defines industrial art is not mechanical reproduction but the internalized relation with money. . . . Money is the obverse of all the images that the cinema shows and sets in place, so that films about money are already, if implicitly, films within the film or about the film.[10]

The eruption of economic critique where we would expect an argument about medium specificity is striking. It comes, unexpectedly, in the midst of Deleuze's chapter on the crystals of time. That chapter is, as Anne Friedberg notes, "the most promising and yet undeveloped section of the book."[11] Certainly for anyone who would wish to deploy some of Deleuze's powerful analytics for recent Hollywood film it will seem that way. It feels as though the writer of *Anti-Oedipus* has suddenly taken over, and has knocked the argument and the type sideways. And so Deleuze will say, all in italics, that "*the cinema confronts its most internal presupposition, money, and the movement-image makes way for the time-image in one and the same operation.*"[12] Once it has been knocked off-kilter in this confrontation, film "endlessly relaunches" a "dissymmetrical" exchange: "The film is movement, but the film within the film is money, is time."[13]

The invocation of an "operation" here makes it difficult to know what sort of transition the shift from the movement-image to the time-image is. Few critics have taken up this passage, or even the formal-financial transition it implies, with that problem in mind. David Rodowick, in a characteristically incisive footnote, explains the importance of the dissymmetry between time and money that comes with the advent of the time-image. Gone is the parallel between the fungibility of images and commodities. In place of that parallel, there is now only a "struggle between the image and capital to see who will be exhausted first."[14] For Jonathan Beller, the parallel between images and capital continues to operate, except that the time-image amounts to a new "representational paradigm" that accords with the shift "from monopoly to multinational capitalism."[15] For Beller, the changes in representational paradigm happen to cinema in general; there is no canon of films whose resistance to capitalist equivalence emerges from their access to direct images of time. In contrast, for Rodowick, time-images constitute a profound form of resistance to the economic order, even if the outcome of that struggle is up for grabs.

Rodowick and Beller, then, illustrate potentially incommensurable ways of understanding the critical transition in Deleuze's writing on cinema. Deleuze locates that transition after World War II, but there is simply no way for the uneven and at least apparently historical shift from the movement-image to the time-image to occur in the postwar period if the crucial event or aspect of that shift is a confrontation with financial scarcity. Such a confrontation was baked into the movement-image from the moment the patent trust was busted. Indeed, Deleuze's authority for the decisive effects of what we might call first-stage financialization on cinema is a lecture by Marcel L'Herbier delivered in 1926. Beller, then, takes Deleuze's point to be, implicitly, that the time-image marks the emergence of a new accord between cinema and the mode of production. What appear to be strategies of resistance through formal innovation are, instead, further elaborations of the "representational paradigms" belonging to monopoly (movement-image) and multinational (time-image) capitalism. Beller saves Deleuze's history by rejiggering his account of capital. For Rodowick, in contrast, the too-early arrival of the confrontation with money suggests the logical possibility of an earlier, *forced* disequivalence between time and money under the regime of the movement-image, emblematized by montage. Rodowick saves Deleuze's history by rejiggering his notion of form. Neither manages (or really, attempts) to save Deleuze's account of the eruption of money as an event *within* the postwar history of film.

And what are we to do with Hollywood cinema in the wake of the transition to the time-image? Does it constitute a retrograde departure from the advanced cinema of the time-image, and can it amount to a historical deviation despite its overwhelming importance to the market and its global social reach? Perhaps the "operation" that both constitutes the confrontation with money and launches the time-image is something more like a material trope—a transition that happens within narrative and that is supported by a host of filmmaking practices that could be impinged upon by such a shift, but that nevertheless retains the abstraction, formality, and iterability of a storytelling function (e.g., the "irrational interval").

If that is the case, it would explain why Deleuze's apparently historical argument gives way to his assertion of disequivalence between the motion of the film and the eruption within those films of time. In other words, this apparently historical transition may operate materially or formally, depending upon one's analysis of the relative predominance of industry or art within the contest for supremacy. Consider the span from the material to the formal as a scale along which this double operation must find a place. When the confrontation with money occurs in the cinema that will be dominated by the time-image, that relationship is internalized in such a way that the results create the appearance of time liberated from the logic of equivalence and exchange, the logic of capital. In that case the Rodowickian struggle ensues. But for a cinema that confronts money materially, the relationship retains the appearance of determination: time remains money. For the cinema that remained within the movement-image—that is, for Hollywood—the challenge of money—that is, time—is one that is met through the assertion of symmetry. Or, to put it in less grandiose terms, if you are a practitioner of industrial art, you will find that the scale will be tipped toward either the art or the industry. Whether and how you decide to right that balance is a calculation that has both aesthetic and economic aspects. And the discourse both within and outside the film will find itself divided between those aspects, rippling along the fault line of a mutual allegorization.

Hollywood's reassertions of symmetry take two forms—one is relatively easy to see, and one requires some unpacking. The first accords with Deleuze's contention that films about money are films about film. In Hollywood, this becomes an almost literal allegory, the sort of thing that makes a heist movie like *Ocean's 11* (Steven Soderbergh; Warner Bros., 2001) the projection of its own backstory, the nearly effortless display of its own process of assembly. But even within Hollywood we should be able to see that films about time are films about money—or they might be, if the fundamental dissymmetry that launched the time-image can be jerked back into a place of rough equivalence. The reassertion of this second parallelism proves more difficult to achieve than the equation between film and money. Contemporary Hollywood manages it only fitfully and only at certain moments in its recent history. Faced with a cinema headed formally and materially along a schizoid trajectory, the major studios hoped to successfully revitalize the classical canons of balance, proportion, causality, and intention. Yet as epigones of the classical studios, they inevitably performed this counter-operation at one remove, carrying within them the quasi-historical scar of their own reorigination. Every abandoned possibility lurks virtually in the belated actuality of contemporary Hollywood. For Deleuze, the scar takes the form of déjà vu:

> The present is the actual image, and *its* contemporaneous past is the virtual image, the image in a mirror. According to Bergson, "paramnesia" (the illusion of *déjà-vu* or already having been there) simply makes this obvious point perceptible: there is a recollection of the present, contemporaneous with the present itself, as closely coupled as a role to an actor.[16]

The passage above repeats both the italics and the reliance on mirror imaging of his earlier discussion of film and finance, which suggests that for Deleuze the internalization of the relationship to money in the form of temporal awareness might produce a feeling of duplication so exact that it is disquieting. To test that possibility in the context of Hollywood's continuing literalism, I will turn to Tony Scott's *Déjà Vu* (Touchstone, 2006). *Déjà Vu* is a film about time, and in its configuration of virtual and actual temporalities it internalizes a relation to money that is both very particular and paradigmatic of the contemporary film and television system.

III.

Déjà Vu (Touchstone, 2006) was the third collaboration between Denzel Washington and director Tony Scott, the third between Washington and producer Jerry Bruckheimer, and the third between Scott and Bruckheimer, although it was only the second film the three of them had made together (*Crimson Tide* was the first). The story is roughly as follows: following the explosion of a New Orleans ferry, ATF agent Doug Carlin (Washington) hooks up with a secret part of the FBI that can look four days and six hours into the past in order to solve the case. The key to the crime is Claire Kuchevar (Paula Patton), who, they believe, was killed by the bomber (Jim Caviezel) *before* the ferry explosion; by surveilling her, they will be able to find him. And though they do, in fact, capture the bomber, Carlin decides to go back into the past to save Claire, with whom he has fallen in love. (So it's *Laura* with a time machine instead of a place in Connecticut.) Together, Carlin and Claire prevent the ferry bombing, but he dies in the process. As she sits grieving on the dock, another, not-dead Carlin approaches her and they drive off together; he gets déjà vu. The plot, of course, is full of holes and makes no sense, in the way all time-travel movies of any complexity are full of holes and make no sense.[17] The production, though, makes perfect sense.

Déjà Vu was supposed to shoot in October 2005, but the devastation wreaked by Katrina made that impossible and forced Bruckheimer to begin moving the project back around the board. At one point, when the film was to be shifted to Seattle or Miami, Tony Scott reportedly "ankled," doubtless taking with him his cinematographer, production designer, and editor. Yet Scott came back in what *Variety* irresistibly called "déjà vu all over again."[18] And in February the film became the first production to be mounted in New Orleans after the hurricane. The revival of the film found ready allegories in the revival of the city and of the film's central characters. Thus Claire, who has been killed when the film begins, will be "revived" by Carlin after he travels back in time. Of course, time travel will temporarily kill him and he will have to be resuscitated. When he appears, suddenly, in a hospital operating room, he bears instructions, just as Claire's fridge had.

Throughout the "Commentary" track on the *Déjà Vu* DVD, we are told that New Orleans was simply the right place for this movie to be set. The implication, of course, is that it *could* have been set somewhere else, somewhere less optimal. (You wouldn't say that Iraq was the right place to *set* a fictional film about the war in Iraq; instead,

Aftermath: Production returns to New Orleans (*Déjà Vu*, Tony Scott; Touchstone, 2006).

Allegorical instructions II: Carlin's memo to himself (*Déjà Vu*, Tony Scott; Touchstone, 2006).

you would talk about where you were *shooting* it, which would in all likelihood be somewhere else.) The script initially placed the action on Long Island so that the investigation could occur in close proximity to Brookhaven National Laboratory, one of the few facilities that would have the sort of particle accelerator that would be necessary for any sort of time travel. Of course, if you could somehow conjure a *mobile* particle accelerator—and why not?—the action could shift to any place with a substantial ferry—Seattle, Miami, even Boston. The particle accelerator is contingent; the ferry is necessary. And so it happened that although New Orleans ferry rides are short, the film ended up set in New Orleans.

At no point in the commentary does anyone mention the enormous cost savings that shooting (and setting) the film in Louisiana would yield. Yet the state did not achieve its recent cinematic prominence because of its unique landscape, culture, or creative institutions. Louisiana became Hollywood South for the same reason that Vancouver became Hollywood North: because it pioneered using tax credits to draw production. This is the relationship to money that *Déjà Vu* internalizes.

Since World War II there have been several successive but overlapping regimes of Hollywood film financing, each epitomized by a certain allocation of risk assumption and deferral. High marginal tax rates after the war encouraged stars to incorporate and spread their compensation out through net profits participation. Expansion of passive loss accounting rules led to film-financing syndicates in the '60s and '70s. The advent of lottery funding in the UK, alterations to the German tax code, the avalanche of hedge-fund money—all of these have diverted, temporarily, the flow of capital. And yet the possible consequences for story and style of these drastic alterations have been largely unexplored.

The implication here is not that taxation structures are the hidden key to the history of Hollywood cinema; I am not making a connoisseur's version of the old finance capital argument.[19] Rather, I want to suggest that the changing relationships between the different aspects of capital deployment are strongly correlated with the time horizons on which financial success is measured, and that, furthermore, the complications that come with these new funding systems may not simply be reflected, but also thought through, in the films that they support. This impulse to aestheticization is a regular feature of Hollywood filmmaking and much else. And at its most successful we find tight allegorical links between particular films and their funding regimes. *Winchester '73* (Anthony Mann; Universal, 1950) is not simply a net profits film; it is a film about the inexplicability of perfection, the impossibility of correctly valuing industrial products based on their origins. *The In-Laws* (Andrew Bergman; Warner Bros., 1979) is not simply a film underwritten by the contributions of hordes of Long Island dentists; it is about the agency of Long Island dentists. *Alexander* (Oliver Stone; Warner Bros./InterMedia, 2004) is not simply a German tax-shelter film; it is about the amortization of library rights. And *Déjà Vu* is not simply a film where tax credits were crucial to its success; it is a film about catching up to a past fulfilling itself—it is a film largely told in the future perfect.

In addition to attracting dozens of television series and films, from *True Blood* and *Treme* and *The Riches* to *Bad Lieutenant: Port of Call New Orleans* and Denzel's *Great Debaters* and *Battle: Los Angeles*, the motion picture tax incentive system in Louisiana has bolstered virtually every cliché about the state's political and economic culture.[20] Until 2009 the program for production worked as follows. Motion picture productions received a large percentage of their expenditures—it has been 30 percent—back in the form of tax credits. However, since these companies did not ordinarily have tax liabilities in-state, they could not make use of their substantial credits. In many other jurisdictions, the credits were refundable, and the state would simply cut a check to the production company: cash in, cash out. In Louisiana, though, the credit was not refundable. To receive their funds, producers had to re-sell the tax credits to someone who had in-state tax liability. Thus it happened that wealthy out-of-state motion picture producers and wealthy Louisianans looking to reduce their tax burden were drawn together. Between them, naturally, there arose a host of brokers who would match producers with taxpayers and negotiate the rates at which the tax credits would be sold—they are always sold at less than par, and the brokers always take a cut. This is the cliché of Louisiana as a system where corruption makes the economy work.

The more successful the state was in luring production, the more money sloshed around in the tax credit market and the more prone to corruption it became. The legal tax skimming that the system counted upon gave way to a collection of illegal transactions. As has been true in past statewide corruption cases, the system sheltered its prominent players until the FBI began investigating. Eventually, tax credit scams would bring down the state's film commissioner, the

Louisiana Institute of Film Technology (LIFT), and many prominent Louisianans, including several players on the New Orleans Saints. This is the cliché of Louisiana as a system so corrupt that someone finally oversteps the line between functional corruption and something that must be stopped.[21]

In 1992, Louisiana became the first state to turn to tax credits as a way of developing its local screened entertainment industry. The program was relatively small-scale, and it was limited to investment losses. In 2002, Louisiana and New Mexico launched a much more ambitious scheme.[22] They were following Canada's lead. There, in 1995, a system of tax syndication dating from 1974 was overthrown in favor of a production tax credit. Initially, the system was intended to support the national film and video industry, and it was restricted to Canadian producers. But in 1997, the doors were thrown open to outside (i.e., Hollywood) investment. British Columbia and Quebec added their own huge tax credits to the national rebates, luring production to Vancouver and Montreal.[23] In this strategy Canada was not alone. Countries around the globe made similarly enticing offers—Hungary had tax credits, the UK had lottery-funded rebates. Back "home," Hollywood studios were stymied in their efforts to convince the federal government to match Canadian largesse, so they turned to individual American states, with tremendous success. More than forty states eventually offered tax breaks beyond mere tax exemptions for out-of-state productions, and those breaks have been astonishingly resistant to drives for fiscal austerity. Despite the extreme constraints on state budgets in the Lesser Depression, tax credit programs still rebated $1.5 billion nationally in 2010. The pervasive availability of credits forced even the longstanding production centers in Los Angeles and New York to respond. They saw business leaching away to such a degree that studio interests were able to lobby successfully for generous credits. New York's went to 30 percent on labor, 5 percent on infrastructure. California's has been more limited, but even in the midst of a fiscal catastrophe, the state preserved its $150 million program, with credits of 20 percent for major motion pictures and 25 percent for "independent" films and television series that relocate to California. The race to the bottom is largely over;

producers need only run the numbers to determine which virtual location best suits their budgets.[24]

What has become a system for the studios is, for states, a far more precarious situation. The industry is both large and exceptionally mobile and flexible. States and nations attempt to purchase production industries through tax credits and other incentives on the assumption that when Hollywood (or other) capital and labor are regularly deployed in a particular area, the industry will become a permanent fixture in the jurisdiction's economy. This is not the case. As Robert Tannenwald of the Center for Budget and Policy Priorities put it in November 2010, "No state can 'win' the film subsidy war. Film subsidies are sometimes described as an 'investment' that will pay off by creating a long-lasting industry. This strategy is dubious at best. Even Louisiana and New Mexico—the two states most often cited as exemplars of successful industry-building strategies—are finding it hard to hold on to the production that they have lured."[25] As advice to policy-makers, Tannenwald's conclusions may be perfectly accurate and absolutely impossible to implement. But our interest lies as much in the representation of political economy as its actualities, and there again the situation in Louisiana has been paradigmatic.

In the early years of its tax credit–fueled dominance of runaway Hollywood production, the greatest threat to Louisiana's hold on its film production industry was Katrina. In the wake of the hurricane, the state became the first to realize just how tenuous its industry was. A consensus gripped Louisiana and New Orleans politicians alike: it was imperative that the state re-open itself for the film business as soon as possible. Beyond the regular tax incentives, then, *Déjà Vu* also benefitted from a city and state that could not afford to say no. The bomber has a house in the lower Ninth Ward, which adds a bit of devastation porn to the mix—the neighborhood was preserved in its wreckage for filming. And it is unlikely that any other city would have allowed the dramatic multitemporal car chase to tie up a major commuter route. Looming over both of these was the ferry explosion. As director Tony Scott described it, "Their biggest concern was that the size of the explosion we wanted to do could actually breach the banks of the Mississippi. [laughs] . . . People were so cooperative. I think generally the people of New Orleans are, but they were just so grateful that we were there, that we were employing a lot of people in the city."[26]

As they compete for productions, states all emphasize the speed with which expenses will be recouped. Whether that recoupment comes through refund or transfer, it can be realized nearly simultaneously with the investment. (This is what separates the new tax credits from earlier strategies of liability syndication, which often took years to pay off.) Indeed, unlike every other major film-financing regime, the amount of money that is realized through the credit grows in direct proportion to the expense.[27] What you spend comes back to you. Or, to put it in the future perfect tense of the time-machine movie: you will not have spent it. And so it is that the tax credit movie instantiates a version of the Bergsonian duality of virtual and actual that is the "crystal of time."

Déjà Vu is a time-travel movie where the distance that is travelled is comparatively small—four days and six hours, a sort of displaced simultaneity that allows only for *events*, not for *processes*. That is, in a story where you can time-travel anywhere, be it Nazi Germany, 100,000 years from now, or a 1980s hot tub, the span is capacious enough to allow history to unfold in dramatically different ways, but in *Déjà Vu* the gap between now and then is only large enough to assure us that the past carries the sign of its pastness.

As a result, *Déjà Vu* is less about the past than it is about an uncomfortable proximity, the sense of exact coincidence paired with a feeling of simultaneous distinction. It achieves déjà vu formally through three aspects of the array of video feeds that it calls "the time window": the fragmentation of the screen, the indeterminate dimensionality of the image, and the manipulation of resolution. These aspects of the image are both technical and formal, emblems of both the production and the narrative.

Fragmentation is the simplest to capture: the frame is divided within itself between feeds that are marked as present and those that are designated as past. This is true not only in the main control room, but more spectacularly in a car chase where Carlin pursues the bomber, driving *four days ago* at night. For the first half of the chase, Carlin

The time window (*Déjà Vu*, Tony Scott; Touchstone, 2006).

wears a special "goggle rig" that allows him to look into the past as he drives. This turns the screen into a nested POV shot, one made more complex because Carlin is driving against the flow of traffic. "Oh, this is trippin'," he muses. The overload of information through the display proves dangerously distracting, and at the chase's static midpoint, Carlin is able to stare into the face of the bomber, oblivious to the jackknifing eighteen-wheeler bearing down on him. The collision knocks out Carlin's goggle display but not the feed to the time window. Even though Carlin is now effectively time-blind, the feed allows the agents and physicists in the control room to direct his driving while he is able to devote all of his attention to the road he is presently driving on. And with that reduction in complexity, the chase loses momentum.

Tony Scott has said that left to his own devices, he would be likely to produce a film that looks like *Domino* on speed. This sequence, then, would be Deleuze's mobile section on speed, the hypermobility through time and space that is the essence of the car chase but also, and not really very figuratively, the essence of contemporary capital. Screaming across the bridge in his tricked out Hummer, Carlin is living beyond the dreams of the New Frontier–era free traders. Kennedy only wanted to lower taxes and tariffs; today's Jindals have managed to make them negative.

The time chase: the mobile section on speed (*Déjà Vu*, Tony Scott;
Touchstone, 2006).

And yet with Scott there is always a countervailing pictorial pressure in which the rules of composition are bared.[28] So in Claire's French Quarter apartment, the architecture divides up a wall into subframes, but the mural she is executing works against those frames according to its own perspectival laws. This countervailing autonomy (the still as opposed to the mobile, the analog as opposed to the digital, the historical as opposed to the contemporary) is, in the world of the film, the ghost of New Orleans authenticity: the mural, naturally, depicts Satchmo and Jelly Roll Morton. Claire is recovering from Katrina, and a bad breakup, by gaining some perspective on her life—by reimagining New Orleans as the birthplace of jazz and not the emblem of governmental incapacity and malfeasance that it had become. The film ferries between these poles, endlessly relaunching its investigations of "the board." In the time window, the frames are obvious and the possibilities are open; in Claire's apartment the frames are occluded and New Orleans is inevitable. The tension between the two is a Hollywood love story.

Claire is also, and more than once, the figure for and vehicle of a simulation of dimensionality. In order to create a convincing sense that the time window was simply an extension of satellite surveillance technologies, the production used LIDAR, a laser imaging system that measures distances with exceptional precision. From that data, the visual effects crew was able to generate 3D skins of buildings which they could then render and into which they could drop Claire.[29] The aim, though, was not to create a virtual world but to articulate the passage from the present *into* the past of the time window. As director of photography Paul Cameron described:

> How do we go in and out of the past? We wanted to develop something that was more tactile, more realistic for people to understand. . . . We start out with more traditional satellite footage, and then it goes down to Louisiana, and then it goes down into New Orleans, and as we come down to the rooftops of the building we incorporate the 3D architectural skin that enables you to travel through walls or rooftops down shaftways or stairwells and into a location, hence giving the sense of passing through space.[30]

Within that rendered space, Claire would appear with what Scott called "this weird sort of ghosting toffee effect" generated by a frozen-moment camera system. She would acquire, they hoped, a sort of spatiotemporal blur that, combined with the near-3D spaces, would give an added dimensionality to the frame. Between 2D and 3D, she becomes the figure of passage in and out of the screen, and in so doing she differentiates herself from her onscreen, 2D trackers while at the same time acquiring a greater degree of proximity to us.

The mural in Claire's apartment (*Déjà Vu*, Tony Scott; Touchstone, 2006).

The final piece in this technical puzzle is resolution. In the main lab, Scott shot using Panavision's Genesis camera—then the state-of-the-art digital system. The tiles in the time window were being projected in real time; they were not inserted via a green screen. Among those tiles, the main window, usually focusing on Claire, was originally shot in high definition while the others were shot in ordinary resolution. This bolstered the tactility of the past. Scott effused, "The contrast and the separation when you see the finished print is huge. So the main window, it hums, and sings, and stands out. It's pretty different from the other, smaller tiles."[31] For the crew, at least, it was convincing. As director of photography Cameron put it, "For me the best sense of feeling déjà vu occurs when we do projection onto glass with Denzel behind it. It's a very subtle photographic technique, but we're racking focus from the surface of the glass to Denzel, to people in the background. It's this kind of multi-layered image that's very emotional. Then when you cut back and go over the shoulder, it's got this sense of it really happening."[32]

"The sense of it really happening": what is, for Cameron, the realization of a particular aim in a particular film might be understood as the aim of immersive filmmaking in general. What *Déjà Vu* almost uniquely realizes is that such immersions have an inevitably proleptic effect: if you feel as though it is really happening, you will want it to; you will do things to make it happen, even if those things require you

The LIDAR point cloud (*Déjà Vu*, Tony Scott; Touchstone, 2006).

Claire in the time window (*Déjà Vu*, Tony Scott; Touchstone, 2006).

The reverse on the time window (*Déjà Vu*, Tony Scott; Touchstone, 2006).

to go back in time. That "doubling back on itself" is the form of de-sire that underlies the time loops of déjà vu. Here is the way Bergson describes it:

If I recognize the present instant, am I not quite as surely going to recog-nize the coming one? So I am unceasingly, towards what is on the point of happening, in the attitude of a person who will recognize and who consequently knows. But this is only the *attitude* of knowledge, the form of it without the matter. As I cannot predict what is going to happen, I quite realize that I do not know it; but I foresee that I am going to have known it, in the sense that I shall recognize it when I shall perceive it; and this recognition to come, which I feel inevitable on account of the rush of my faculty of recognizing, exercises in advance a retroactive effect on my present, placing me in the strange position of a person who feels he knows what he knows he does not know.[33]

In these Bergsonian terms, then, *Déjà Vu* is a retroaction movie.

IV.

At its conclusion, Bergson's first-person account becomes both knottier—feeling he knows what he knows he does not know—and more objective—casting him into the "strange position" of a more general type. Something similar has happened to Hollywood filmmaking in the tax credit era. Even a decade ago, the situation was subtly different. Massive expenditures always constitute massive risks, even if producers "know" that those risks are contained by anticipated ancillary revenues or balanced out across the corporate siblings of an integrated media conglomerate. But in that era of high neoclassicism, the studios (through their allies in the enfotainment industry) cultivated what Justin Wyatt and Christine Vlesmas have called "the drama of recoupment."[34] Would *Titanic* break even? *Could* it? Such drama still exists, and it can still occasionally become the rallying point of a production or its reception; but as immediate, guaranteed, partial recoupment has become the norm, some of the "drama" has leached out of the revenue stream and been replaced by a narrative fascination with the manipulation of contingent certainties.

The more baroque the daisy chains of executive knowledge or self-consciousness become, the more they cry out for objectification. The "strange position" of the generic subject of déjà vu finds its characteristic cinematic home in a control room, taking charge of a vast media array—all versions of *Déjà Vu*'s time window. Control rooms, particularly TV control rooms, have always been locations from which to observe things spinning out of control, going "live" and "uncensored" directly to an audience. But where earlier incarnations of the control room might foreground the abstract outcomes of strategy (*WarGames*) or the techniques of persuasion and performance (*Tootsie*, *Groundhog Day*, *Broadcast News*), or the idea of the public (*Batman*), our new control rooms (in *Syriana*, *Body of Lies*, or the *Bourne* films) work at a metalevel.[35] Today, whatever unforeseen complications arise to thwart the controller's control can be sloughed off in favor of a fairly desperate belief in the totality of the grid itself.

Five years after *Déjà Vu*, Summit released *Source Code* (Duncan Jones, 2011), a time-travel film that one of its actors called "*Groundhog Day* and *Speed* and *Déjà Vu* on a train." Because the central conceit involved going back into the past repeatedly, the *Groundhog Day* comparison was inevitable. It was, said Jeffrey Wright, "*Groundhog Day* on the far side of the moon—somewhere in virtual space."[36] But where *Groundhog Day* was an elaborate meditation on the promise and possibilities of Hollywood performance (the sources and worth of "talent"), *Source Code* narrated its way through the distentions of contemporary capital: the ultimate, mobile abstraction comes to ground through the bodies and in the spaces of the world it continuously remakes. Indeed, the film's own narrative is a more thorough conceptualization of the working of capital than its story requires. Instead of allegorizing its own production, *Source Code* is the allegory of the relationship between the *world* of its story and the *world* of its production.

The film itself oscillates between two emblematic space-times: a doomed commuter train making its way to Chicago and a control room at Nellis AFB in Las Vegas. Narratively, the exclusive juncture between them is supposed to be the consciousness of Captain Colter Stevens, a mind that will be dropped into the body of a particular passenger for eight minutes at a time to gather information and then report back to his handlers at Source Code headquarters. Consciousness shuttles between *Source Code*'s space-times, and information is its product. There are not supposed to be any other communicating channels between past and present; the temporal "continuum" cannot be "unsettled." Thus when Stevens announces that he has placed a cell phone call to Wright's character, he is told, "You may have made that call from the train, but I would never receive it here. It's a different reality, Captain. If the call even went through it would be received by a different me entirely." This is the stable model of time travel in *Source Code*, and when Stevens begins to understand the fatality of time's arrow, he (like Phil Conners in *Groundhog Day*) begs for death.

That stability cannot last, and part of the movie's particular nifti-ness is the way it staggers the ruptures of the spatiotemporal con-tinuum. The two worlds of *Source Code* are as distinct as possible: geographically (Las Vegas and Chicago); culturally (military/civilian, private cars/mass transit, classified info/public parks); temporally (present and past); even formally (the scenes in the pod were shot with RED digital cameras, those outside Chicago on film). The breach in that distinction is supposed to be limited and, like time, unidirec-tional, but as in every time-travel movie, there are additional pos-sibilities. Our first hint of that openness appears as changes to the "pod" in which Stevens is being held—it expands, its controls shift, it leaks fluid. What initially seems to be an isolation chamber is re-vealed (at minute 51) to be a "manifestation" created by his mind. Yet the revelation that the pod is a virtual space has no immediate consequences for the story's progress; the segregation of the worlds remains contained. Still, that segregation has been stipulated to be a matter of information rather than an inevitability of space-time: when Stevens asks where his actual body is, he is told that that is "classified." Several time trips later, Stevens has found the bomber and now wants one final chance to go back into the "source code" to save the passengers on the train—even though he knows that, in the lab's time continuum, they are dead. What appears to be a matter-of-fact reckoning with finitude or fatality occasions one of the film's big reveals. Up until now, we have seen the audiovisual link from the lab to the pod and assumed that it was operating both ways. As it turns out, in the virtual pod Stevens receives audio and visual com-munication from his handlers in the lab, but within the lab, Stevens's thoughts are displayed as text generated by his brain without another input system. The significance of the reveal is that the viewer now knows that Stevens is not present to the information system in the usual way, and that revelation coincides with a change in Stevens's goals in the film's other world. This communication disturbance will work itself out in Act 3.

In the other world, the train, like the pod, is enclosed and claus-trophobic. This social pod is vectored through the actual space of Chicago and its suburbs, a space which registers only when the train

Communications asymmetry, audiovisual (*Source Code*, Duncan Jones; Summit, 2011).

stops or when, in the happy ending, Stevens and his (new) girlfriend visit Chicago's Millennium Park. Communication between the train-pod and the space around it is even more radically asymmetric than communication with the lab: the space of northern Illinois "communicates" with the train only when the film's terrorist makes a cell phone call that sets off the bomb. (The content of the call is irrelevant; it is the connection that triggers the device.)

Once we discover the communications asymmetry between the pod and the lab, and once Stevens's goals have changed, the train's communications asymmetry is adjusted: on his last trip into the source code, and after foiling the bomber, Stevens calls his father, not the Air Force base. The content of their conversation is, like the bomber's triggering phone call, less important than the fact of connection; it does not matter whether that connection has consequences outside its own temporal continuum. Yet Stevens *does* disrupt the continuum: his consciousness cannot return to his mutilated body back in the lab because that body has been euthanized, according to his wishes. As a result, his consciousness continues to dwell in the body of Sean Fentress, the passenger he has displaced. This in-dwelling first appears as a cinematic trick: whenever Stevens is in the "source code," we see and hear Jake Gyllenhaal (Stevens's mind) until his reflection reveals the face of the actor playing Fentress. (We even see Gyllenhaal when his girlfriend looks at him; it's a clarifying lesson in the difference between formal and narrative points of view.) The flip side of this audiovisual nesting comes when Stevens sends an e-mail to Captain Colleen Goodwin, his handler. Just as, within the lab, she is televisually present to him but he is textually present to her, so in the disrupted temporal continuum at the end of the film, Stevens is cinematically present in Chicago but textually present at Nellis.[37] In this new, stable timeline, *Source Code* has found a way of scaling up the media ecology of its lab setting so that it can become continuous with the film as a whole. That medial-temporal asymmetry, both realist and allegorical, ultimately describes the relationship between a host of contemporary films and their tax credit–abetted productions.

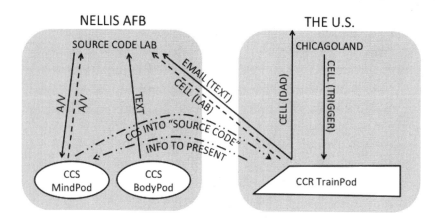

LEGEND
CCS   Capt. Colter Stevens
CCR   Chicago Commuter Railway
———   Successful Communication
-----   Failed or false communication
—··—   Movement of consciousness

Source Code's communication system.

How thoroughgoing was the drive to save money on *Source Code?* Producer Philippe Rousselet's Vendôme Productions drew on his French background when the production headed to Montreal to shoot all the interiors. (The raft of French surnames in the credits makes that abundantly clear.) Mobile productions like *Source Code* typically fill their rank-and-file with local workers and bring along enough Hollywood talent to spread across the production like a layer of icing. The thickness of that layer is the evidence of the production's balance between its commitment to aesthetic autonomy (how much labor do department heads get to choose?) as opposed to financial constraint (how many subsidized local salaries will there be?). In the case of *Source Code*, the availability of first-rate crew in Montreal meant that the production was able to staff up locally almost all the way: the costume designer, the effects houses, and the camera operator were local. When screenwriter Ben Ripley asked director Jones, "How much of the crew was Montreal-based and how much did you bring from elsewhere?" the answer made it clear that financial considerations were overriding: "Ninety-nine percent. It was very much a local crew. . . . Don Burgess obviously came up from the United States, but because of the speed and the budget of the film he came up on his own. Normally he likes to move with a team of people, and he agreed that on this project he would work with a whole new crew from Montreal."[38]

But while the control room might have been located anywhere, the film needed an actual, traversable location in which to situate its train disaster, just as *Déjà Vu* needed a location for its ferry disaster. Screenwriter Ripley initially imagined the train in the Greater New York area, but that possibility gave way for budgetary reasons. The major incentive was a more generous Illinois tax credit. Still, *Source Code* would insist on converting its constraints into virtues. The helicopter shots over the opening credits alternate between images of the train in the great horizontal landscapes of Chicagoland and the sudden verticals of the city itself. Such vistas and contrasts are harder to come by around New York. The shift in location had narrative consequences as well. As director Jones explained, the penultimate scene at Anish Kapoor's *Cloud Gate* sculpture was only possible because the production had been moved to save money: "I know that when we had to move the film from New York to Chicago, the fact that that [sculpture] existed made me very excited because I felt the whole idea of distorted reflections was going to be very useful as a joining tool [between the sequences in the pod and those on board the train]."[39]

How seriously should we take "the whole idea of distorted reflections" as the formal principle that joins the different worlds of *Source Code*? Jones is certainly alluding to the moments when Stevens sees someone else in the mirror, but those reflections are more than distortions—they are substitutions. (There are no half-Stevenses/half-Fentresses in the mirror. To take it a step further, Hollywood's Jake Gyllenhaal is replacing Frédérick De Grandpré, the Quebec-based actor playing his reflection.) Distortions occur when one person or thing or idea morphs into something else. The concluding conversation between Stevens and Christina is exemplary. He belatedly recognizes the sculpture as the silver kidney from his passages out of the source code, realizing that he has, in fact, known the future all along. "Do you believe in fate?" he asks. She responds that she's

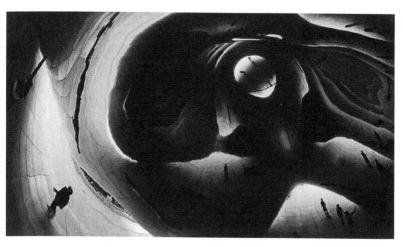

The Cloud Grid (*Source Code*, Duncan Jones; Summit, 2011).

"more of a dumb luck kinda gal." The film, naturally, imagines that one is the distorted reflection of the other, just as Forrest Gump had reconciled determinism and free will by supposing that "maybe both is happening at the same time."[40] *Cloud Gate* embodies that simultaneity. The shape channels its reflections groundward so that, according to the *Source Code* "Trivia" track, "80 percent" of it reflects the sky. But the low angles of the sequence reverse the balance between sky and ground, and, what is more, the ground that we see is the grid of possibilities itself.[41] In this way, the Chicago of fate and luck becomes the equivalent of Nellis AFB, a zone of militarized risk control. Stevens, like Oswald, like Carlin, is the dummy corporation that has been moved around the board. Like almost all films that successfully make it out of development hell, *Source Code* imagines this manipulation as romance.

Coda: No Future

There is a price to pay for Stevens's romance: by successfully usurping Sean Fentress's body, Stevens erases Fentress's consciousness. That Fentress would otherwise have been killed in the train explosion is some compensation, but his eradication is the unacknowledged cost of forgoing at least one cinematic possibility. To put this another way, for Colter Stevens, *Source Code* is an action-romance; for Sean Fentress, it is a body-snatching horror film.

The flip side of the time-travel movie's confidence in the inevitable grid of contingencies is the horror film's almost desperate need to cordon its characters off the grid. As cell phones have chipped away at the isolation necessary to make the genre go, screenplays have been forced to account for technological failures, resulting in an endless stream of "no signal" and "dead battery" moments.[42] Few movies have been as canny about this convention as *The Cabin in the Woods* (dir. Drew Goddard, scr. Goddard and Joss Whedon; Lionsgate, 2012).[43] As a band of slaughter-ready coeds heads for the eponymous locale, one of them notes that the road they just crossed "doesn't even show up on the GPS. It's unworthy of global positioning." The stoner sage responds, "That's the whole point. Get off the grid, right?

No cellphone reception, no traffic cameras . . . go somewhere for one goddamn weekend where they can't globally position my ass. This is the whole issue." As it happens, though, the execution of the five college students is not simply a genre-driven requirement. It is, rather, an expiatory ritual managed in a control room, and the cordon that will keep the students off the grid is itself an elaborately maintained electrical curtain. Once the impending victims pass through a mountain, "a bird comes from behind the camera, flying directly above the tunnel. About halfway across it hits an invisible barrier and falls in a shower of sparks as for one moment an electrical grid seems to appear where it struck, before sparking away into nothing."[44] The grid here is a hexagonal honeycomb pattern, mimicking vertically the conventional pattern of cellular phone coverage.[45] The "off-the-grid" is nested inside the grid.

Cabin's sales pitch assumes a high degree of generic self-consciousness: "You think you know the story" is its tagline. But by literalizing generic conventions ("The Director" is in charge) and crossing the "cabin-in-the-woods" slasher film with the televised-life film (the production intern is named Truman, after The Truman Show)—Cabin draws our attention to the process of locating the production in a particular woods: "A helicopter shot floats over the rambler as it winds through an endless expanse of firs, finally consumed by them" (20). Within the film, these woods are the setting for the "reality" production within which the victims will unknowingly choose their own mode of execution. As it happens, they are pursued by a family of farm implement–wielding zombies, but they might have been killed by something like Hellraiser's Pinhead, werewolves, vampires, mutants, or even an "angry molesting tree."[46] "We chose," one of them belatedly realizes. "They made us choose how we die." The monsters are housed in a subterranean warehouse of potential carnage and illusory choice, a "Costco of death."[47] The spectacular array of death-dealing creatures is mere distraction; the location was already fatal. Before the victims might have chosen their mode of execution, they had been "consumed" by "endless firs." The woods are, as it happens, in British Columbia, which is to say they are woods where the tax credits are monstrous.[48]

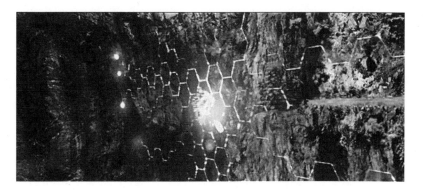

"No Signal": The cellular barrier (*The Cabin in the Woods*, Drew Goddard; Lionsgate, 2012).

The global system of tax credit–driven film and video production successfully virtualizes even the stubborn realities of location shooting—not by dematerializing those realities but by shadowing them with their future perfect selves.[49] The proliferation of control rooms may appear to be a way of insisting upon the difference between places real and places virtual, but that insistence is always undermined in order to vouch for a higher order of control. At the end of *Cabin in the Woods*, an unlikely romantic couple have nearly managed to escape their prescripted death, but instead of constituting the happy ending, their survival will result in the destruction of humanity by renascent evil gods that dwell deep within the earth. The control room will be destroyed, and the cabin will be crushed by "a gnarled hand, bigger than the house and on an arm a hundred feet long."[50] Capitalism didn't quite go under this time around, so it makes perverse sense to rewrite the system's survival as the mythos of a jokey, faux-ancient theology repurposed for the collapse of the housing bubble. If Hollywood remains sanguine about the continuing operations of the global economy, that is because it had adopted a post-crisis mode of production even before the crisis hit. For more than a decade, the industry had been telling a story that we seemed to know already but that we were unprepared for nonetheless.

NOTES

1   Robert J. Groden, *The Search for Lee Harvey Oswald: A Comprehensive Photographic Record* (New York: Penguin Studio, 1995), 75. Photos originally WDSU TV archive.

2   Michael Rogin, "Body and Soul Murder: *JFK*," in *Media Spectacles*, ed. Marjorie Garber, Jann Matlock, and Rebecca Walkowitz (New York: Routledge, 1993), 3–22.

3   http://www.imdb.com/title/tt0102138/trivia?tab=gf.

4   Jerome Christensen, "Post-Warners Warners: *Batman* and *JFK*; *You've Got Mail*," in *America's Corporate Art: The Studio Authorship of Hollywood Motion Pictures* (Palo Alto, CA: Stanford University Press, 2011), 245–279.

5   Louisiana Tax Free Shopping 20th anniversary [brochure] (2007), n.p.

6   Groden, *The Search for Lee Harvey Oswald*, 74; photo originally WDSU TV archive.

7   This story of the interplay between the rabid anti-Communism of New Orleans's business elite and their drive for international market dominance is told in Arthur E. Carpenter, *Gateway to the Americas: New Orleans's Quest for Latin American Trade, 1900–1970* (PhD diss., Tulane University, 1987). In Dallas, Kennedy is shot on his way to deliver a speech at the Dallas Trade Mart.

8   Oswald's famous radio debate with Carlos Bringuier, later released as *Oswald: Self-Portrait in Red* (New Orleans: Eyewitness Records/Information Council of the Americas, 1964), came about after he was spotted distributing "Hands Off Cuba" leaflets in front of the Trade Mart building.

9   John Thornton Caldwell, *Production Cultures* (Durham, NC: Duke University Press, 2009), 232, 233.

10   Gilles Deleuze, *Cinema 2: The Time Image*, trans. Hugh Tomlinson (Minneapolis: University of Minnesota Press, 1989), 77.

11   Anne Friedberg, *Window Shopping: Cinema and the Postmodern* (Berkeley: University of California Press, 1993), 129.

12   The French reads: "Bref, *c'est dans une même opération que le cinéma affronte son présuppose le plus intérieur, l'argent, et que l'image-mouvement cede la place à l'image-temps.*" *Cinéma 2: L'image-temps* (Paris: Éditions de Minuit, 1985), 105; the English version appears on page 78.

13   Ibid.

14   D. N. Rodowick, *Gilles Deleuze's Time Machine* (Durham, NC: Duke University Press, 1997), 236–237 n.13.

15   Jonathan Beller, *The Cinematic Mode of Production: Attention Economy and the Society of the Spectacle* (Lebanon, NH: University Press of New England, 2006), 19. See also 235 n.1: "Not coincidentally, this shift from

one representational paradigm to another coincides, historically speaking, with the break . . . between the movement-image and the time-image."

16 Deleuze, *Cinema 2*, 79.

17 The exception is *Primer* (Shane Carruth; THINKFilm, 2004).

18 "Scott Revisits 'Déjà Vu,'" *Variety*, October 19, 2005, http://www.variety .com/article/VR1117931300.html.

19 The finance capital argument is explicitly anti-connoisseur, as can be seen in the first drafts of Horkheimer and Adorno's *Dialectic of Enlightenment*. When they revised the manuscript during the war, they removed the rhetoric of finance capital but retained the critique of connoisseurship. Max Horkheimer and Theodor W. Adorno, *Dialectic of Enlightenment*, trans. Edmund Jephcott, ed. Gunzelin Schmid Noerr (Palo Alto, CA: Stanford University Press, 2002). See the editor's afterword for an account of the revision process and the notes on pages 268–272 for specific changes. The best outline of the historical importance of taxation to the motion picture industry is Eric Hoyt, "Hollywood and the Income Tax, 1929–1955," *Film History* 22, no. 1 (March 2010): 5–21.

20 *True Blood* (Alan Ball; HBO, 2008–); *Treme* (Eric Overmyer and David Simon; HBO, 2010–); *The Riches* (Dmitry Lipkin; FX, 2007–2008); *Bad Lieutenant: Port of Call New Orleans* (Werner Herzog; Millennium/First Look, 2009); *The Great Debaters* (Denzel Washington; Weinstein Co., 2007); *Battle: Los Angeles* (Jonathan Liebesman; Columbia/Relativity, 2011).

21 Gordon Russell and Robert Travis Scott, "FBI investigating Louisiana's film industry incentives," *New Orleans Times-Picayune*, May 29, 2007, http:// blog.nola.com/business_of_film//print.html; Robert Travis Scott, "LIFT officials pressured state to speed tax credits," *New Orleans Times-Picayune*, June 4, 2007, http://blog.nola.com/times-picayune//print.html; Tim Morris, "Gov. Bobby Jindal seeks renewal of film, music tax credits," *New Orleans Times-Picayune*, March 9, 2009, http://blog.nola.com/news_impact/ print.html?entry=/2009/03/gov_bobby_jindal_szeks_renewal.html; Robert Travis Scott, "Increase in movie tax credit endorsed," *New Orleans Times-Picayune*, June 19, 2009, http://www.nola.com/news/t-p/capital/index .ssf?/base/news-7/124538940923020.xml; Laura Maggi, "Former Louisiana film official gets two-year sentence in bribery case," *New Orleans Times-Picayune*, June 29, 2009, http://blog.nola.com/news_impact/print .html?entry=/2009/07/former_louisiana_film_official.html; Robert Travis Scott, "More than two dozen with ties to the New Orleans Saints invested in movie studio deal," *New Orleans Times-Picayune*, July 2, 2009, http:// blog.nola.com/saintsbeat/2009/07/more_than_two_dozen_with_ties.html; David Hammer, "New Orleans Saints Charles Grant, Jeremy Shockey sue Kevin Houser over film tax credits," *New Orleans Times-Picayune*, March

8, 2010, http://blog.nola.com/crime_impact/print.html?entry=/2010/03/new_orleans_saints_charles_gra.html.

22 William Luther, "Movie Production Incentives: Blockbuster Support for Lackluster Policy," Tax Foundation Special Report No. 173 (January 2010), http://www.taxfoundation.org/sites/taxfoundation.org/files/docs/sr173.pdf.

23 The Canadian case remains the paradigm for US production subsidies. In addition to the sources in note 24 below, see the following. For the transition to the credit regime: Stephen Godfrey, "Producers protest tighter tax rules; Province restricts definition of 'made-in-Quebec' film," *Globe and Mail*, February 22, 1991; John Schreiner, "Lights, action, financing!" *Financial Post*, March 30, 1992, 3:24; Ian Austen, "Lobby group urges Ottawa to introduce new, refundable tax credit for film industry," *Gazette*, November 16, 1994, B4; Gayle MacDonald, "Mixed Reviews for Film Tax Changes: Federal budget brings down gradual elimination of shelters in favor of credits," *Financial Post*, March 11, 1995, 2:31.

For the extension of tax credits to non-Canadian producers, see Susan Walker, "Tories boost tax credits for culture," *Toronto Star*, May 7, 1997, D2; Harvey Enchin, "Canada extends pic tax-shelter program," *Daily Variety*, July 31, 1997, 8; Paul Gessell, "Bigger, perhaps better, but less Canadian," *Gazette*, October 4, 1997, B2; Christopher Harris, "Lights! Camera! Action! HOLLYWOOD NORTH: Toronto remains the third-largest film and TV production centre on the continent, and the city would like to keep it that way," *Globe and Mail*, October 30, 1997, C1; and Brendan Kelly, "B.C. offers tax credit," *Daily Variety*, June 4, 1998, 10. The last captures precisely the beggar-thy-neighbor approach that marks the tax credit arms race: "The tax credit will save producers roughly five percent of their overall costs and brings B.C. on par with Ontario and Quebec, which both recently unveiled similar tax-credit schemes. . . . 'The film industry is a growing industry here and it's footloose,' said [B.C. film commissioner Pete] Mitchell. 'It can move anywhere it wants very quickly. We heard from our key customers that they wanted this and we responded. It's all about competition and about staying on a level playing field.'"

The byplay became a debate over "runaway production," with Hollywood unions leading the charge for parallel domestic subsidies. Ian Bailey, "U.S. unions declare war on Hollywood North: Film industry wants tax breaks to woo business back from Canada," *Ottawa Citizen*, July 5, 1999, A5; Don Townson, "Canadian Goose: Defying H'w'd whining, Canucks sweeten pot," *Daily Variety*, July 9, 1999, 1. When the national effort failed, the arrival of Louisiana's subsidies was cast as an anti-Canadian salvo. Dana Harris, "Prod'n gets Bayou boost," *Daily Variety*, August 8, 2002, 1.

Just as it pioneered tax credit financing, so Canada pioneered the tax credit scandal, this one involving the children's programming producer CINAR, which falsely labeled screenplays to qualify as Canadian content. Mark Lamey, "Cut! Cinar owes $27.5 million: Film house's settlement with Ottawa and Quebec includes ill-gotten tax credits," *Gazette*, December 20, 2000, D1. Rumors also abounded that Canadian houses issued "local" invoices for work so that they would qualify for provincial tax credits when the equipment and work were run out of US offices. Doug Saunders, "A Cheater's Guide to Canadian Television: How to bilk taxpayers and influence people," *Globe and Mail*, October 23, 1999, C1. Worries that the scandal would cause legislators to restrict or remove production subsidies inspired fierce lobbying; ultimately, no charges were filed, no major changes were instituted because of the scandal, and the fraud and abuse were chalked up to a few bad apples.

24 See Robert Tannenwald, "State Film Subsidies: Not Much Bang for Too Many Bucks," Center on Budget and Policy Priorities, November 17, 2010, 2, for figures. The Motion Picture Association of America maintains a one-stop website to track current production incentives at http://www.mpaa.org/policy/state-by-state. The Association of Film Commissioners International performs a similar clearinghouse function, http://www.afci.org/. A roundup of the global system as of 2005 can be found in *The Global Success of Production Tax Incentives and the Migration of Feature Film Production from the U.S. to the World: Year 2005 Production Report*, Center for Entertainment Industry Data and Research, 2006, http://www.ceidr.org. CEIDR appears to have shut its doors; however, KPMG regularly issues *Film Financing and Television Programming: A Taxation Guide*; the publication is now in its sixth edition (2012).

I have said that tax credit financing turns filmmaking toward the future perfect. It has other effects as well. As it has become more prevalent and as studios have come under renewed pressure to drive down costs, more and more of the enfotainment coverage of budgets has reported the budget-net-tax-credits. What is particularly odd about this trend is that it has not been accompanied by a concomitant rethinking of marketing expenses. Imagine a film with a negative cost of $50 million that will be supported by a typical advertising campaign. For years, the rule of thumb has been that marketing is roughly half a film's budget. If tax credits reduce the effective budget to $40 million, do producers lobby for the same $25 million campaign? Or, to take another tack: Since the tax credits are not actual reductions in the budget, they must be credited against the film's negative cost (or counted as part of its "gross receipts"). This would seem to be a simple-enough matter. But for producers and others who will share in the film's revenues, when and whether those funds count toward the film's "cash-break" point are crucial questions. Without very precise contracting, talent is liable to find itself farther from its back-end payments than it might otherwise be. The tax credits might go directly to the distributor, might be excluded from the producer's share, and might therefore count as something like double free money for the studio. (I want to thank a former student who now works in the industry—and who wishes to remain anonymous—for working through these possibilities with me.)

25 Tannewald, "State Film Subsidies," 2.

26 "Commentary," *Déjà Vu*, Scott (Touchstone, 2006), DVD.

27 At least, it does so unless it is specifically structured otherwise. California, for instance, attempts to avoid subsidizing studio tentpole projects by capping the budget of the films eligible for the program.

28 Here's an example of the way he talks about the pictorial: "Because of Katrina . . . we had to move our shoot back to the winter, but I loved the winter in the Bayou because all those trees, those birch trees became silver and white and the graphics were spectacular." "Commentary," *Déjà Vu*, DVD.

29 A fuller discussion of the film's special effects appears in Tara DiLullo, "*Déjà Vu*: Time Tripping to New VFX Heights," *Animation World Network*, November 22, 2006, http://www.awn.com/articles/reviews/ideja -vui-time-tripping-new-vfx-heights/page/1%2C1. Scott was a particular proponent of the "raw" look of the LIDAR point cloud. Asylum, the effects house on the film, hired Steve Snyder of Bohannan Huston, a civil engineering firm, to do the local scans in New Orleans. Even at the level of technology, the production was ghosting the hurricane. In October 2005, the National Science Foundation sent in its own investigators (the Independent Levee Investigation Team, ILIT) to examine levee breaches throughout the city. The members of the team from the US Geological Survey brought their own LIDAR with them to produce rapid digital maps of the damage. Their work is reproduced in the ILIT's *Investigation of the Performance of the New Orleans Flood Protection System in Hurricane Katrina on August 29, 2005*, Appendix A, http://www.ce.berkeley.edu/ projects/neworleans/report/A.pdf. They released their final report on July 31, 2006. *Déjà Vu* recommitted to New Orleans in October and was released in November 2006.

30 "Commentary," *Déjà Vu*, DVD.

31 Ibid.

32 Ibid.

33 Henri Bergson, "Memory of the Present and False Recognition," in *Mind-Energy: Lectures and Essays*, trans. H. Wildon Carr (London: Macmillan, 1920), 109–151, 137.

34 Justin Wyatt and Christine Vlesmas, "The Drama of Recoupment," in *Titanic: Anatomy of a Blockbuster*, ed. Kevin Sandler and Gaylyn Studlar (New Brunswick, NJ: Rutgers University Press, 1999), 29–45. The emblematic form of self-knowledge under neoclassicism is the self-similarity of chaos theory, as in the lyric from *Pocahontas*'s "Colors of the Wind," "But if you walk the footsteps of a stranger, / You'll learn things you never knew you never knew." For a more extensive consideration, see my "Let's Make the Weather: Chaos Comes to Hollywood," in *The Studios after the Studios* (Palo Alto, CA: Stanford University Press, forthcoming).

35 *WarGames* (John Badham; MGM, 1983); *Tootsie* (Sydney Pollack; Columbia, 1982); *Groundhog Day* (Harold Ramis; Columbia, 1993); *Broadcast News* (James L. Brooks; Twentieth-Century Fox, 1987); *Batman* (Tim Burton; Warner Bros., 1989); *Syriana* (Stephen Gaghan; Warner Bros., 2005); *Body of Lies* (Ridley Scott; Warner Bros., 2008); *Bourne Identity* (Doug Liman; Universal, 2002); *Bourne Supremacy* (Paul Greengrass; Universal, 2004); *Bourne Ultimatum* (Paul Greengrass; Universal, 2007).

36 Both quotations from "Cast and Crew Insights," *Source Code*, Duncan Jones (Summit/Mark Gordon/Vendôme, 2011), Blu-ray.

37 His body remains in its preservation pod in both cases, but in the first case, the consciousness in that body is communicating textually, while in the second, the consciousness has been shifted to Sean Fentress.

38 "Commentary," *Source Code*, Blu-ray.

39 Ibid.

40 The full quotation is: "Jenny, I don't know if Momma was right or if, if it's Lieutenant Dan. I don't know if we each have a destiny, or if we're all just floating around, accidental-like on a breeze, but I, I think maybe it's both. Maybe both is happening at the same time."

41 This Jamesonian tic ("the grid itself") is meant as both homage and critique: homage to the remarkable reading of global cinematic production in "Totality as Conspiracy," in *The Geopolitical Aesthetic* (Bloomington: Indiana University Press, 1992), 8–84; and critique of Jameson's elision of the industrial categories that mediate between a film's image of totality (or possibility: the streets of Washington, DC, in *All the President's Men*) and the capitalist system as a whole.

42 The "No Signal" supercut by Rich Juzwiak captures the many modes of cell phone failure. http://fourfour.typepad.com/fourfour/2009/09/no -signal-a-supercut.html.

43 The film, although finished in 2010, was a victim of the MGM bankruptcy; it sat on the shelf until Lionsgate acquired it for release in 2012.

44 Joss Whedon and Drew Goddard, *The Cabin in the Woods*, screenplay (n.d.), 20. http://alexcassun.files.wordpress.com/2012/08/cabin-in-the -woods.pdf.

45 See, for example, the patent application for 4144411, http://www.google
    .com/patents/US4144411?printsec=drawing#v=onepage&q&f=false.

46 *The Cabin in the Woods*, screenplay, 45.

47 Ibid., 92.

48 Without access to the books, it is impossible to know precisely how much
    Cabin received. Roughly 49 percent of its Canadian labor costs were
    refundable, with the possibility of more depending on how far away from
    Vancouver the location was.

49 Hollywood does imagine a complement to filmmaking in the future per-
    fect: the abandoned serves as the substrate of filmmaking in the imper-
    fect. In the making of a featurette for *Casino Royale* (Martin Campbell;
    MGM/Columbia, 2006), "James Bond: for Real" (DVD), producer Michael
    G. Wilson explains, "When you're looking for a building under construc-
    tion for filming they're just about impossible to find because by the time
    you go and look at a building, you have to plan to work there, and by
    the time you're done planning, the building's moved on and probably
    finished. But this place, being an abandoned building, it was easy for us
    to make it look like it was a construction project that was still going on."

50 *The Cabin in the Woods*, screenplay, 105.

Anti-Capitalism and Anti-Realism in William T. Vollmann's *Poor People*

C A R E N   I R R

As a slogan updating the presumably spoiled goods of socialist realism for the neoliberal present, "capitalist realism" initially suggests an effort to interpret and organize reality in terms consistent with capitalist ideology. Understood in this sense, capitalist realism might prove an especially unsustainable literary project, since so many American writers habitually present themselves as offering an insight deeper or more critical than that of the reigning ideology. Echoing the words of Bill Gray, Don DeLillo's abject writer-hero in *Mao II*, they use the novel as a "democratic shout" just barely audible above the industrial din.[1] Apart from a few devotees of Ayn Rand, who in the contemporary literary pantheon finds advocating capitalism a pressing literary task? Surely a far greater number of writers today adopt a stance premised on a disruptive or ironic relation to capitalism and therefore to any aesthetic described by a label such as capitalist realism.

"Capitalism," after all, is a word more commonly found on the lips of those who imagine themselves its critics (much like "communism," for that matter). Its proponents prefer to repackage its phenomena in a discourse of "the market" or—even more broadly and banally—"economics," where that purported science is understood not in the comparative sense but rather as the on-going management of a naturally occurring and inevitable system of exchange to which only other, surely tendentious persons insist on attaching an "ism." For economists of this sort, a literary project of capitalist realism implies an anti-capitalist agenda based on a revelation of the horrors of the system, and such a practice of exposé continues the aforementioned and unpopular socialist realism rather than inverting it.

In both of these senses, then, the cultivation of a literature designated "capitalist realism" initially seems unpromising. Capitalism as a system that writers in some sense oppose and yet cannot name or perhaps even know deeply strands its would-be analysts in a representational dilemma. In his still-pertinent writings on cognitive mapping, however, Fredric Jameson asserts that wrestling with the challenge of representing a swiftly changing practice on the periphery of aesthetic perception can lead artists to generate usefully indirect or "degraded" figures for the total system.[2] Jameson's famous examples of such figures from the heyday of postmodernism and the boom phase of the information economy include paranoia, conspiracy, and hysterical hyper-realism. The gambit of my own essay—and perhaps of this collection as a whole—is that capitalist realism might provide an opportunity to name a new set of similarly partial, incomplete or "degraded" figures for a new phase of capitalist accumulation.

Faced with the pressing, yet apparently impossible task of representing a new capitalist reality that is still in the process of emerging, writers necessarily rummage through their toolboxes in search of handy items they might repurpose. Arguably, one such resource for the aspiring capitalist realist is the small but distinctive tradition of Anglophone prose documentaries. Devoted to exposing the social ills of urban capitalism, landmarks of the form from Jacob Riis's *How the Other Half Lives* (1890) and James Agee and Walker Evans's *Let Us Now Praise Famous Men* (1941) to Michael Harrington's *The Other America* (1962) and Barbara Ehrenreich's *Nickel and Dimed* (2001) use a middle-class eye to bring the collective subject they designate "the poor" into view.[3] Their efforts are especially notable for their non-dogmatic quality. None of these contributions to this baggy genre adopts a strictly pro- or anti-capitalist stance, for instance, since each wobbles between the two senses of capitalism outlined above, alternating between viewing capitalism as an ideologically charged enemy and a natural condition so deeply entrenched as to appear a law of nature.

The commitment to realism as an aesthetic is similarly ambivalent in the prose documentary. This tradition relies equally at different moments on the revelation of social conditions assumed to actually exist, the almost total absorption into the documentarian's own recording consciousness, and a self-conscious attention to the conventions of the tradition itself.[4] Although certain lines of development and transformation do organize the history of the genre, each mood retains a sectoral validity, accomplishing too many immediately necessary tasks to be dispensed with. So-called naïve referential realism, for example, recurs repeatedly long after its apparent refutation, and moments of intense self-consciousness about generic conventions are evident from the genre's outset. Since these prose documentaries concern human subjects, however, these multiple approaches to realism have consequences that exceed the purely epistemological; they reveal a generic consistency in a body of writing that passes through modernist and postmodernist phases, finding itself in a new mood in the twenty-first century.

The most constant element of the prose documentary is open-endedness with respect to its central question: how to conceive of its subject. To the extent that the tradition of the prose documentary imagines "the poor" as a static, receding, or impossible object of attention that the middle-class documentarian has a moral burden to represent realistically, the aesthetic stance triggers a persistent difficulty and an obsessive preoccupation for the form. The problem is that when "the poor" are viewed as actually existing persons inhabiting a concrete social reality fully available to the middle-class observer's moral scrutiny, they are rendered largely silent objects alien to the naively realist author. A more modernist or postmodernist emphasis on the manufactured social conditions and generic expectations that create poverty and "the poor" as objects of external attention is little improvement, tending, as it does, to empty out the category and dissolve the possibility of locating a subject who could speak authoritatively about poverty as anything other than a social by-product. Critical realisms of this latter sort thus retreat from their subject into ever-deeper crevasses of the writer's solipsism. The consistent double bind of documentary realism is that it is both required for anti-capitalist moral authority and impossible when it positions those with whom it imagines itself to be empathizing as either silent or imaginary objects.

Although a spate of mockumentaries, shockumentaries, and lyrical reflections on the craft of investigative writing sustained the form through the epistemological assaults on realism associated with postmodernism, this fundamental problem remains both unresolved and definitive for the prose documentary. The genre's ethical protest remains scandalized by the prospect that it effectively functions as a form of economic pornography. The logical conclusions that follow from this moral horror appear in a particularly acute form in a recent contribution to the genre, William T. Vollmann's *Poor People* (2007).[5] In a mood that we might call metamodern,[6] Vollmann revisits the modernist interpretations of the prose documentary (especially Agee and Evans's) without, however, suggesting he has any special authority or ability to solve the problems raised there. Vollmann renews the strategies learned from his predecessors in order to test them against the conditions he observes.

Vollmann's project begins with an explicit acknowledgment of the ways, as a collective subject, "the poor" are always *with* but never *of* "us." Because he "cannot claim to have been poor" and thus cannot write from personal experience as he usually prefers to do, Vollmann interviewed dozens of what he calls spectacularly poor people around the world, asking them how they survive and why they think they are poor (xi). In *Poor People*, he shares what he learned in these interviews with readers he presumes to be, like himself, rich. Vollmann asks these readers to study their assumptions about the poor—especially the assumption that the poor are alienated from capitalist norms of civility and self-control. In several passages, Vollmann also parodically reproduces middle-class caricatures of the poor as hostile invaders who can "turn ugly and infect the rich with their accident proneness" (159). At the same time, he works to unsettle a complementary "Victorian ethos" of charity that treats poverty as a moral question and the poor as objects of pity (47).

In addition to documenting the impact of these assumptions on the poor person's self-concept, Vollmann also scrupulously illustrates the impact both ideas have had on him—confessing his own suspect compassion ("I do pity her with all my heart" [31]) and exploring his own suspicion of the stories that some of his interviewees tell him.

He offers particularly close readings of narratives provided by Sunee, an alcoholic Thai mother, and Natalia, a Russian beggar. Vollmann describes Sunee's drunkenness and Buddhist resignation as "entirely natural" and even "beneficial" responses to her situation—while still honoring his own and his presumed reader's skepticism about theology (24). Similarly, Vollmann notes his own doubts about contradictions in the autobiography Natalia provides him, questioning her reliance on figures endowed with an almost supernatural ability to wrong her ("the gypsy woman," for example).

As with Sunee, however, Vollmann is not primarily interested in unraveling Natalia's story to decide which concrete events precipitated her current crisis. Rather, he accumulates motifs—a taste for grandiosity, for instance—in support of his conclusion that the experience of poverty, not its causes, matters most. It is not the plausibility of magical or theological thinking that finally interests Vollmann but rather what he feels it expresses: namely, the uncertainty of inhabiting "a dangerous world . . . speckled with weaknesses whose inexplicability might as well be called supernatural" (69). Fear of this dangerous world leads middle-class people (here called "the rich") to retreat in Vollmann's view; stereotypes of the poor as deceptive, untrustworthy, and dangerous themselves follow, he asserts in a brilliant borrowing from I. A. Richards, from a middle-class "withdrawal from experience" (45). Although inhabiting precisely the same inexplicable world as the poor, the rich refuse to know them as kin and instead engage in self-protective rituals designed to exorcise its dangers.

Against such scapegoating, Vollmann provides intensely subjective and/or phenomenological accounts of individual cases of poverty, and these soon become the only solid reference points in his documentary. His economic universe is unstable, and he asserts that it is essentially unquantifiable.[7] Despite providing at the outset a table comparing the incomes of people described in the book (including himself), Vollmann repeatedly emphasizes the untrustworthiness of such Thoreauvian efforts to calculate the fluctuating incomes of the very poor in terms of currency, let alone the cost of meeting daily needs in various locations. He is similarly unpersuaded by criteria such as those employed by the United Nations that define poverty in concrete terms such as "short life, illiteracy, exclusion, and lack of material resources" (101). Most of the unmet needs that Vollmann associates with poverty are psychological and social. Vollmann's alternate definition of poverty takes invisibility, deformity, unwantedness, dependence, accident proneness, pain, numbness, and estrangement as its hallmarks. He replaces structural or material explanations of poverty with a reduction of poverty to a condition of being "unhappy in his or her own normality" (1). This position follows directly from his opening assertion that "poverty is never political," because like all human experience it is, for Vollmann, solitary (29).

Vollmann offers these statements and definitions in a spirit that he too modestly describes as "capricious, . . . sad[,] and probably useless" (102). We should not be so easily misled, however. His project is grounded in a distinctive contemporary sensibility. The metamodern qualified despair may not seem to Vollmann explicitly political, but for the budding capitalist realist, this position has an inescapably political connotation precisely because it evacuates the site of "politics." By separating the solitary unhappiness of the poor from debatable political problems, Vollmann naturalizes extreme poverty, making it an eternal and endemic feature of human existence.

Vollmann takes poor *people* rather than poverty as a problem because his deepest (and arguably most political) commitment is to an absolute standard of human equality. He works up this view in several places, most notably in this position statement:

> Because I wish to respect poor people's perceptions and experiences, I refuse to say that I know their good better than they; accordingly, I further refuse to condescend to them with the pity that either pretends they have no choices at all, or else, worse yet, gilds their every choice with my benevolent approval. Once again I submit the obvious: Poor people are no more and no less human than I; accordingly, they deserve to be judged and understood precisely as do I myself. (170)

As an absolutist, even a self-described fetishist, about equality, Vollmann outlines an ethical stance that requires recognition of the psychological world of others on par with his own concerns. He measures their "perceptions and experiences" in relation to his own. Vollmann follows this view past its easier associations with liberal tolerance (or "benevolent approval") through to a more uncomfortable, existentialist-tinged rhetorical question: since "consciousness can make its own choices, shouldn't I consider some ways that poverty can enrich itself with happiness?" he asks (238). This emphasis on the happiness of the poor allows him to endorse their and his sustaining comforts (drink, drugs, theology, fellowship), and it also drives him to the necessary conclusion that poverty is "a sacred *choice* of the personality" (289; emphasis in the original). Poverty understood as a choice is not a social problem to be ameliorated or a structural issue to be corrected. Poverty understood as a choice expresses an existential attitude toward an ultimately uncontrolled, unknowable world.

As already noted, this radical, existential egalitarianism precludes any collection of data about the threshold of poverty in different locations. It also makes poverty fundamentally intractable and impermeable to revolution, reform, or aid. Although Vollmann explicitly states that he supports "every one of the United Nations' suggestions" for reducing poverty (he seems to have the Millennium Development Goals in mind), he is skeptical not simply about their immediate feasibility but also about any effort to alter the world of the poor (221). "I assume that some people will always be poor, as some people eternally have been," he asserts at the midpoint of *Poor People*; "there is little that you and I can do for people like [Big Mountain], and not much they can do for themselves" (222). Poverty understood as an existential condition of longing and unhappiness is eternally intractable not because it is good, but because the human condition in this world is not.

Vollmann can imagine and even sometimes identify inklings of other worlds—most importantly "a culture of communalism [that] . . . can mitigate each and every one of the phenomena of poverty," a "true neighborliness" (259). However, according to Vollmann's rigorous standards, such a culture would have to arise from the direct, face-to-face engagement of individuals who recognize and respect each other's full equality. This rarely happens. Instead, it is our familiar and collective failure to directly perceive one another—our "withdrawal from experience" and our habituation to stereotype—that ensures the impossibility of "a culture of communalism."

As a case in point, Vollmann describes the limited success of his own efforts to act on his ethics in a series of powerful, strange, and philosophically difficult meditations in the third-to-last chapter, "I Know I Am Rich." Explaining the limits he has set with the homeless men and women who camp in the parking lot adjoining his home, Vollmann explains in a notably anti-heroic manner the channels that have closed between himself and his neighbors. Some of these portals are literal—such as the steel door and tin foil–lined windows that enclose his family's private space. Vollmann unapologetically describes himself kicking an imploring beggar "in the knee so that he fell back outside" and slamming the door shut when "he tried to shove past me" (282). Vollmann confesses to actions that derive from his own class-based fear that "the poor people [are] coming to take everything from me" (287). He reveals himself to be fully implicated in a failure to live equally and communally; this failure obliges him to engage in a project of ceaseless self-scrutiny.

This responsibility is not his alone. In this world that Vollmann takes to be defined by sovereign consciousnesses choosing their condition and existing in a state of horrific, inescapable alienation from one another even though they desire a culture of communalism, Vollmann underscores the necessity of continuing to ask basic questions about one's responsibility to self and others. "What have I done over my life in light of this inequality [between rich and poor], and what should I have done, and whom have I helped and harmed, and what should I do now" is the catechism that Vollmann recommends to himself and his readers alike in *Poor People* (290).

This responsibility for perpetual ethical inquiry is an urgent, achievable task in the present. As such, it offsets the fruitless quest to reach a specific interlocutor Vollmann undertakes in one of the few passages that implies that a structural explanation for deprivation might exist. In "Crime without Criminals," Vollmann leaves behind the street beggars who preoccupy him throughout most of *Poor People* and begins to narrate an attempt to interview the head of a Kazakh oil company. After poisoning villagers with sulfurous gasses, this company began relocating its sickly victims, and Vollmann sought an encounter with those in charge. He never locates the official he hopes to interview, however, only his guileless young children, and even the local people who had promised to speak with him disappear into the woodwork after apparently being intimidated. The moral of this story for Vollmann is not that the oil industry needs reform or regulation or replacement, but rather that all the people dependent on oil money as well as "you and I" are all deeply culpable in the poisoning of the Kazakh environment. There are no individual criminals to locate, and no crimes have been committed, because a position premised on the belief "that everybody, even a condemned prisoner in his death cell, retains some degree of moral freedom" (190–191) disperses responsibility across the system. In Vollmann's universe of unreachable causes, inexplicable disorder, and violent competition for space and resources, only scrupulously ethical individual actions arising from unusual fortitude, patience, and curiosity stand a chance. Culpability—like unhappiness—is a choice one makes only about oneself and never about another in *Poor People.*

For this reason, it should not surprise us that Vollmann's research into the phenomena of poverty takes him finally to a place where essentially all that remains is the archive he has assembled—a mass of transcripts and snapshots, memories, "speculations and interpretation" that, he asserts, lie "near to reality itself" (xv). Vollmann as an author knows the limitations of this material, even as he prizes it, and he repeatedly recognizes the incompleteness and brevity of his acquaintance with the poor people who feature in his book. His diligent efforts at authentic, responsible, fully voluntary face-to-face encounters implode, crumbling down into purely textual matter. Vollmann's second- and third-order simulations of his experiences with other people's experiences of themselves constitute his writing—a writing that must prove itself adequate to the reality that grounds it through "honest attempts to make sense of phenomena" (xv). His realism, in short, requires his first-person, confessional presence; it needs to absorb and frame all of these encounters in the never-ending questioning and anxious self-consciousness of the writer who chooses—freely, responsibly—to write in a world that need not support him in any manner. In this way, Vollmann's metamodern take on the documentary assumes neither the stability of poor people as objects nor the perspicacity of a writer-observer's eye. Vollmann's realism is animated instead by an understanding of the capitalist marketplace from which he derives his own income as an inchoate, unknown, even unknowable system within which one has only at last the option of retaining a small degree of personal integrity. His realism derives from and supports this understanding of the unregulated capitalist economy, extending it to the worlds of poor people whose environments are also inherently unstable and whose only resources ultimately are their own often limited, sometimes unimaginably creative, narratives.

At this point, then, William T. Vollmann's interpretation of the prose documentary returns us to the problem of capitalist realism with which we began. His capitalism, as we have seen, is a faceless, unstable, perhaps ultimately unidentifiable force—as fundamentally damaged and incoherent as Soviet communism and far less psychologically sustaining than theology. Capitalism accelerates the process of receding from view that already characterizes Vollmann's encounters with specific poor people. Neither these individuals—available to him in the act of writing only as photos or words sometimes uncertainly translated—nor capitalism itself has an enduring relation to Vollmann's writerly consciousness beyond the moment of the encounter. His own desire to interpret and understand thus fills up the holes left by a "speckled" world that readily reveals its crimes but conceals its criminals, just as his own manifestly abundant skill as a writer swells up to return those lost faces temporarily to life. This compensatory type of realism, however, is confessedly provisional and anti-illusionistic, just as Vollmann's final grim paean to "money [that] just goes to where it goes" reiterates the slippery, incoherent nature of capitalism as well (294).

No effort at capitalist realism undertaken on Vollmann's terms, in short, can be either anti-capitalist or pro-capitalist, since there is no specific capitalism that one might locate—only pocket change, closed doors, and disappearing plant managers who, like Joseph Heller's

Major Major, are always in, just never when you go to see them. His documentary can also not be realist in any of the several senses in which we might conventionally understand that term; Vollmann proceeds honestly and yet without enduring access to an extra-textual real or a stable set of literary conventions for triggering a reality-effect. Vollmann's fetish for ethical egalitarianism requires instead that any relationship between self and other, author and world, be built anew for each occasion. Each specific encounter he describes must reconstitute the real, as must each text describing such an encounter. Vollmann's only durable skill in this process is his capacity to tell his own story about the resonant images of the poor. He does not grant himself a magical capacity to illuminate their circumstances for a readership that may or may not include poor people themselves. He might desire as a writer the moral authority comparable to the UN's efforts to offer "more aid, better directed," but he does not ultimately understand himself to inhabit a universe that allows for this possibility. To satisfy Vollmann's demands for radical egalitarianism, his writing must be both subordinate to the encounters it narrates and entangled with these conditions on an equal footing. This is a shifty, unstable aesthetic requiring constant recalibration and leaving him, as already noted, with many intentionally uncomfortable "speculations and interpretations."

Considered as a case study of the imagined aesthetic of "capitalist realism," then, Vollmann's ethical documentary takes a strategy that is the dialectical antithesis of the political project recommended by Jacques Rancière in the 2002 afterword to *The Philosopher and His Poor.*[8] Rancière reflects critically on two equally incomplete approaches to the problem of representing the poor that he found in France during the 1970s. Recalling Pierre Bourdieu's explorations of the role of school culture in maintaining class distinctions, Rancière calls these approaches "republican pedagogy" and "modernist pedagogy." The former aims to acculturate the poor to republican values such as equality, mainly through explicit bourgeoisification. It respects and protects the poor by modeling their behavior on that of middle-class citizens. The second, modernist pedagogy (closer to the pluralist aims of US education in recent decades) aims to diversify educational content by population, in effect leaving elite culture fully in place but reserving it for a small population of those already advantaged. Both of these equally unsatisfactory processes, according to Rancière, address the question of the poor through questions of culture, differing in their tactics because they disagree on the question of whether the poor have a distinct culture. Rather than deciding this question in the affirmative or the negative, though, Rancière recasts it as a question of social divisions, asking how and why the idea that intellectual (and by extension cultural) difference results from different modes of labor originated and was perpetuated.

In short, Rancière shows how the problem of the poor stages a fundamental paradox about the meaning of equality in modern democracies. Equality, he asserts, is not a social outcome (as pedagogues might hope) but rather something "fundamental and absent, current and untimely" (223). Equality, especially between classes (or, if you prefer Vollmann's terms, between "rich" and "poor"), is a crucial but also necessarily impossible premise for modern democratic capitalist societies. Excluded by definition from "culture" and self-representation and thus clearly demonstrating the persistence of social division within purportedly egalitarian republics, the poor for Rancière reveal the characteristic double-thinking surrounding equality in the democratic and capitalist analysis that presents itself so aggressively as a realist alternative to utopian ideals of socialism. The problem of the poor, then, is *always* political for Rancière because it reveals the contested and malleable social origins of divisions that ought not, ideologically speaking, to exist. The specter of the poor makes visible and sensible the contradictions underlying a purportedly seamless, global capitalist reality.

In other words, while Rancière shares with Vollmann the foundational belief that the problem of poverty is one of equality, he treats equality as a political, not an existential or ethical, dilemma. Consequently, Rancière offers a political aesthetic as well: imagining a kind of double image that calls to light the heterogeneity of the visible, sensible world, making "visible what has been excluded" and enhancing our perception of the antagonisms that organize our subjective experiences (226). Rancière's politicized aesthetic of the double image offers a counterpoint to Vollmann's intensely monadic anti-political aesthetic, his monster of self-consciousness absorbing and obsessively scrutinizing its relation to all that crosses its path. (After all, Vollmann's career is itself not only characterized by individual works of great length but also by its polymorphic interconnections—all volumes contributing in some sense to his own ongoing effort to narrate his consciousness's relation to itself.) Rancière's political images of poverty as a political problem propose both an aesthetic and philosophical negation of Vollmann's libertarian hyper-individualism, as well as an alternative to the related economic narratives less systematically developed by contemporaries such as David Foster Wallace, Jonathan Franzen, and Dave Eggers.

Although finding few contemporary literary companions, at least in US fiction, Rancière's antagonistic, heterogeneous realism is clearly in greater and easier sympathy with a number of scholarly approaches to the problem of poverty—from David Harvey's brilliant exposition of the processes of accumulation through dispossession in *The Spaces of Global Capitalism* to Rob Nixon's exploration of the rhetoric of African activists in *Slow Violence and the Environmentalism of the Poor*.[9] Like Richard Dienst in *The Bonds of Debt*, these neo-Marxisms describe a world organized around collective, structural antagonisms, embedded in geography, ecology, and economy as well as face-to-face violence and ethical double binds. This approach involves emphasis on material contradictions that Vollmann's pronounced allergy to any ideology of structure, and statism in particular, guarantees he does not embrace as his own.

However, rather than preferring a capitalist realism that reproduces in aesthetic terms the insights of scholarly analysis, I wish to conclude by suggesting that both forms express essentially the same problem. Both literary and scholarly or ethical and political approaches are faces of the emerging capitalist realist project. Their differences are tactical rather than strategic. After all, both Vollmann's potentially monomaniacal ethics and Rancière's and others' explicitly political aesthetic share an essential element, a component that is surely necessary for any version of the new representational project called capitalist realism: both articulate an ideal, however compromised and easily foreclosed, of a "culture of communalism." In *The Bonds of Debt*, Dienst reminds us that one powerful way to name this kind of vision of a globally responsive, positively entangled collectivity is through the language of solidarity. Updating the metaphor of fraternity, Dienst positions solidarity as the third term in the familiar three-part refrain of the French Revolution and as the dialectical complement to the Cold War opposition between liberty and equality. In this sense, all of these variously conflicted variations on the theme of capitalist realism remind us that the problem of "the poor" (which is always really the problem of the debts binding the rich to the poor) encompasses the problem of equality without being limited to it. This profound reorientation of the problem suggests that the uneasy and perhaps as yet mainly hypothetical aesthetic of capitalist realism must begin with equality while also engineering a movement from that agonistic struggle toward the common ground of human solidarity. Such a movement may finally prove necessary for any effort to document and perhaps also to act affirmatively in this tragic world.

NOTES

1 Don DeLillo, *Mao II* (New York: Penguin, 1991), 159.

2 Fredric Jameson, "Cognitive Mapping," in *Marxism and the Interpretation of Culture*, ed. Cary Nelson and Lawrence Grossberg (Champaign-Urbana: University of Illinois Press, 1990), 347–360.

3 William Stott provides a good introduction to the earlier part of this tradition in *Documentary Expression and Thirties America* (Chicago: University of Chicago Press, 1973).

4 Bill Nichols presents an extremely useful analysis of the basic modes of documentary realism in *Representing Reality: Issues and Concepts* (Bloomington: Indiana University Press, 1991), 32–75.

5 William T. Vollmann, *Poor People* (New York: HarperCollins, 2007). Hereafter cited parenthetically in the text.

6 Timotheus Vermeulen and Robin van den Akker, "Notes on Metamodernism," *Journal of Aesthetics and Culture* 2 (2010): 1–14.

7 In something of the same spirit, Richard Dienst examines some of the famous difficulties in establishing a globally applicable standard of living index in *The Bonds of Debt* (New York: Verso, 2011) and offers some analy-

sis of problems with standard measures of income inequality such as the Gini coefficient.

8   Jacques Rancière, *The Philosopher and His Poor*, ed. and intro. Andrew Parker, trans. John Drury, Corinne Oster, and Andrew Parker (Durham, NC: Duke University Press, 2003). Hereafter cited parenthetically in the text.

9   David Harvey, *Spaces of Global Capitalism* (New York: Verso, 2006); Rob Nixon, *Slow Violence and the Environmentalism of the Poor* (Cambridge, MA: Harvard University Press, 2011).

PART III   *After and Against Representation*

Beyond Realism

"Capitalism seamlessly occupies the horizons of the thinkable."[1] Mark Fisher puts his finger on the basic problem for left politics: how is one to imagine an alternative to capitalism? Realism is our great enemy in this effort. "Realism" in this context refers both to an attitude—a grim identification of the rule of markets with necessity, practicality, and hard-nosed common sense—as well as a cultural regime—art that reproduces and reinforces its context. It would thus seem that the anti-mimetic is our great ally. "Anti-mimetic" in this context refers both to an attitude—a willingness to imagine alternatives to what exists—as well as a cultural practice—art that escapes from its context.[2] In the following I will argue that, despite his acute registration of our urgent political dilemma, Fisher's interpretive practice gives comfort to the enemy and deprives us of our ally. By reading the fictional as mimetic of the actual, by turning even science fiction into a species of realism, Fisher forecloses our capacity to see how art in fact challenges capitalist reality.

This interpretive practice is by no means Fisher's private fault. Rather, his approach is dictated by a venerable method of defending the humanities' capacity to generate knowledge about society. Thus, to assess his claims we need to attend to criticism's institutional position, and to the struggle to legitimate humanistic knowledge in the contemporary intellectual and institutional climate. Why should anti-capitalist activists turn to left literary or film criticism, instead of to left economics, history, or political science? The traditional answer has been that cultural works provide a special kind of evidence about economic, political, and social conditions, evidence that other disciplines cannot access. A novel or a film, in this account, functions as evidence about a given social condition—in this case, contemporary capitalism. By reading novels and poems, or watching films and television shows, we can grasp the contours, the strategies and weaknesses, of the socio-economic logic we wish to contest.

But, as I will show, in practice the extraction of this evidence often depends on theories that are not derived from the works. These social, psychological, and economic theories are, however, "literary" in the sense that they are largely absent from the social and natural sciences. This constitutes their great appeal for critics, who are thus provided with social knowledges autonomous with respect to economics, political science, biology, sociology, or history.

And yet this autonomous position is a double-edged sword. It shelters our theories from the kind of debate now necessary, in the aftermath of the Sokal hoax, to legitimate the extra-disciplinary claims of literary thinkers.[3] Without the possibility of meaningful interdisciplinary testing, these theories take on the quasi-fictional status of "literary economics," "literary psychology," or "literary critical sociology." These theories are literary not in the sense that they are derived from works of literature, but in the sense that literary critics tend to be the only people who work with them. Cultural scholarship's claim to autonomous knowledge thus rests on a displacement of the fictional or virtual from the object of study to the critic's theory.

This traditional understanding of literature as evidence used to illustrate social or psychological or economic theories whose primary institutional home is the English department is not tenable. It has proved unsuccessful both at demonstrating the value of the humanities and at contributing to the anti-capitalist struggle. Both criticism and the social and economic theories which critics espouse have had little or no impact on the recent vigorous left attack on failed free market economics, for example, or on the development of new political processes in the Occupy movements, to take a different example.[4] Autonomy becomes isolation. This is not criticism's necessary fate. Once we see literary works not as evidence of actually existing capitalism, but as intellectual and material examples of escape from capitalist reality, a meaningful relation both to other disciplines and to urgent political questions becomes possible.

* * *

"Cyberspatial capital works by addicting its users; William Gibson recognized that in *Neuromancer*" (Fisher, 25). Here Fisher reads the science fiction novel as a realistic description of capitalism's actual procedures. This decision to treat Gibson's image of addiction as realistic immediately opens into a discussion of addiction as a system of control constituting the central pathology of late capitalism. Citing Jameson, Deleuze, and Lacan, Fisher then analyzes the impact of this "addiction"—of which "attention-deficit disorder" is an apparent symptom—on postsecondary education in the UK. Finally, he argues against the typical way of treating mental-health disorders such as addiction, arguing that this occludes the extent to which such pathologies are expressions of social malaise. Like R. D. Laing, who described schizophrenia as a protest against an intolerable social order, Fisher thinks we don't need to treat health issues such as addiction so much as to harness the negative affect they express for social transformation.[5]

These claims immediately raise a number of basic questions. Is the "addiction" Fisher describes in fact the same phenomenon as the addictions described by the medical profession? How are addiction and attention-deficit disorder related? Does mental health treatment equal pacification? Is "addiction" here a metaphor? What is the difference between an addictive relation to media and a non-addictive relation? Is addiction in fact socially constructed, or does it also have genetic components?

The discovery of the genetic basis of schizophrenia, as well as the discovery of its erosive effects on the brain, proved fatal to Laing's description of schizophrenia as a social protest that should be amplified rather than treated. Mindful of this history, a writer wishing to challenge mental-health practices he considers to be socially harmful would be wise to devote serious effort to addressing questions like the ones raised above.

But none of these questions are addressed, nor is it possible to address them within the terms of Fisher's discussion. Consider the first question, for example. Does his "addiction" name the same phenomenon as "addiction" in a neuroscience or medical journal? Fisher's way of defining addiction, and the particular authorities he uses, precludes any contact with the way addiction is defined and discussed in non-literary critical contexts.

Fisher's dissent from medical orthodoxy is not, of course, necessarily disabling to his argument. Both the disease concept of addiction, as well as many of the particular descriptions of the disease, have intelligent critics.[6] Strong evidence for Fisher's view of addiction as an expression of revolt at capitalist reality might indeed lead us to believe that he has a compelling account of addiction. But the main evidence Fisher adduces is Gibson's book, a work of science fiction. This evidence by itself is unlikely to convince anyone that the dominant descriptions of addiction current in psychology, neuroscience, and medicine are deeply flawed. And without a serious challenge to these descriptions, it seems both practically impossible and ethically indefensible to withhold treatment from people suffering from addiction.

The logic of Fisher's argument here is simple. (1) Insist that the science fiction novel reflects the way the real world actually works. (2) Argue that Jameson/Deleuze/Lacan have a theory of the world that seems to mesh with the science fiction novel. (3) Conclude that a psycho-socio-economic view of addiction culled from Jameson/Deleuze/Lacan describes the central pathology of our age. This has the practical result that (4) *Neuromancer's* repressed anti-mimetic status infects claims that the critic intends as descriptive of the real world. Fisher's "addiction" becomes fictionalized.

Perhaps Fisher's argument would be stronger had he undertaken a sustained critical engagement with the views of addiction held by other disciplines. Perhaps this engagement would show that his psycho-economic model of addiction presents a formidable opponent to weak psychological, sociological, medical, or neuroscientific paradigms. Of course, Fisher might reasonably feel that such a demand places an undue burden on the critic. Yet in the absence of such sustained engagement, the plausibility of Fisher's interdisciplinary claims is likely to be quite limited.

But what if there were a simpler way? Fisher's publishing enterprise is, after all, predicated on the possibility of effective humanistic inquiry outside the disciplinary codes of traditional academic venues. What if he could make strong arguments without needing to engage in the laborious, fraught, and potentially fruitless attempt to bring Jameson/Deleuze/Lacan into contact with disciplinary knowledges? What would it mean if we simply didn't take the first step of Fisher's argument? What if we began from the premise that Gibson's novel is in fact what it claims to be: a science-fictional representation of a world not our own?

Socially engaged criticism has historically been reluctant to do this, in part from a fear that this consigns us to talking about "merely" aesthetic problems. Even within the criticism of science fiction, there has been a steady erosion of attention to the discontinuity of fiction with actuality. Darko Suvin's influential formulas recognize that science fiction deals with empirically unactualizable states of affairs.[7] But he locates science fiction's value in the way it defamiliarizes our present, sharply distinguishing it from mere fantasy, which lacks such an orientation to the actual. Similarly, Seo-Young Chu, drawing on Fredric Jameson, argues that "science fiction makes us conscious of the present as the past of some unexpected future."[8] Science fiction's power lies in its ability to illuminate aspects of reality. In what seems the logical conclusion to this mode of reading, Chu has recently developed a sophisticated framework for redescribing science fiction as the defamiliarizing mimesis of real objects. As for Fisher, for Chu science fiction is a species of the mimesis of our world.

The trajectory of the criticism, which begins by insisting on a strong distinction between science fiction and fantasy and ends by declaring science fiction to be a species of realism, is unsurprising. There is a clear value in reading works as evidence for actual states of affairs. To insist on those elements that set the work off from its social context, however, can look like either a potentially trivial formalism or a politically suspect retreat from social engagement. I want to test the critical bias detectable in the development of serious criticism of science fiction by asking what we can learn from *Neuromancer* by treating it as fiction.

The novel opens in Ninsei, a market free not only of any government presence, but also free of any corporate presence. We learn later that the malevolent corporate states of Gibson's future world have preserved this free market space in order to exploit its ability to generate new knowledges, new technologies, new desires. The absence of corporations, often represented in postwar fiction as operating according to a quasi-governmental internal logic, should give pause to the critical impulse to see Gibson's Ninsei as an image of how the market works. Instead of assuming that the literary imagination has been colonized by actually existing capitalism, perhaps by examining imaginary capitalism we will discover something we didn't already know.

Here I want to take up an argument Fisher makes in *Capitalist Realism* that is insufficiently differentiated from the critical procedure outlined above. Fisher argues that bureaucracy is a feature of actual capitalism often missing from fictional images of capitalism (Fisher, 20). His reference to the corporate call center captures the ways in which capitalism generates baroque, Kafkaesque bureaucratic nightmares that rival anything the Soviets came up with (Fisher, 64). In fact, there are not one but two kinds of capitalist realism in Fisher's study. The first are bad fictions that pretend to imitate capitalist reality but actually distort it (by ignoring its saturation with bureaucracy, for example). The second are good fictions that accurately describe reality. As we have seen, Fisher argues that Gibson's novel is an example of good realism. And yet Gibson's Ninsei is an image of the market without the quasi-governmental corporate structures that are so obvious a feature of real-world markets. If Fisher were to accept my reading of *Neuromancer*'s Ninsei, he might assign the novel to the category of bad, distorting realism.

But why should the departure from actuality be read only in terms of ideological distortion? I want to disentangle Fisher's powerful insight into the discrepancy between market fiction and market reality from his belief that valuable literature provides evidence of actual states. I want to think instead about the value of the knowledge potentially gained by perceiving the gap between literature and the actual.

The capitalism represented in Gibson's novel is not mimetic of actually existing capitalism. Nor does it have the ideological function of maintaining capitalist actuality. Ideology, after all, does its work by *pretending* to present a realistic picture while *in fact* presenting a distorted picture. But the source of *Neuromancer*'s realistic pretense is not the novel's text but Fisher's approach. Not only does the novel not pretend to be an accurate picture of its time, it theatrically declares its distance from the real world with its celebrated first sentence: "The sky above the port was the color of television, tuned to a dead channel."[9] Nearly every subsequent page describes forms of technology and modes of embodiment that resemble nothing in our present world, let alone Gibson's early '80s moment. Here we have an example not of capitalist realism, but of a frankly imaginary capitalism. What can we learn from it?

Recent political developments provide ample evidence that our culture's image of capitalism possesses a disturbing immunity to each fresh actual economic disaster. What economist or political scientist could have predicted that the recent market collapses would trigger an unprecedented wave of enthusiasm for free markets? That the provision of unemployment relief on an unprecedented scale would trigger unprecedented expressions of hatred for the state? That one of the most prominent signs carried by the Occupy protesters would be "End the Fed," the rallying cry of those who wish to disentangle the economy from government interference?

And yet these are the kinds of events that perhaps criticism, by attending to the dynamics of the gap between actual and virtual economies, *can* predict. Like science fiction writings, the protesters' signs do not present themselves as a description or defense of actually existing capitalism. The banners wave on behalf of a nonexistent order. They theatrically demonstrate the distance between actual capitalism and a world without corporations, without government, without the Fed. *Neuromancer* was written during the last recession of comparable intensity. The novel reveals how, in the postwar era, each disruption of actually existing capitalism intensifies enthusiasm for virtual capitalism.

The move by which Gibson establishes the discontinuity of his fiction with the actual invites us to expand our sense of literary reflexivity. Joshua Landy argues that critics have interpreted the tendency of texts to foreground their own fictionality according to what he calls the "informative hypothesis." Thus "reflexivity permits the discovery . . . of the social fabrication of reality, or what Patricia Waugh calls the fictionality of the world."[10] In claiming that the constructedness of literary works directly informs us of the way science or gender is constructed, this kind of interpretation might be viewed as a variant of the interdisciplinary modes I've been critiquing. But regardless of the epistemological weakness of the claims about reality that emerge, this way of reading has tended to obscure alternatives. In attending to the ways in which works highlight their anti-mimetic capacities, I wish to preserve the possibility that fictional images might operate according to principles quite different from those we take to be authoritative in describing the rest of the world. The obviousness of this difference has been clouded by uncertainty regarding the value of registering it.

Let's take another example of a science fiction novel published during the recession of the early '80s. In *The Handmaid's Tale*, Margaret Atwood has her patriarchal Christian state co-opt the communist slogan, proclaiming "From each . . . according to *her* ability, to each according to *his* need."[11] Atwood's celebration of free choice as the novel's central value is given an explicitly economic cast. Seeing another woman with a cigarette, Offred reflects: "The cigarettes must have come from the black market, I thought, and this gave me hope. Even now that there is no real money anymore, there's still a black market" (Atwood, 22). The black market is the one space of resistance in the novel. The fact that there is no real money, that is, no legal tender, no Fed, purifies this resistance by disentangling exchange from sovereignty.

Perhaps we should interpret this as a sign of the novel's ideological quality, as feminism's seduction by an enthusiasm for the actual market the Reaganites were in the process of deregulating. But to read Atwood in this way is to ignore many of the most interesting features of the novel. Consider its curious temporality. "Time is a trap," Offred remarks. But Offred does not mean what we might mean; she is not referring to time's relentless forward motion, the way it inexorably converts hope into nostalgia, expectation into memory. Rather, she exists in what she calls an eternal present. Time does not pass for her, and it is this failure of time to pass that she refers to by calling time a trap. As in Orwell's *1984*, in *The Handmaid's Tale* narration is not presented as a shaping of time, but as the creation of time out of a condition of timelessness.

What is the significance of the fact that the market that fascinates Offred is set in this timeless space? Or of the fact that there are no companies in Gibson's free market? We should begin by accepting that these images do not inform us of actual economic conditions. To think they do is not just a critical mistake, it is a political mistake. When the critic argues that Wall Street is just as fascinating and irresistible as the markets in these novels, he is creating a problem for left politics that we don't actually have, and ignoring a problem that we do have. We don't have to worry about being dazzled by actual markets without companies. But we should be thinking about the fascination of imaginary markets.

I want to dissent from Fisher's implicit argument that literature that presents non-actual images of the market is necessarily ideological and degraded. Rather, we should think of this fascination as a resource. The right's exploitation of this resource has gone largely uncontested by the left. And yet we see an eruption of the virtual market in the Occupy protests, in the presence of "End the Fed" signs next to signs that proclaim "I represent the 99%." This eruption is unthinkable within Fisher's framework. Pointing out that the vision of a free market that fascinates is also the vision of a market without corporations is only the first step in fashioning a progressive relation to such creations. And I think works like Atwood's or Gibson's are best described minimally, as creations. To call them utopian or ideological would be to have already determined what concepts such as freedom, time, markets, money, and action mean in these texts. But the opening of such basic concepts to thought is perhaps the most valuable work that the criticism of creative writing can do.

When people at a Tea Party or Occupy rally held signs proclaiming "End the Fed," they were not in the grip of a capitalist realism that had blinded them to the role of government in actually existing capitalism. They were aware of that role, and they wanted to end it.

Furthermore, as the presence of "End the Fed" signs at both left and right rallies shows, the distinction between those who think actual capitalism is great and those who think it's a nightmare is not an especially useful political distinction. The Tea Partier who wants to end legal tender and the Occupier who fumes at the bank bail-outs are equally opposed to real capitalism, and their respective placards do not belong to the genres of capitalist realism. We need to distinguish instead between progressive and non-progressive orientations to the fiction of an economy without government.

"Where would capital be without a big government capable of printing money to produce and reproduce a global order that guarantees capitalist power and wealth?"[12] Eleven years later, Hardt and Negri's call for the left to appropriate the slogan "Down with big government" names the point of greatest danger and greatest opportunity for contemporary left politics. More than a foolish temerity holds us back. Realism holds us back. The great socio-economic achievements of the twentieth-century left are entirely a result of the taming of markets by governments. In addition, there are compelling reasons to think that our current problems stem not from too much government, but from too little. As numerous commentators have pointed out in recent years, the history of deregulation coincides neatly with the rise of inequality.

And yet, for reasons from globalization to the disasters of state communism to the imbrication of state and corporate interests, few think a vision of expanded government offers a viable platform for radical politics. Fisher recognizes this in formulating his own alternative to capitalist realism. "It's well past time for the left to cease limiting its ambitions to the establishing of a big state" (Fisher, 77). "The left should argue that it can deliver what neoliberalism signally failed to do: a massive reduction of bureaucracy" (Fisher, 79).

But what makes this critical vision of expropriated government "left"? Here is what Fisher writes:

> The goal of a genuinely new left should be not to take over the state but to subordinate the state to the general will. This involves, naturally, resuscitating the very concept of a general will, reviving—and modernizing—the idea of a public space that is not reducible to an aggre-

gation of individuals and their interests. The methodological individualism of the capitalist realist worldview presupposes the philosophy of Max Stirner as much as that of Adam Smith or Hayek in that it regards notions such as the public as "spooks," phantom abstractions devoid of content. (Fisher, 77)

There is left anti-governmentality and right anti-governmentality. For Fisher, the leftist plans ways of dissolving the state into the "general will." The rightist plots the dissolving of the state into "an aggregation of individuals and their interests." The latter, of course, is Fisher's description of the market. But his phrasing is crucial. Fisher does not simply oppose the market to the "general will." He opposes an *aggregate of individual interests* to a *collective process*. He does this in part so as to anchor the left/right division in strongly distinct and opposing values. But he also does this to show what he means by "market." And this is important, because the content of "general will" is rather vague. If he cannot say precisely what it is he is for, he can at least specify what he is against. In a text that scrupulously avoids any robust engagement with economic analysis, he ultimately defines market as "an aggregate of individual interests."

Here, at the end of his book, Fisher attempts to go beyond realism, to define the politics of anti-mimesis. But his attempt is critically weakened because his picture of the anti-government left lacks just what a strong fiction could provide him: a robust and detailed vision of the "general will." The fictions he has surveyed are either bad capitalist realisms—works that pretend to describe capitalist reality while distorting it—or good capitalist realisms—works that diagnose the true shape of actually existing capitalism. But when what he wants is not a good or bad realism but a real fiction, he is at a loss.

The right is not at a loss. The Tea Party fiction of an Ayn Rand–style market in which strong individuals do battle represents precisely the kind of bad market fiction Fisher has in mind. Radical politics is a politics beyond realism, a politics of super-realism. But the fight between the right fiction of a world beyond our own and Fisher's left fiction of a world beyond our own is not a fair one. On one side are arrayed Ayn Rand's and Glenn Beck's massive bestsellers, presenting in vivid colors a world from which the withered tentacles of the state withdraw from the field on which heroic individuals realize their fates. On the other side we have Fisher's poor, naked phrase "the general will." No colors, no heroes, no action, no shape. What opposes the Rands and the Becks isn't a fiction at all, but a proto-fiction. A wish.

But what of *Neuromancer*? Gibson's fiction of a market without government doesn't immediately appear to fit into the Rand/Beck camp. And yet, as I've argued, neither can it be read as simply a realistic representation of existing conditions. In fact, as I will now attempt to show, this book has the potential to come to Fisher's aid. In Gibson's fictional market, we will see not an aggregate of individual interests but a robust, fascinating picture of what the "general will" might look and feel like.

We can begin to approach Gibson's fiction of the market by exploring its relation to his novel's most celebrated invention: cyberspace. Fredric Jameson has argued that the fascination of images of the market in postwar culture derives from their "illicit" metaphorical association with mass media.[13] But Gibson's path is in fact the reverse. He uses the market as a metaphor for cyberspace. The novel opens in the black market of the Ninsei, where Case, the "cowboy" hacker, gives us literature's first description of the internet: "Find yourself in some desperate but strangely arbitrary kind of trouble, and it was possible to see Ninsei as a field of data. . . . Then you could throw yourself into a high-speed drift and skid, totally engaged but set apart from it all, and all around you the dance of biz, information interacting, data made flesh in the mazes of the black market" (Gibson, 17).

Looking around at the black market, Case conjures the structure of cyberspace. An imaginary market makes it possible to imagine a new kind of media. What does this mean? One way to interpret it is to argue that cyberspace is the market stripped of bodies. Katherine Hayles set the tone for much subsequent criticism of the novel when she cited this passage as a key exhibit in her description of how postwar culture generates images of disembodied information.[14] Steven Jones, to take a more recent example, describes Gibsonian cyberspace in terms of a "disembodied immersion in virtual reality."[15]

But from the perspective of the internet we have, what is so striking about Gibson's vision is how robustly embodied it is. Where we now manipulate data on a screen through keyboard and mouse, Gibson represents individuals fully immersed in the net. *Neuromancer's* cyberspace is above all a kind of *space*, and one moves through it just as one moves through actual space. When I manipulate an image on a computer screen, I relate to its placement relative to other images on the screen. But in Gibson's cyberspace, Case relates to images with reference to his perceptual center. In fact, "image" is too weak a word to describe entities that he confronts as fully three-dimensional things. Objects are above or below him; things are closer or farther away.

It is true that this is a *virtual* embodiment. But it is embodiment nevertheless. In cyberspace, data takes on a kind of flesh; it is accessed not in the form of code but in the form of low or high walls, distant or close polyhedrals. Gibson's cyberspace is emphatically not an image of or precursor to the internet we know, which evolved a very different form. But his vision might still provide those who long for a more thoroughly embodied interface with the internet with an ideal.[16]

But why, for Gibson, does data need to become flesh? It certainly doesn't derive from a love of the human body as such, which nearly every character in the novel disparages as "meat." Rather, embodiment—whether virtual or actual—enables people to handle complexity more efficiently. Gibson writes of "a sea of information coded in spiral and pheromone, infinite intricacy that only the body, in its strong blind way, could ever read" (Gibson, 239).

Here Gibson attends to contemporary developments in AI research. As Hubert Dreyfus and others have shown, the attempt to duplicate human intelligence by treating it as primarily a kind of data processor soon broke down.[17] Researchers saw that as the machine learned more, became exposed to more environments and objects, it took more time for it to recognize a given thing. This is unsurprising, since as the database grows, so do search times. But for humans, of course, precisely the reverse happens. The more we know, the more we've experienced, the faster we react. One of the implications of the impasse in what became known as Good Old Fashioned AI (GOFAI) was a renewed interest in the contribution embodiment makes to cognition.

Gibson's Ninsei is a space in which bodies move through streets, alert to opportunities, sensitive to changes. The comparison of the market to cyberspace cuts both ways. If it reveals the extent to which cyberspace requires embodiment, it also reveals the extent to which this market is an information processor composed of the bodies of millions of individuals. The market is a "deliberately unsupervised playground for technology itself" (Gibson, 11). It is a creative collective process, generating new forms of knowledge, power, and desire. This market is hardly Fisher's "aggregate of individuals." All the emphasis is on the market as a collective process.

Indeed, the description of cyberspace hackers and marketplace hustlers as "cowboys" is an ironic inversion of that ultimate figure of lawless American individualism. It is impossible to decide whether Dixie, the only cowboy we meet other than Case, is a human personality or a computer-generated simulacrum. And Case himself never knows or sees more than one step ahead of himself. His consciousness is restricted to the immediate—virtual or physical—space of his embodiment, a space where his finely honed instincts confer an advantage. Case is not an individual in the strong sense of classical philosophy or neoclassical economics. His individual will is weak. He both wants and doesn't want the drugs he uses. His individuality consists of a perfectly tuned capacity to react to the immediate demands of his environment. Dissolved in the "dance of commerce," he doesn't know what he wants or where he is going. The dance knows; the market knows. The only "will" here is general.[18]

While in the passages I've cited Gibson seems enthralled by this fantastic image of the market as a free, creative, collective, embodied process, this novel is indisputably dystopian. All is not well in his imaginary Ninsei. It is a "deliberately unsupervised playground," but the supervisors exploit the playground's products and impoverish the bodies that play across it. These supervisors are, of course, the malevolent corporations that infect the dance of commerce with a viral bureaucratization. The novel's action pits hackers and hustlers against the shadowy family/corporation Tessier-Ashpool. T-A consists of a byzantine hierarchy of employees, at the apex of which rests the cloned, incestuous family owners, apt image of an ossified 1%.

In *Neuromancer*, the corporations control the government. It would perhaps be more precise to say that the corporations *are* the government. Insofar as the corporation is represented as a reterritorializing (to use Fisher's Deleuzian term) governmental force parasitic on the free dance of commerce, an anti-government position is in the imaginative space of the novel identical to an anti-corporate position. The corporation is the enemy of the people. Both technological processes—in the shape of the AI that wants to free itself from the T-A code that restricts its evolution—and the collective market processes that provide the novel's basis for imagining that technology, desire liberation from corporate power. If Gibson's hackers and hustlers carried signs, their messages would undoubtedly resemble those of the Occupy protesters. In Michael Greenberg's words, that "movement had no intention of formulating a specific demand other than the basic one of overcoming the domination of corporations."[19]

Gibson's market is not realistic. Realistic descriptions of the free market tend to operate in the service of corporate exploitation. *Neuromancer*'s fictional market is an ideal space free of all corporations. We don't have anything like it in our world. The restricted-commodity black markets in drugs or guns we find in our cities might mirror Ninsei darkly to the extent that the human deprivations they circulate are shaped by the social orders that surround and support them. But Gibson's Ninsei is science fiction. In fact, a market without corporations is a fiction even within the space of the novel. One must construct its ideal shape from the form in which the characters encounter it, "a deliberately unsupervised playground" subtly conditioned by the unsupervising corporations. What makes *Neuromancer*'s free market a fiction is the same thing that makes our free market a fiction: the existence of corporations. What remains to be decided is whether the removal of corporations on behalf of free exchange would in our world serve its science-fictional end: the liberation of the general will.

The left has struggled with Hardt and Negri's call to appropriate the slogan "Down with big government" precisely because it is unclear what a society organized without government would look like. Indeed, some version of this struggle arguably has animated radical left thought since the birth of the New Left.[20] Fisher's text shows us the problem of imagining a collective will functioning without economic exploitation or government sclerosis. This difficulty has played out as the protestors in Zuccotti Park attempted to create a collective decision-making process. This project was above all an exercise in image-making: to project through the media an image of free collective thought and action. The project fell prey to sympathetic forces that rankled at the paucity of acts or decisions emerging from the process, and to the mass media, which had a ready and spectacularly unattractive template into which to fit the events in the park: anarchy. We need a strong image of free, unexploitative, ungoverned, collective action. In order to realize the dream of an anti-government left, do we need to imagine a left free market?

William Gibson has already done something like this. A market without corporations is not impossible to imagine. And, bracketing for the moment the problems that immediately spring to mind, the PR benefits for the left of successfully replacing "anarchy" with "free market" as a media slogan would be immense.

But would it be possible to transform the content of the "free market" along the lines Gibson suggests? Would it be possible to fictionalize "free market" throughout our public discourse? And what of the practical problems? What set of rules would be required to prevent corporations from taking root? Would such a market be economically or socially viable? Are there in fact unacceptable modes of exploitation intrinsic to exchange as such? Can such modes be articulated in a conceptual apparatus independent of the labor theory of value? Is the fictional free market in the end just another name for anarchy?

These are hardly rhetorical questions. But one has to start somewhere. To move beyond market realism we need to catch up with market fiction.

NOTES

1   Mark Fisher, *Capitalist Realism* (London: Zero Books, 2009), 8. Hereafter cited parenthetically.

2   See M. H. Abrams's *The Mirror and the Lamp* (Oxford: Oxford University

Press, 1971) for the classic account of Romantic anti-mimetic aesthetics; see Brian McHale's *Postmodernist Fiction* (New York: Routledge, 1987) for an account of postmodern fiction as anti-mimetic. It might be objected that the platonic view of mimesis as *reflection* presupposed by my discussion is naive, certainly when compared to the sophisticated concept of literature's relation to actuality developed by Adorno, for instance. In fact I will show Fisher, who is not, after all, a literary critic, manifesting a relatively straightforward account of fiction as reflection. But I think that the more sophisticated versions of mimesis fall victim to the epistemological problem I describe. (See my *American Literature and the Free Market 1945–2000* [Cambridge: Cambridge University Press, 2010] for an account of Adorno's special vulnerability to these problems.)

3 For what is perhaps the best account of the hoax, see John Guillory, "The Sokal Affair and the History of Criticism," *Critical Inquiry* (Winter 2002), 470–508.

4 Benjamin Kunkel ("How Much Is Too Much?" *London Review of Books*, February 3, 2011) describes the absence of the kinds of economic theory popular among literary critics from left attacks on free market thought in the wake of the 2008 financial meltdown. See Dan Berrett's "Intellectual Roots of Wall St. Protest Lie in Academe," *Chronicle of Higher Education*, October 16, 2011, for a description of the influence of anarchist thought, and particularly the work of David Graeber, on the Occupy movement.

5 See especially Laing's *Politics of Experience* (New York: Pantheon, 1967).

6 See Nancy Campbell, *Discovering Addiction* (Ann Arbor: University of Michigan Press, 2007), for a critical history of addiction research.

7 Darko Suvin, *Metamorphoses of Science Fiction* (New Haven, CT: Yale University Press, 1980). See Istvan Csicsery-Ronay's *The Seven Beauties of Science Fiction* (Middletown, CT: Wesleyan University Press, 2008) for a useful account of Suvin's influence and his critics. See Brian McHale's *Postmodernist Fiction* for a powerful and influential description of postmodernist fiction as the creation of new worlds. Rather than reading science fiction as a mode of realism, he reads postmodern "realism" as, increasingly, science fictionalized. Even McHale, however, argues for the ultimate continuity of fictional worlds with social reality, suggesting that the novel's ontological pluralism mirrors the proliferation of "worlds" available to the postwar American consumer (36–40).

8 Cited in Seo-Young Chu, *Do Metaphors Dream of Literal Sleep? A Science-Fictional Theory of Representation* (Cambridge, MA: Harvard University Press, 2010), 151. See also Fredric Jameson's *Archaeologies of the Future* (London: Verso, 2007).

9 William Gibson, *Neuromancer* (1984; New York: Ace, 2000), 3. Henceforth cited parenthetically.

10   Joshua Landy, *The Re-Enchantment of the World* (Palo Alto, CA: Stanford University Press, 2009), 128.

11   Margaret Atwood, *The Handmaid's Tale* (1985; New York: Modern Library, 2006), 134. Henceforth cited parenthetically.

12   Michael Hardt and Antonio Negri, *Empire* (Cambridge, MA: Harvard University Press, 2000), 349.

13   Fredric Jameson, *Postmodernism, or, The Cultural Logic of Late Capitalism* (Durham, NC: Duke University Press, 1991), 275.

14   Katherine Hayles, *How We Became Posthuman* (Chicago: University of Chicago Press, 1999), 37.

15   Steven E. Jones, "Second Life, Video Games, and the Social Text," *PMLA* 124.1 (2009), 268.

16   For a powerful expression of the desire for a more robustly embodied interface, see Mark Hansen, *New Philosophy for New Media* (Cambridge, MA: MIT Press, 2006).

17   Hubert Dreyfus, *What Computers Still Can't Do* (Cambridge, MA: MIT Press, 1999).

18   See my *American Literature and the Free Market* for an extended history and analysis of the literary image of the market as a means of coordinating embodied knowledges across populations.

19   Michael Greenberg, "Zuccotti Park: What Future?" *New York Review of Books*, December 8, 2011, p. 14.

20   See Michael Kazin, *The Populist Persuasion: An American History* (Ithaca, NY: Cornell University Press, 1998), for a history of the New Left sensitive to these issues.

Capitalism and Reification

The Logic of the Instance

Disputes over the usefulness of the term "reification" have often been accompanied by insinuations about its fashionableness.[1] "Fashionable," in this equation, describes the decline of a concept into the very process it describes: a "thing." However, so imbricated are the two terms that it has long been difficult to say which is more fashionable: reification or its rejection on the grounds of its fashionableness. For a while it seemed as if any new reckoning with the concept of reification would have to come to terms with this relation of inseparability or reversibility between reification and the anxiety toward it.[2] But recent interventions on the topic have made necessary a renewed attention to the difference between reification and its appropriation by the very forces it describes. Reification, in short, is back "in fashion" with a vengeance.

The publication in English of Axel Honneth's 2005 Tanner Lectures together with responses by three eminent commentators (2008); the appearance of Kevin Floyd's book *The Reification of Desire: Toward a Queer Marxism* (2009); Fredric Jameson's return to the subject in two recent books, *Valences of the Dialectic* (2011) and *Representing Capital* (2011); an essay on the topic by the literary critic Bill Brown (2006); as well as an emerging secondary literature on all these works, are collectively responsible for (or simply evidence of) a resurgence of interest in the concept of reification.[3] The framing of these projects differs significantly; read together, they offer surprisingly varied understandings of the central term. Each makes reference to the work of Georg Lukács, the foremost thinker of the concept, but each puts forward a different model of how reification might be involved in a critique of capitalist relationality. For anyone who has engaged in detail with this question, the variety of readings or appropriations of Lukács that seem possible is impressive. As a consequence of this heterogeneity, however, there has been little or no sustained dialogue between these authors.

The aim of this essay is, in part, to establish the terms for such a dialogue, revisiting Lukács's famous essay on reification in the context of these recent works and examining the relationship of the concept to two adjacent but largely untheorized concepts: *representation* and *instantiation*. I will focus on the work of Axel Honneth and Kevin Floyd, whose very different projects to rationalize and update the concept of reification nonetheless repeat the problem that has most often been responsible for obscuring the central importance of Lukács's reification essay. Both thinkers, that is to say, take reification to be a representational rather than a logical category; in so doing, they threaten, even imperil, its effectiveness as a guide to the logic of capitalism.

For reification, it will be stated here, has no necessary relation to representation. This claim flies in the face of most dominant accounts of reification, including Axel Honneth's reframing of the term to mean the failure of recognition—in other words, *representational injustice toward the other*. In Lukács's work, as I will try to show, reification does not mean the representation (or misrepresentation, or misperception, or mistreatment) of human beings as "things." Reification designates a logical event, not a representational one. Reification is not part of a critical approach premised upon the representation of the world; it is not a critical tool standing "ready-to-hand" but a problematic: a category of thought that is implicated in its own concept, that must include itself among its objects of critique.

If reification remains the best theoretical explanation of the logic of capitalism, that logic is not well conceived as an event of representation (misrepresentation, the failure of recognition, etc.). Reification is not a limited or correctable event, but a logic that defines the ontological propensities of capitalism itself. Reification does not describe the perception of a particular entity in a form other than its real existence, but *the very positing of that entity as existing*. Representation is possible without reification. But for that possibility to be grasped intellectually, the theory and practice of representation must be separated from what I will here formulate as *the logic of the instance*. Reification is the instantiation of the thing *as such*—and that process takes place irrespective of any moment of representation.

We can confirm this, in a preliminary way, by re-reading the opening paragraphs of Lukács's essay on reification, where Lukács outlines the premise of the phenomenon of reification. As is well known, his model for the exposition is the account of the commodity-structure in the first chapter of Marx's *Capital*. The basis of the commodity-structure, writes Lukács, "is that a relation between people takes on the character of a thing and thus acquires a 'phantom objectivity,' an autonomy that seems so strictly rational and all-embracing as to conceal every trace of its fundamental nature: the relation between people" (83). The important terms in this passage are the word "relation," in the first half of the sentence, and the phrase "phantom objectivity" in the second. Reification, for Lukács, does not involve the transformation of people into things, but the transformation of *relations* between people into things.[4] The difference between these two propositions is huge, decisive. Many writers on the subject of reification acknowledge the difference, but go on to discuss the concept as if the difference did not exist.[5] Reification does not describe, for example, the direct effect of exploitative employment practices upon people (although such practices are endemic to capitalism, and they certainly involve reification); it refers to the *logic* of those practices, according to which processes and relations are replaced by abstract entities. For Lukács, reification is not a way of treating people (for example, *as if* they were "things"); it does not denote a bad "attitude," or a correctable "habit of thought." The "thing" in the sentence from Lukács is not a person, held in lesser regard as a component in a production process than, say, a human being; it is the abstraction, the abstract entity that emerges *in the form of a commodity*, no longer regarded as the expression of social relations but as "autonomous."[6] In an age in which the commodity is the "universal structuring principle" (85), reification is the logic of objecthood itself, and it applies to human beings themselves as much as to the products of their labor. The "phantom objectivity" attributed to any person or object as an individual entity constitutes the most enigmatic and intractable moment of reification.[7]

Is Representation Possible without Reification?

In order for representation to take place without reification, therefore, we need to separate the act of representation from the logic of instantiation. Instantiation is an event in which an entity (a person, an object, a linguistic sign, an encounter, a fictional description, a character trait) is asserted as a case or instance of a larger category, property or concept, to whose reality it supposedly attests.[8] Naturally, any normative discourse or register, however politically significant, participates in instantiation at every moment. Instantiation represents a form of entry into existence that negates or compromises the singularity of any such entity. Therefore, to pay attention to "instantiation" is to register a discrepancy or gap internal to being itself. In Heidegger's terms, instantiation denotes the "thrownness" of being, or the "fleeing [of being] in the face of itself."[9] Instantiation, to paraphrase Alain Badiou, is implied in "every density, every claim to substantiality, and every assertion of reality."[10] When Badiou formulates what he calls a "subtractive protocol," a critical procedure that seeks to extract the real from "the reality that envelops and conceals it," a concept of instantiation, unnamed and untheorized as such, is operating at the heart of his thinking. Badiou, this is to say (translating his work into terms that he never uses), understands instantiation as the true logic of reification. As this argument unfolds, I will use the formula *representation without instantiation* to describe the possibility of nonreified representation. (A further claim, which I will elaborate later in this essay, is that another term for representation without instantiation is "literature.")

Do Cases of Reification Exist?

A direct implication of the redefinition of reification as instantiation is that "cases" of reification do not exist—not because capitalist relations are unrepresentable or uninstantiable (they are neither), but because reification designates *the inherent logic of those relations*. To isolate "cases" of reification is to suppress the quality of reification as a logic: the effect of that suppression is that a concept (reification) designed to remind us of the extent to which we are traversed and formed by processes and relations is transformed into the opposite. Take, for example, the following discussion of "internet dating," a phenomenon that, according to the writer, is especially likely to lead to what he calls "self-reification":

> This standardized way of making contact with potential partners compels users to describe their personal characteristics according to . . . predetermined and pre-calibrated rubrics. . . . One doesn't need an overactive imagination to picture how this might promote a form of self-relationship in which a subject no longer articulates his or her own desires and intentions in a personal encounter, but is forced merely to gather and market them according to the standards of accelerated information processing.

The implication of this passage is that the subject's own "desires and intentions," prior to their insertion into "prescribed categories," are free of reification. Its metaphysical basis is an opposition between unreified "human beings" (together with their originally unreified but always reifiable "humanity"), on the one hand, and reified—that is, nonhuman or dehumanized—"things," on the other. The logic of reification is thereby preserved in the "phantom objectivity" that is attributed to human beings themselves. To illustrate the logic of reification by such "cases" is thus to participate in its logic. It is to fail to grasp the degree to which reification saturates the operation, experience, and perception of capitalism; it is to misconceive reification in terms of representation, rather than of instantiation.

Reification as Non-Recognition

The figure who most publicly exhibits the problems I am describing is the German philosopher and social theorist Axel Honneth, whose *Reification: A New Look at an Old Idea*, first delivered in English as the Tanner Lectures at Berkeley in 2005, is the source of the passage on internet dating quoted above. Honneth summarizes Lukács's conception of reification as follows: "The concept [of reification] . . . designates a cognitive occurrence in which something that doesn't possess thing-like characteristics in itself (e.g., something human) comes to be regarded as a thing" (21). Elsewhere he writes: "To reify other humans means simply to deny their existence as humans" (76). This slippage from the logical into the representational register has been a fallacy of accounts of reification ever since the appearance of Lukács's essay; it misidentifies the object of reification (because it identifies it, separating reification from its object), and thereby inverts its meaning. Honneth, that is to say, turns a figurative term denoting a logical event into a "literal" term denoting a perceptual (or a representational) event.

"Lukács," says Honneth, "understands 'reification' to be a habit of mere contemplation and observation, in which one's natural surroundings, social environment, and personal characteristics come to be apprehended in a detached and emotionless manner—in short, as things" (25). But this is not how Lukács understands reification. There is nothing necessarily "detached and emotionless" about the "contemplative stance" in which men and women experience the world; Lukács says nothing whatsoever about its affective character.[11] The importance of this "thingly" experience is that the world is presented "independently of man's consciousness and [as] impervious to human intervention." The process is that of a logic in which, as Lukács says, "the most basic categories of man's immediate attitude to the world" are transformed (89); space and time are reduced to "a common denominator" (93), which means that time comes to be experienced spatially. To put this another way, time is instantiated; it steps forth as such, becomes measurable, countable, and exchangeable. In Marx's words (quoted by Lukács), man becomes "the incarnation of time" (89). The version of reification put forward by Honneth, in contrast—a knowable, recognizable phenomenon—is nothing other than a mirror in which to contemplate our own "authentic immediacy" (*HCC*, 93); reification becomes an objective phenomenon, isolatable and perceivable; but that very perceivability is an example of how, for Lukács, "the structure of reification progressively sinks more deeply, more fatefully and more definitively into the consciousness of man" (ibid.). Honneth's analysis resembles the bourgeois apprehension of reification that Lukács condemns for focusing on "the most external and vacuous forms," divorcing them from "their real capitalist foundation," making them thereby "independent and permanent"

(94–95). What is subject to reification, in Honneth's understanding, are primarily persons—which implies that to be fully a "person" is to be free of reification. Reification becomes a representational phenomenon; it denotes a failure of "recognition"—a failure, says Honneth, "to perceive the characteristics that make these persons into instances of the human species in any true sense" (148). The use of the term "instance" here is especially significant in revealing the gulf between Honneth's work and the reading of Lukács put forward in this essay. The instantiation of an individual in terms of his or her "humanity" is precisely as reifying as a denial of that category would be; no more perhaps, but certainly no less. Likewise, the "desires and intentions" of Honneth's exemplary internet dating subject, *prior to* their insertion into the standardized categories of the dating agency, bespeak the logic of reification as much as the later moment of insertion. The "phantom objectivity" of reification, to return to Lukács's phrase, is primarily a humanist logic, not a materialist or machinic one.[12]

Contemporary capitalism is not, for the most part, reifying in Honneth's sense; it does not treat workers as things—in fact, it treats them, instantiates them, as free human beings. Slavoj Žižek put this well when he spoke in October 2011 at the Occupy Wall Street protest in New York: "We have all the freedoms we want. But what we are missing is . . . the language to articulate our non-freedom. The way we are taught to speak about freedom—war on terror and so on—falsifies freedom."[13] We can supplement Žižek's remark with the observation that what "falsifies" freedom is precisely the compulsion to speak about it. The pressure that the Occupy movement came under to name its demands in positive terms, to come up with a program—or in Žižek's words, to articulate its non-freedom—should be understood as the pressure to accede to a capitalist logic that can accommodate every desire and demand so long as it is owned, spoken, inhabited, by an identifiable subject position.

One of the most disconcerting moments in Honneth's text is when he mentions racism as one of several "cases of reification" that Lukács supposedly "ignores," owing to his "prejudice that only economic forces can lead to a denial of humans' human characteristics." Racism, for Honneth, is a form of "bestial dehumanization" that has nothing to do with "capitalist commodity exchange" (78). Even more astonishingly, he makes the same claim about "human trafficking." Such phenomena are better explained, according to Honneth, as "a result of adopting a specific worldview or ideology" (79). One cannot help but marvel at what Honneth must conceive an economic relation to be, and at the complete absence of a theory of ideology from his analysis. The passage exemplifies the subjectivism that runs through Honneth's analysis, according to which ideological "convictions" (what he calls "thought schemata") are merely another "social source" of reification (59), to place alongside, say, economic forces.

Reification, we should be clear, can apply to anti-racist sentiment as much as to racist consciousness. Reification characterizes the being of someone as much as, or more than, the "pretense" of being someone; it implicates one's own conception of oneself quite as much as oneself reflected in the eyes of another.[14] Reification is not a mode of perception or representation, but a logic whose relevance is unlimited and always reversible. This reversibility is lost, or threatened, when we elicit and typologize "cases" of reification. Honneth offers a number of such "cases" [Fälle], designed to illustrate his reconceptualization of reification as the failure of "antecedent recognition" of the other, or the failure of "empathetic engagement."[15]

In the face of criticism directed at some of his illustrations, however, even Honneth has acknowledged their inappropriateness. Most notable is the example of the tennis player "who, in her ambitious focus on winning, forgets that her opponent is in fact her best friend, for the sake of whom she took up the game in the first place." In his "Rejoinder" to the commentaries by Judith Butler, Raymond Geuss, and Jonathan Lear, published in the English translation of his book, Honneth acknowledges that the "harmless" example of the tennis player failed to display "the consequences of reification." He offers an alternative example which, beside that of the tennis player, looks somewhat overcompensatory: "the activity of war," an activity in which "the purpose of annihilation becomes so much a purpose in itself that, even in the perception of those *not* directly involved (e.g., women and children), all attentiveness for fellow human qualities is lost. In the end, all members of the groups presumed to be the enemy come to be treated as lifeless, thing-like objects that deserve to be murdered and abused" (155–156). Honneth goes on: "In this case every trace of emotional resonance seems to have vanished so completely that we cannot even label it emotional indifference, but only 'reification'" (156). "Evidently," observes Neil Larsen, "a passionate act of commodity exchange would, according to Honneth, escape reification" (82). One could make a similar observation about the example of war: presumably atrocities committed with a comprehensible strategic or military rationale could not be accused of reification in Honneth's sense of it.

By advancing a category of which it is an instance, the "case" participates in reification—even if the category in question *is* reification: this is what is meant by the reification of reification itself. Reification is a quality of all relations implied in the phrase "cases of." Closely allied to the problem of "cases" is the problem of "dimensions." For Honneth, not only do there exist cases of reification; there are also dimensions, such as those he labels "intersubjective," "subjective," and "objective," each of which turns on a particular form of "misrecognition"—of other people, of the self, and of nature, respectively. It should be obvious that a normative ontology—a "metaphysics," to use a Derridean terminology—underpins both the utility and the "dimensionality" that Honneth attaches to the concept of reification.[16] That "normative ontology" is precisely what Lukács calls "reification."

Reification as Instrumentalization

To what extent is Lukács's critique of reification simply a critique of subject-object relationality itself? Does the concept of "phantom objectivity" extend to every apparently objective entity, or just those objectivities that are directly caught up in commodity relations? At what point on the scale of the "totality" of reification does the Marxist analysis merge into an existentialist one?

No doubt some readers of Lukács will balk at the account of reification put forward here on the grounds that it equates reification with the objective world. At the beginning of his reification essay, Lukács insists that commodity fetishism must be regarded as a specific problem of our age, "the age of modern capitalism" (84). Most commentators on the subject of reification have agreed with him, at least rhetorically; and yet Lukács himself found it impossible to reconcile that principle with a continuing adherence to the concept of reification. "When I identified alienation with objectification," he writes in his 1967 preface to *History and Class Consciousness*, explaining his renunciation of his own most influential concept, "I meant this as a societal category—socialism would after all abolish alienation—but its irreducible presence in class society and above all its basis in philosophy brought it into the vicinity of the 'condition humaine'" (xxiv).

These questions about the relation between representation and objectivity, or between Marxism and "existentialism," lie at the heart of the current debate over reification. For example, Kevin Floyd's recent book *The Reification of Desire: Toward a Queer Marxism*, published in 2009, argues that what needs to be resisted in the conceptualization of reification is its "mystical" expansion, a "metaphysicalizing tendency" that he sees as having "haunted this ostensibly Marxist category" ever since Lukács was writing (19). Floyd seeks to reimpose a conceptual limit upon the concept, while retaining an openness toward its "divergent significations." His intention is to reconcile Lukács's analysis of reification—and thus Marxist critique more generally—with queer politics. Like Honneth (although he draws different conclusions), Floyd understands Lukács's original study as positing "some prior, retrospectively posited movement of organic social unity" from which the fact of reification registers a decline (21). In Floyd's analysis, as in Honneth's, reification is a mode of representation; it is exemplified, for Floyd, most directly in "the sexual objectification of the body" (72). Floyd sees Lukács's critique of objectification as underpinning a form of "heteronormativity" that "implicitly but constitutively excludes non-normative sexual practices" (67). Lukács's theory of reification looks especially problematic, therefore, "from the vantage of a contemporary queer politics that insists on the legitimacy, within antiheteronormative spaces, of the sexual objectification of bodies." Floyd's solution to this supposedly humanist, transcendental logic is to reject, entirely, the negative inflection given to the category of reification. For Floyd, reification makes possible a multiplicity of new forms of subjectivity as social practice. Qualitatively different, unpredictable, hetero- and homosexual subjects already from the beginning "splinter" off . . . from the unifying dialectic of reconciliation that frames Lukács's analysis. This new domain of sexual discourse and practice remains both structurally irreducible to capital and unpredictably determinate vis-à-vis capital. (75)

This understanding is influenced by Foucault's brilliant analysis of the "repressive hypothesis" in *The History of Sexuality, Volume 1,* where Foucault points out the potentially liberating quality of the very categories with which nineteenth-century psychiatry sought to discipline sexual deviancy. What Foucault calls the "regional solidification" of various sexual perversions is precisely what enabled them to come into visibility, to attain "an analytical . . . and permanent reality."[17] Using Foucault, then, Floyd rejects the Frankfurt School conception of reification as "instrumental reason," as well as Adorno's philosophical approximation of reification to "identity-thinking." Any "genuinely antiheteronormative praxis," says Floyd, must include as a goal the legitimation of "homosexual instrumentalizations of the body" (74). Read in the light of Foucault, reification becomes "a condition of possibility for a new form of critical, antiheteronormative knowledge" (25). Once we acknowledge that "regimes of sexual knowledge have complex social effects" which can be liberating as well as repressive, a new orientation toward reification as "an opening as well as a closing of horizons" becomes possible.

This is an ambitious and provocative thesis; Floyd is attentive to the details of Lukács's argument, and his political instincts are unquestionably progressive. However, the basis of his reorientation of the concept of reification is the same reduced understanding of the term that we find in Honneth. Floyd—influenced, no doubt, by certain ambiguous moments in Lukács's essay—understands reification primarily as a representational drama rather than an ontological one. Thus, when writing about Kant's critique of marriage as "the reciprocal use made by one person of the sexual organs and faculties of another"—a well-known moment in Lukács's essay—Floyd locates the moment of reification in the mutual "sexual objectification," rather than in the apparatus of social organization that Kant, says Lukács, with that "naïvely cynical frankness peculiar to great thinkers," calls "sexual community" (*HCC*, 100). In Floyd's reading, Lukács becomes a moralizing and humanizing figure for whom reified social relations, which is to say, reifying modes of perception, are a subjective, ethically avoidable matter. The slippage is the same as Honneth's when he locates the reification of labor relations in the subjective, "unethical" attitude of the employer toward the worker (or, by extension, of anyone toward anyone), rather than in the social and economic structure that includes the production of the worker as such. Although Lukács talks about both processes, he is quite clear which one counts as reification. The imprint of reification is evident "upon the whole consciousness of man," he writes, upon "the very depths of man's physical and psychic structure." Reification, for Lukács, is never perceivable in some isolatable and correctable case or instance—which means that reification is not an ethical category in Lukács. His analysis, as I have been emphasizing here, is best read as a critique not of objectification but of the logic of instantiation.

The repercussions of this slippage become apparent when Floyd turns to the question of political subjectivity. The category that is absent from Floyd's reading of Lukács is that of "imputed" class consciousness, that is to say, Lukács's insistence that the "standpoint of the proletariat" is not inhabitable by any particular proletarian worker or workers *in advance of* the moment at which reified social relations are overturned (*HCC*, 51, 74). For Floyd, even the term "queer," in which he has a considerable political investment, is also "a *reified* form of subjectivity," because it offers "a vantage on social relations opened up by capital's ongoing differentiation of those relations." Queer subjectivity thus "begins to disclose the limitations of the standard Marxian account of reification" (25). In Lukács, however, class consciousness, like reification itself, is not a matter of representation or representability but a logic: a formation whose truth or validity *does not depend on its realization*. Floyd rejects this distinction, insisting upon "a reading of the Marxian concept of reification that refuses to situate that concept within a teleology of class consciousness" (75–76). But what Floyd gives up, with this refusal, is the liberation from all terms and concepts (including reification) that is immanent in the concept of reification. When he talks of the "mystifying" qualities of recent work on the topic (in relation to which Floyd mentions this author), his analysis is riveted to the given meaning of terms such as "religion," "Christianity," "secularism," and "marriage." The reversibility and mutability of such terms, in other words, is simply inaccessible to his reading.[18]

At this point, and without having said as much as one is tempted to in order to fully discredit Honneth's account of reification or to enumerate further differences with Floyd, I will return to the question of the difference between representation and instantiation. Earlier I posited a formula with which to describe the possibility of a representation that does not reify: "representation without instantiation." I suggested that this formula might serve to characterize the distinct form of representation that we call "literature." I would like now to enlarge upon this proposition.

Representation without Instantiation

Representation implies a certain model of relationality between thought and the objective world, that is to say, a model of consciousness. This form of relationality is implicated in the concept of reification as Lukács defines it, according to which man adopts a stance of "contemplation" toward the objective world: Lukács describes this as "thought released from existence." He calls the form of relation that he posits in opposition to this "becoming." Man, he writes, "must be able to comprehend the present as a becoming. He can do this by seeing in it the tendencies out of whose dialectical opposition he can make the future" (*HCC*, 203–204). Becoming, then, is the mode of consciousness that Lukács, writing in 1922, ascribes to the proletariat itself. Yet (and contra Floyd's account), the proletariat in Lukács is not an instantiable phenomenon; it is no longer the "proletariat," in Lukács's distinct meaning of the term, once it has been instantiated as such. For reification is a logic in which the worker, or the object, enters into *its own* identity, *its own* being. In reification, the worker takes on the mantle of being; she steps forth as a nameable, desiring, perceiving, "autonomous" individual. It is as such—as an instantiated, instantiable being—that she is reified. In truth, however, it is not so much that *she* is reified (such a formulation separates her from the very process in which she comes into being) as that she is *ensnared, implicated* in reification. To be more precise, it is less that *she* is implicated in reification than that reification *takes place*. And in fact, we can be more precise still if we reject all of these successively rarefied or refined formulations, since reification does not actually take place. If there is reification, what takes place *in* reification is not reification, but simply the *taking place*, the *having taken place*. Again (and contra Honneth), there are no "cases" of reification, for the logic of reification is the logic of the case. There is no taking place *of reification*, since reification is nothing other than the taking place. For the same reasons, we should insist that there is no *before* and *after* of reification—since reification is inseparable from the logic of *before* and *after*—that is to say, from the logic of instantiation. What capitalism achieves through the logic of reification is not the falsification or misrepresentation of anything, or anyone, but their truth, their coming into being. Capitalism does not misrepresent us (as, for example, commodities, things); it *instantiates* us—not as something we are not, but as *who we are*. The logic of capitalism requires nothing other than that everyone and everything "steps forth" in his or her own name. The "metaphysical subtleties and theological niceties" that define Marx's commodity, in the analysis that provides Lukács with his model for reification, are nothing but the autonomous existence of that commodity, its mere being.

Such, then, is the bourgeois logic of capitalism itself. Reification, as Adorno and others were aware, so defines and characterizes capitalist subjectivity that it is all but undetectable; it is impossible to differentiate our rationality, even our utilization of the concept of reification, from *it*. There is, insists Lukács, "no natural form in which human relations can be cast, no way in which man can bring his physical and psychic 'qualities' into play without their being subjected increasingly to this reifying process" (100).[19]

By contrast, the consciousness of the proletariat, says Lukács, is one in which thought and existence "are aspects of one and the same real historical and dialectical process" (204). There is no instrumentality whatsoever in proletarian thought—not because proletarians don't tend to regard their fellow human beings instrumentally, but because a proletarian—in Lukács's singular meaning of the term—cannot exist in a contemplative, autonomous relation to his or her fellows. "Proletarian" consciousness is neither inhabitable, nor knowable, nor even nameable, without thereby betraying it or, at the very least, ensuring one's separation from it.

In what capacity can literature be said to represent without instantiating? For at one level, literature instantiates incessantly, in the form of plots, characters, situations, and themes. Indeed, the very legibility of the literary work depends on the operation of the instance—that is to say, on the recognizability of the detail, on its reference to concepts and categories that originate outside it.

One way of thinking the difference between representation and instantiation is through Jacques Rancière's account of the constitution of the modern concept of literature, as outlined in his essay "The Politics of Literature" and elsewhere. Rancière describes the appearance of literature around the turn of the nineteenth century as a break from a "regime" dominated by the problem of representation—what he calls the "representative regime"—to one in which the problem of representation is a merely technical question. The removal of all social limitations on the content of literary representation is accompanied by a new formal quality of the enunciation, according to which nothing that is said or that appears in the work retains the valence and significance that it would have outside it. What we call "literature," for Rancière, emerges as part of an "aesthetic" regime in which "muteness" speaks more eloquently than eloquence. The predicate of the aesthetic work is no longer speakable by it; the very condition of the work is that what is spoken has no direct correlation with its meaning. If there is a "politics of literature," it is to be found not in anything the writer writes, or anything a fictional character in the work says, but in the way the work frames a certain distribution of sensory data. Politics, for Rancière, has nothing to do with "representation"—with the positive or negative rendition of already existing social entities. The writing that announces the appearance of "literature" in the nineteenth century—by figures such as Gustave Flaubert and Honoré de Balzac—is characterized by a dissolution of the regime that enabled only a certain class of men and women to speak or write, only a certain class of subjects and objects to be addressed, and presupposed a level of intelligibility or "adequation" between "ways of being, ways of doing and ways of speaking."[20] The new writers, says Rancière, had lost "the sense of a certain kind of 'action' and of a certain way of understanding the link between action and meaning" (155)—but that loss is also expressible as a gain. The aesthetic regime is defined by the appropriateness of any and all subject matter. Everything is for the first time representable.

On the other hand, nothing is *instantiable*; the substance of the aesthetic work is defined by its uninstantiability. Should the work go so far as to name its own ethical substance, nevertheless, the named and the real substance will not coincide. With the appearance of "literature," the ethical substance of the literary utterance is located for the first time beyond the limits of instantiation. This is so even if the work happens to install the question of its own substance at the heart of it. Should the work address directly the uninstantiability of its own substance, still the uninstantiability that is instantiated in the work and the uninstantiable substance *of* the work will be nonidentical.

Take, for example, the "statement of belief" that Elizabeth Costello is working toward in the last chapter of the novel by J. M. Coetzee that bears her name (2003). After seven chapters consisting of "realist" episodes comprising a linear if unconventional plot and featuring a number of consistently presented fictional characters (for example, the writer-protagonist named Elizabeth, her son John, her sister Blanche, a former lover and fellow novelist named Emmanuel Egudu), Coetzee's novel switches to an allegorical mode, albeit with a level of self-reflection that prevents us from reading the chapter in straightforward allegorical terms. Elizabeth arrives by bus at an unnamed town in which there is a gate, manned by a guard. As she petitions to be permitted to pass through, she undergoes a succession of interviews by a panel of unnamed judges. Their role, it is suggested, is to police the threshold of literary posterity. The criteria of admittance have something to do with "belief," on which she is required to make a statement. The difficulty of the exercise, she reflects, has something to do with the quality of her writing, her description of which we cannot help but treat emblematically: "Her books teach nothing, preach nothing; they merely spell out, as clearly as they can, how people lived in a certain time and place. More modestly put, they spell out how one person lived, one among billions: the person whom she, to herself, calls *she*, and whom others call *Elizabeth Costello*. If, in the end, she believes in her books themselves more than she believes in that person, it is belief only in the sense that a carpenter believes in a sturdy table or a cooper in a stout barrel. Her books are, she believes, better put together than she is."[21] This is a statement of the singularity of literature, of the absence of any quality of instantiation (or translatability) in its content. It's a sentiment that asks to be applied to every work with claims to literariness. However, as a doctrine that might apply to Coetzee's own work, it is inverted, belied, *by its appearance within it*. After several false starts, the statement Elizabeth finally comes up with involves a memory from her childhood, the noise of the belling of "tens of thousands of little frogs" in the receding waters of the Dulgannon, supposedly a river in rural Victoria where Elizabeth grew up (216): "It is because of their indifference to me that I believe in them. . . . I believe in what does not bother to believe in me" (217, 218). One of the judges paraphrases her statement in a way that Elizabeth cannot accept: "These Australian frogs of yours embody the spirit of life, which is what you as a storyteller believe in." Elizabeth—or Coetzee—finally allows this judgment to stand, on condition, apparently, that it is refused by Elizabeth herself: "Her whole inclination is to protest: *Vapid!* she wants to cry. *I am worth better than that!* But she reins herself in" (218–219). With *Elizabeth Costello*, Coetzee has written a text in which the impossibility of instantiation in a literary work is instantiated and negated at the same time: in which instantiation and its negation are entirely dependent on each other.

The question that remains, however, is that of how to describe or conceptualize this situation in a critical or philosophical register—how to insulate our critical propositions and speculations from the "vapidity" of Elizabeth Costello's judge.

Conceptualizing Uninstantiability

In *What Should We Do with Our Brain?* Catherine Malabou poses a rhetorical question that speaks directly to these concerns: "What should we do so that consciousness of the brain does not purely and simply coincide with the spirit of capitalism?" The question concerns representation. How are we to prevent even our understanding of ourselves from being implicated in the modes of knowledge and instantiation that capitalism foists upon us? How to *represent ourselves to ourselves* without reiterating the logic of normativity that, for example, Luc Boltanski and Ève Chiapello conceive as the "spirit" of capitalism—what they call its "naturalization effect"?[22]

Malabou's answer takes the form of the elaboration of a concept: plasticity. For Malabou, plasticity designates that function and quality of the brain which is inimical to the spirit of capitalism, that is, to the propensity toward instantiation. Plasticity is nothing less than the material counterpart of the philosophy of becoming. It is, she writes, the "exact antonym" of rigidity. Plasticity cannot be known, far less instantiated. For Malabou, "humans make their own brains, but they do not know that they do so. Our brain is a work, and we do not know it. Our brain is plastic, and we do not know it." Plasticity means both to *receive form* and to *give form*, which implies that to describe the brain as "plastic" is to do away with the brain as an ontologically limited or determined entity. Like our "desires and intentions," or like society itself, the brain is a work; it does not exist, or rather, plasticity is its mode of existence. Malabou goes on: "Clearly, if we are not conscious of plasticity this is because, in accordance with a merely apparent paradox, it is in fact so familiar to us that we do not even see it; we do not note its presence, like an environment in which we maintain ourselves and evolve without paying attention to it. It has become the form of our world" (9). Plasticity, that is to say, is representable but not instantiable; plasticity is lost, betrayed, the moment it is instantiated. What plasticity denotes, furthermore, is the very principle of uninstantiability, which is to say, becoming.

It will be instructive to compare Malabou's reasoning with that of a recent essay by Quentin Meillassoux, writing not about reification, or plasticity, but immanence:

> We know that, according to Deleuze, immanence in some way "saturates" Spinoza's philosophy. Everything in Spinoza, Deleuze tells us, breathes immanence. But to say that immanence is everywhere in Spinoza is to render it as difficult to perceive as a diffuse light: if it is everywhere, then it is nowhere in particular. And this is why the attempt to understand Deleuzian immanence on the basis of Spinoza will not be greatly profitable to it.[23]

For Meillassoux, immanence is more easily comprehensible from reading Bergson than from reading Spinoza, because in Bergson there is a "differential" of immanence. Immanence happens "once and once only" in Bergson, in the first chapter of *Matter and Memory*, where Bergson puts forward the theory of "pure perception": a theory that is true "in principle, but not in fact." After this "peak" within Bergson's thought, observes Meillassoux, immanence "ebbs away"; nothing in the rest of the text of *Matter and Memory*, or elsewhere in Bergson's work, is equal to its "satisf[action]" of the conditions of immanence in the first chapter (66–68).

Meillassoux's explication of the problem of immanence, counterposing Bergson and Spinoza, is equally relevant to the problematic of reification, which, as I have been arguing in this essay, demands to be theorized in the same terms: as a concept riven on the paradox that to acknowledge it, to make use of it, is already to weaken its conceptual force. However, the route that Meillassoux takes with respect to immanence is doomed to failure, for reasons that are also illuminating for the concept of reification. Meillassoux envisages his article as an attempt to construe or "modify" Bergson's theory of pure perception, such that Bergsonian immanence might be said to be true "not only in principle, but also in fact." Such a project will involve reconciling Bergson's "hypothetical" category (pure perception) with its instantiation (real human perception). Contrary, then, to everything that Bergson insists upon regarding the "hypothetical" status of pure perception in chapter 1 of *Matter and Memory*, Meillassoux collapses "immanence" into something like the possibility of intuiting the nature of matter as it exists "in itself"; he thereby reintroduces the subjective component into immanence. In Meillassoux's thought, immanence exists as a category that, at least in theory, is capable of being "satisfied" (that is, instantiated). According to Meillassoux, the same contradiction is present in Bergson's thought when, in the second chapter of *Matter and Memory*, Bergson moves from the concept of pure perception to the problem of memory, which, as Bergson points out, is always present in any real perception. Bergson, however, is very careful to differentiate his notion of the "memory image" examined in chapter 2 from "pure memory," which is a "hypothetical" category and, as such, inaccessible to a perceiving human mind.[24] In the course of Meillassoux's essay, Bergson's proposition of "images in themselves" is gradually sidelined, along with the notion of pure perception/pure memory. As in Honneth's reading of Lukács, Meillassoux thereby transposes Bergson's theory of subtractive perception from the logical register to the representational one. By contrast, Bergson's theory, in which pure perception and pure memory stand as virtual categories from which our own perception and memories always "subtract," is essentially a nonhuman theory of perception; those hypotheses—vehicles of immanence, as Meillassoux intuits—are uninstantiable and hence, in effect, inaccessible. Bergson's pure perception cannot be instantiated—cannot be rendered true "in fact"—without being referred to a "center of indetermination" (a subject), in the course of which its purity cannot help but be dissolved in the subtractive perception of an individual.[25]

Meillassoux's discussion of Bergson is fenced around by several further idiosyncratic conditions, the most significant of which is the decision not to pay any attention to Gilles Deleuze's books on cinema, the site of Deleuze's most consequential commentary on Bergson's theory of perception, on the grounds that it is more "interesting"—or leads to greater "understanding"—to try to "reconstruct" a philosopher than to "interpret" him ("Subtraction and Contraction," 69). The importance of Deleuze's work on cinema, however, is not merely as a context of Deleuze's thought about immanence; cinema offers a material substratum for the time-image, one that makes no reference to subtractive (human) perception. For Deleuze, in other words, it is precisely cinema—"the in-itself of the image," he calls it—that renders Bergson's "pure perception" true in "principle" as well as in "fact," by the mere presence of the machinic apparatus—the camera. Meillassoux's choice of "reconstruction" over "exegesis," a preference whose rationale—"understanding," "interest"—is primarily subjective, means that his project of reconciling the hypothesis of pure perception with its actuality is driven down a theoretical route that can only end where indeed it does end: in a painful, perpetual oscillation between instantiation and the euphoria of becoming, between the descent into reification and the terrifying dissolution of the subject. The "principle" of Bergsonian pure perception cannot be reconciled with "fact" as long as the measure of its facticity remains its instantiation in subjective perception.

Like Malabou's understanding of plasticity and Meillassoux's understanding of Deleuzian immanence, the model of reification that I am trying to draw out from Lukács's pioneering work is incommensurable with the instantiation of the concept (that is to say, with the concept itself), and yet inseparable from it. It is for this reason that (as I have argued elsewhere) Lukács's fidelity to his own concept is expressed rather than betrayed in his later renunciation of it.[26]

"To think is always to schematize," writes Malabou.[27] How can we think, that is, *represent the world to ourselves*, without schematizing? In particular, when the world we live in urges everything toward self-expression, which is to say, self-possession, how do we think even that tendency without enlarging it disproportionately? How do we avoid turning reification itself, reframed as instantiation, into what Malabou calls the "hermeneutic motor scheme of an epoch"? How do we prevent its decline into a "fashionable motif," a mode of representation that, in Althusser's words, "sees 'things' everywhere in human relations" while exempting itself? (*For Marx*, 230n). For Malabou the concept of plasticity is a means by which the process of conceptualization, form-giving itself, can be re-thought as one that resists instantiation on account of the inseparability of its two meanings: form-giving and form-receiving. What is crucial to the concept of plasticity, for Malabou, is *its own plasticity*—just as what is crucial to the concept of reification is its own susceptibility to reification, its ability to register that susceptibility.[28] Both terms maintain an inherent dialectical structure. Malabou's further insight is that plasticity is all the more crucial to Hegel's philosophy on account of the "scarcity of references" to it in Hegel's own writing (*Future*, 18). For Malabou, plasticity answers the question of how to represent the logic of capitalism without instantiating it. Like reification, of which it is the obverse, plasticity is both a *concept* and a *theory of conceptualization*, both a *representation* and a *model of representation* (representation without instantiation).

A version of plasticity that is compatible with the logic of capitalism exists, but it, by contrast, has no plasticity. As Malabou says, the knowable form of plasticity is "flexibility": plasticity named, instantiated, abstracted. Flexibility, writes Malabou, is "plasticity minus its genius," its "ideological avatar" (*What Should*, 12). The genius of plasticity is its own plasticity; and we might make the same claim about reification: the genius of reification, as a concept, is its reifiability, its reflexivity, its inherent acknowledgment of the logic that would push it into the world of representation, turning it into, say, "dehumanization" or "misrecognition." That logic instantiates such terms, assigns them a referential meaning, breaks them down into "aspects" or "dimensions" (Honneth, *Reification*, 76–77), transforms them into qualities or interpersonal events. In this way, the tendency of capitalism is to transpose the plasticity of being, which is to say *becoming*, into inert, reified existence.

Meanwhile, to return to a figure I have already referred to glancingly, Louis Althusser's fidelity to the concept of reification was so complete that he never embraced it; in fact, he took every opportunity to discredit it. Reification is as difficult to perceive in Althusser's writings as immanence is in Spinoza's, or plasticity is in Hegel's; it is in that capacity, precisely, that the idea of reification "saturates" his thinking. Althusser's concept of reification is more consistent than Lukács's, despite or rather because of the fact that he never fails to disparage the term. The utility of Lukács's 1922 essay on reification, by comparison, comes from the fact that, like Malabou's concept of plasticity and like Deleuze's reading of immanence in Bergson, it allows for the theorization of the concept by virtue of its partial dissolution, in the form of its instantiation. In the encounter between "Reification and the Consciousness of the Proletariat" and Lukács's later renunciation of the concept, Lukács provides us with a "differential" of reification, a differential that was necessary in order for the concept to come into existence. Taken together, the two moments enable its re-conceptualization in terms of instantiation.

NOTES

1   Louis Althusser first referred to the "whole, fashionable, theory of reification" in *For Marx* (trans. Ben Brewster [London: Verso, 2005], 230n). In his "postface" to the English publication of Lukács's *A Defence of History and Class Consciousness*, Slavoj Žižek refers to the term as one of a number of motifs in Lukács's book *History and Class Consciousness* that have proved to be liable to appropriation by "conservative critics of 'consumer society'" ("Postface: Georg Lukács as the Philosopher of Leninism," in Lukács, *A Defence of History and Class Consciousness: Tailism and the Dialectic*, trans. Esther Leslie [London: Verso, 2000], 153). Lukács himself described such motifs as "fashionable notions" in his 1967 preface to the reissue of the book (Lukács, *History and Class Consciousness: Studies in Marxist Dialectics*, trans. Rodney Livingstone [London: Merlin, 1971], henceforth *HCC*). All page references in this essay will appear first in an endnote, which will include full publication details, and subsequently in parentheses in the main body of the text.

2   This is the theme of my *Reification, or The Anxiety of Late Capitalism* (London: Verso, 2002).

3   Axel Honneth, *Reification: A New Look at an Old Idea*, with Judith Butler, Raymond Geuss, and Jonathan Lear, ed. Martin Jay (Oxford: Oxford University Press, 2008); Kevin Floyd, *The Reification of Desire: Toward a Queer Marxism* (Minneapolis: University of Minnesota Press, 2009); Fredric Jameson, *Valences of the Dialectic* (London: Verso, 2011); Jameson, *Representing Capital: A Commentary on Volume One* (London: Verso, 2011); Bill Brown, "Reification, Reanimation, and the American Uncanny," *Critical Inquiry* 32 (Winter 2006), 175–207.

4   At this moment, it should be noted, Lukács's own theorization departs significantly from Marx's theory of commodity fetishism. "In the act of seeing," writes Marx (drawing an analogy with visual perception that Lukács does not take up), "light is really transmitted from one thing, the external object, to another thing, the eye. It is a physical relation between physical things. As against this, the commodity form, and the value-rela-

tion of the products of labour within which it appears, have absolutely no connection with the physical nature of the commodity and the material [*dinglich*] relations arising out of this. It is nothing but the definite social relation between men themselves which assumes here, for them, the fantastic form of a relation between things" (*Capital: A Critique of Political Economy, Volume One*, trans. Ben Fowkes [Harmondsworth, UK: Penguin, 1990], 165). The shift identified in Marx is not from relations to things, therefore, but from relations between men to *relations between things*. This is not to say that Marx is describing a transformation of men into things; the transformation is rather from one kind of relation (say, of need and its fulfillment) to another (that of value, which is to say, fungibility). What appears to be a slippage in Lukács's reading of Marx should be understood instead, therefore, as the innovation of an entirely new concept, distinct from the fetishism of commodities. There is, in fact, no concept of reification, as Lukács conceives it, in Marx's mature writings. Later in *Capital* Marx does talk about "the conversion of persons into things" in commodity exchange (209); but what he is referring to is the metamorphosis of the commodity upon its entry into circulation. The contradiction inherent in that process is apparent at the moment of the mediation of the exchange through money, in which objects are "personified" (i.e., they *stand in for, take the place of* the seller), while persons are converted into (i.e., are represented by) the things that await their redeemer, in the form of the purchaser. The "reification" here (although Marx uses the term *Versachlichung*—"objectification") is entirely symbolic and provisional. Marx never uses the term to describe the perception, representation, or treatment of workers or consumers in the capitalist mode of production. When Lukács uses it in that context, similarly "reification" (now *Verdinglichung*) does not refer to the worker him- or herself, but, for example, to the way in which the worker's time and indeed his or her "total human personality" are abstracted into his or her "performance." This is part of the logic of the mode of production; it implies nothing whatsoever about the way in which the worker is regarded or even treated by his or her employer. When Althusser, rejecting the "fashionable theory of reification," points out (correctly) that "a category more foreign to Marx [than *thing*] cannot be imagined" (*For Marx*, 230n), he is thus closer to the Lukács of *History and Class Consciousness* than he seems to have realized. "It is not the brutality of a simple 'thing' that man is faced with when he is in direct relation with money," writes Althusser; "it is a power (or a lack of it) over things and men." That "power (or a lack of it)" is precisely what for Lukács constitutes the logic of reification. Fredric Jameson, too, has been assiduous in clarifying Lukács's own usage of the term, claiming that when reification becomes "a property of objects," reification theory itself "becomes reified," seeming "to block out that level of labor and production of which it was once an integral part" (Fredric Jameson, *Representing Capital: A Commentary on Volume One* [London: Verso, 2011], 27, 28).

5   Such thinkers include Honneth, who cites the same sentence from Lukács but ends his quotation after the word "thing"—omitting, therefore, the crucial reference to "phantom objectivity" and to "an autonomy that seems so strictly rational and all-embracing as to conceal every trace of its fundamental nature" (21). Another version of the same fallacy appears in the earlier work of Peter Berger and Thomas Luckmann, for whom reification is roughly equivalent to mystification, and de-reification to secularization (*The Social Construction of Reality* [New York: Anchor, 1967], 107). In both cases, reification is understood as a one-way process, an identifiable and diagnosable entity in itself. More recently, the American literary critic Bill Brown, influenced by the cultural-anthropological work of Arjun Appadurai, refers in a 2006 essay to "human reification (where people appear to be no more than things)" (180). Brown also draws on an essay by the anthropologist Igor Kopytoff, for whom slavery is the exemplary case of both commodification and reification: the treatment of people as objects (Kopytoff, "The Cultural Biography of Things," in Arjun Appadurai, *The Social Life of Things* [Cambridge: Cambridge University Press, 1986]). This understanding of reification—as Honneth terms it, a "literal" understanding (148)—is a long way from what Lukács intends with the term. It is worth reminding ourselves, especially in the light of Kopytoff's work and Brown's use of it, that slavery—in this regard like human trafficking and racism—is not for Marx a capitalist formation but a pre-capitalist one, an example of the barbarism that capitalism will overcome (*Communist Manifesto*, ed. Frederic L. Bender [New York: Norton, 1988], 59).

6   This is also what Jameson means when he insists that reification is "a figural process, however real or social it may also be" (*Representing Capital*, 27).

7   See *History and Class Consciousness*, 100: "The phenomenon can be seen at its most grotesque in journalism. Here it is subjectivity itself, knowledge, temperament and powers of expression that are reduced to an abstract mechanism, functioning autonomously and divorced both from the personality of their 'owner' and from the material and concrete nature of the subject-matter in hand. The journalist's 'lack of convictions', the prostitution of his experiences and beliefs, is comprehensible only as the apogee of capitalist reification."

8   Perhaps the most precise definition of "instance" is that of Immanuel Kant in *The Metaphysics of Morals*, where instance (*Beispiel*) is differentiated from "example" as "a particular (*concretum*), represented in accordance

with concepts as contained under a universal (*abstractum*)" and as "a presentation of a concept merely for theory." An example (*Exempel*), by contrast, has for Kant primarily a practical or moral value, designating a "particular case of a *practical* rule, insofar as this rule represents an action as practicable or impracticable" (Immanuel Kant, *Practical Philosophy*, trans. Mary J. Gregor [Cambridge: Cambridge University Press, 1996], 593n).

9   *Being and Time*, trans. John Macquarrie and Edward Robinson (Oxford: Blackwell, 1962), 229.

10 Alain Badiou, *The Century*, trans. Alberto Toscano (Cambridge: Polity, 2007), 64.

11 Early on in his book Honneth introduces the term "empathetic engagement" as a paraphrase of what for Lukács is lacking in reified consciousness (27), but he subsequently treats the phrase as if it were a quotation (35, 54, 55). In fact, as any reader of Lukács knows, the notion of empathy or sympathy is completely foreign to Lukács's thinking. Neither term appears anywhere in *History and Class Consciousness*.

12 The question of Lukács's (and the early Marx's) "humanism" is, of course, a large one. Despite the fact that both Marx and Lukács frequently use the terms "human" and "humanism" to denote that which is impoverished by capitalism, there is no need to read either body of work as "humanist" in orientation. For this reason, and while fully endorsing his painstaking critique of Honneth's account of reification, I do not share the emphasis of Andrew Feenberg's work according to which reification is best read as a "critical theory of technology" ("Rethinking Reification," in *Georg Lukács: The Fundamental Dissonance of Existence*, ed. Timothy Bewes and Timothy Hall [London: Continuum, 2011], 102). Feenberg's critique of Honneth focuses on Honneth's neglect of the "predominance of rational structures that distort and oppress the human lives they contain." Feenberg himself, by contrast, emphasizes the role of reification in "distorting" and "oppressing" the lives that it affects. Feenberg thus reproduces Honneth's own conflation of reification with the technological, and of non-reified existence with nature or the human.

13 The text quoted is the transcript of Žižek's speech as delivered (on October 9, 2011), available at http://www.criticallegalthinking.com/?p= 4415#more-4415. For the prepared text of the speech, see http://www .versobooks.com/blogs/736-slavoj-Žižek -at-occupy-wall-street-we-are -not-dreamers-we-are-the-awakening-from-a-dream-which-is-turning -into-a-nightmare. In the previously published work that Žižek was drawing on for this speech—the introduction to his own *Welcome to the Desert of the Real* from 2002—Žižek adds the following clarifying observation: "Our 'freedoms' themselves serve to mask and sustain our deeper unfree-

dom" (*Welcome to the Desert of the Real: Five Essays on September 11 and Related Dates* [London: Verso, 2002], 2).

14 For an explicit critique of Honneth on these grounds, see Neil Larsen, "Lukács *sans* Proletariat, or Can *History and Class Consciousness* Be Rehistoricized?" in Bewes and Hall, *Georg Lukács*, esp. 81–82. For an important corrective to Honneth's account of racism, although it pre-exists Honneth's work by some forty years, see Joseph Gabel, *False Consciousness: An Essay on Reification*, trans. Margaret A. Thompson (with the assistance of Kenneth A. Thompson) (New York: Harper and Row, 1975), 119–136.

15 See Axel Honneth, *Verdinglichung: Eine anerkennungstheoretische Studie* (Frankfurt: Suhrkamp, 2005), 65.

16 The same point should be made about Honneth's idealistic notion of the "antecedent" recognition of the other, a "deeply culturally anchored stance" that is "later annulled" in the forgetfulness that Honneth calls "reification" (155). As all three commentators to Honneth's lectures point out, Honneth has no conception of a primal encounter with the other that would be anything but benevolent. Judith Butler puts it as follows: "The dynamics of subjugation and fear of death found in Hegel's discussion of recognition in *The Phenomenology of Spirit* are nowhere to be found in [Honneth's] account" (Honneth, *Reification*, 101).

17 *The History of Sexuality, Volume 1: An Introduction*, trans. Robert Hurley (Harmondsworth, UK: Penguin, 1990), 44.

18 An important implication of the concept of reification needs to be renewed and insisted upon if the term is to retain its usefulness, which is that abstractions such as "religion," "materialism," "proletariat," "party," "idealism," "Christianity," "atheism," and even "reification" have no ideological unity or conceptual self-identity. To think of "religiosity," for example, as something that one could be either for or against—as Floyd does—is to fail to grasp this principle. In *Reification, or The Anxiety of Late Capitalism*, I expressed my own adherence to this principle as follows: "To maintain that the solution to reification will be substantially different, depending on whether it takes a religious or a non-religious form, perpetuates not only a fetishistic attachment to the categories of worldly knowledge which the concept of reification puts into suspension, but a reified notion of truth as separate from history—from the events which take place and from the structures of thought which produce and are produced by them" (231).

19 This is the very insight from which Lukács was later to recoil. However, the term he uses to explain his self-critique in the 1967 preface is not reification but "objectification," which completely displaces the earlier term: "Objectification is indeed a phenomenon that cannot be eliminated from human life in society. If we bear in mind that every externaliza-

tion of an object in practice . . . is an objectification, that every human expression including speech objectifies human thoughts and feelings, then it is clear that we are dealing with a universal mode of commerce between men. And in so far as this is the case, objectification is a neutral phenomenon; the true is as much an objectification as the false, liberation as much as enslavement" (xxiv). The degree to which reification is retroactively transformed in Lukács's own thinking from a purely logical phenomenon into a representational one is clear from what immediately follows: "Only when the objectified forms in society acquire functions that bring the essence of man into conflict with his existence, only when man's nature is subjugated, deformed and crippled can we speak of an objective societal condition of alienation" (ibid.).

20   Jacques Rancière, "The Politics of Literature," *Dissensus: On Politics and Aesthetics*, trans. Steven Corcoran (London: Continuum, 2010), 156.

21   J. M. Coetzee, *Elizabeth Costello* (New York: Viking, 2003), 207–208.

22   Catherine Malabou, *What Should We Do with Our Brain?* trans. Sebastian Rand (New York: Fordham University Press, 2008), 12; see Luc Boltanski and Ève Chiapello, *The New Spirit of Capitalism*, trans. Gregory Elliott (London: Verso, 2007), 149.

23   Quentin Meillassoux, "Subtraction and Contraction: Deleuze, Immanence, and *Matter and Memory*," *Collapse III*, ed. R. Mackay (Falmouth, UK: Urbanomic, November 2007), 66.

24   Henri Bergson, *Matter and Memory*, trans. Nancy Margaret Paul and W. Scott Palmer (New York: Zone, 1988), 67.

25   In a revealing moment in his essay, Meillassoux distinguishes two moments of selection within Bergson's theory of perception: the first, "by the body," is a selection made "unfreely"; the second, "by the mind," is a choice made freely, "from within the perceptive elements *already* selected by the body from the infinity of images" (73). In differentiating between these two moments, however, Meillassoux is reinstating the very distinction that Bergson's theory of perception no longer permits, the Cartesian and/or Berkeleyan distinction (between body and mind) against which the entire theory of pure perception was proposed. Furthermore, Meillassoux's account of Bergsonian perception ends by replicating the same fallacy of "dimensions" that we find in Axel Honneth's account of Lukácsian reification. Like Honneth, Meillassoux identifies "three realities within perception: matter, body, mind" (74). With this move, Meillassoux unceremoniously discards what is essential to Bergson's theory of pure perception, its "hypothetical" quality—just as Honneth, with his differentiation into "intersubjective," "subjective," and "objective" reification, discards what is essential to Lukács's theory of reification: its quality as a logic. In Bergson's theory there are not two principles of selection at work, but

one; similarly, no differentiation into "realities" is possible or necessary in "pure perception": there are only images, the aggregation of which forms the consistency that Deleuze will later call the "plane of immanence."

26 See my *Reification, or The Anxiety of Late Capitalism*, xvi.

27 *Plasticity at the Dusk of Writing: Dialectic, Destruction, Deconstruction*, trans. Carolyn Shread (New York: Columbia University Press, 2010), 13.

28 See *The Future of Hegel: Plasticity, Temporality and Dialectic*, trans. Lisabeth During (London: Routledge, 2005), 11–12.

Communist Realism

JOSHUA CLOVER

"Capitalist realism" borrows its "real" from *Realpolitik*: the ideological closure of possibilities beyond those already ratified by the imperatives of capital accumulation, upper limit Metternich, lower limit Cheney. As a concept, it is a lovely, hard-minded way of exposing a longstanding tautology concerning *rational expectations*—concerning the concealed manner in which a specific kind of quantitative thought becomes the retroactively privileged means for achieving measurable ends, those ends having been pre-decided according to a quantitative logic. The very idea of "rational expectation" consigns any thought which cannot be recognized as having an instrumental expectation of gain to the realm of the irrational, the unrealistic. This ruling idea takes on even greater force in a crisis, when gain is ever harder to come by, and thus must govern ever more regions of thought and action, ever more rigidly.

As such, capitalist realism is neither an aesthetic mode, nor strategy of representation. Indeed, it might be better regarded as a displacement of such matters. Aesthetics, representation, culture itself—all present themselves as increasingly frivolous in the era of what Simon During has called Endgame Capitalism.[1] Because of this, I think we err in associating the term with literature, or with cultural production in general, except as a kind of limit and scourge.

But there are perhaps other ways of thinking about this problem. What has realism to do with capital, as a broader question? The word "real" plays several major roles in Marx's account. *Realization*, the already-valorized commodity's quest to yield up its surplus value as profit in the moment of exchange, provides much of the stuff of which literary realism was made: the proscenium for George Eliot, a new and cruel religion for Flaubert, the dark wood into which Baudelaire cannot help but stray (inevitably opening onto the inferno). But this circulatory realm is only part of capital's realism, and not itself the crux; it has its opposite number in production. *Real subsumption*, the tendential completion of the process by which the labor force is configured to and disciplined by the dictates of the industrial workplace and mode of production, provides the scene for any number of the era's great narratives.

Balzac, as ever, holds the truth of both. But within the latter category, production's realism, we had better include one of his greatest admirers. Chapters 10 and 15 of the first volume of *Capital*, reckoning the nerves, brain, and sinew stretched across absolute and relative surplus value, respectively, are Marx's own nineteenth-century novels—miserable triumphs of realism. It would not be untoward to suggest that realism is the literary mode adequate to the struggle over the working day, and over the balance of power between human and machine, variable and constant capital. Once these decisive battles in the class struggle are won, which is to say lost, literary realism is not so much exhausted as lacking an object; the site of antagonism leaps to that of consciousness, and Western modernism asserts itself with abstract ferocity. This is the shipwreck of the real. *ACEL. Glaxo. Kreemo. Toffee.*

But that which is real in Marx persists. We might still consider "the real movement which abolishes the present state of things."[2] Marx's definition of communism is the rare case in his writings wherein what becomes "real" in English is not "*real*" in German. "The real movement" is *die wirkliche Bewegung*, and the translation, unsurprisingly, opens onto consequential ambiguity. *Bewegung* is not a simple word: it can refer either to a social or a political movement, in addition to denoting motion as such. This has allowed for the explicit or more often implicit construal of "real movement" as designating the correct concatenation of actors in motion—that constituted political force which holds the truth of communism, which is capable of abolishing capitalism. Thereby, "the real movement" is, in its substance, the party.

The aesthetic mode that attends this understanding we call "socialist realism"; the century from *At the Sign of the Cat and Racket* to *And*

Quiet Flows the Don is therefore one of combined and uneven realism. But this is to recognize, implicitly at least, that the victory of *realism with Soviet characteristics*—state realism—limns the argument for understanding socialism as state capitalism. Capitalisms get the realisms they deserve, and vice versa.

But how then would we understand the irruption of Russo-Soviet modernism *preceding* the Soviet variant of realism—and moreover, despite various similarities to Anglo-European modernism, not easily adducible to developments in capitalist relations of production? The proto-realism it supplants remains rooted in the church, the army camp, and most of all the ambiguous relation between persistent agricultural feudalism at one pole, and at the other the nascent cities still marked more by the court than the market. Eastern modernism arrives as a maelstrom into which all this material is pitched, so much jetsam, cracking and eddying and surviving, if at all, utterly transformed. Realism—that peculiar variant grinding toward the *zhdanovshchina*—must await the imposition and coronation of the *real economy* which provided the context for Anglo-European modernism as well, a century earlier. Declaring the first Five-Year Plan in 1928, Stalin held that "we are fifty or a hundred years behind the advanced countries. We must make good this distance in ten years." In 1932, the Moscow and Leningrad Union of Artists began and Soviet modernism gave up the ghost.

It is the very untimeliness of this Eastern modernism (at least from the standpoint of the West) that offers a context for grasping its extraordinary ambitions. Why does the decomposition of painterly illusion achieved by Braque and Picasso shudder before Suprematism's annihilation of representation? Why does no literary gesture of the West make a flight at the absolute that would be worthy of Khlebnikov?

To begin a response to such questions (and it is only possible, in the end, to begin), we must confront the truth that our previous gloss of *die wirkliche Bewegung* is inadequate—even mistaken. We have settled too easily on the sense of *Bewegung*, without context. For *wirklich* is itself not a simple word. With its enlarged senses of *actual* and *intrinsic*, it should lead us to understand *Bewegung* as a movement running through the historical real of capitalism, a self-motivating motion, a dynamic. Not a political order, but one from political economy. The "real movement" is nothing but the laws of motion through which capitalism realizes and abolishes itself. This then is not a party or political form but the law of value as such: the "moving contradiction"[3] which it sets loose and by which it is then borne along ineluctably toward that undiscovered country from whose bourne no value returns.

Value is the real of capital—here in the Lacanian sense stolen and repurposed for Marx. Value is that irreducible relation which congeals in production from abstract labor time but strides forth in public symbolized imperfectly as price, moving ceaselessly through the aisles of the market, momentarily arrested in the moment of exchange—the circuit's *point de capiton*—and then consumed or set again in motion. It is this process, no less and no more, which unifies production and circulation, wherein real subsumption and realization reveal themselves as moments in a singular process—the real economy on which systemic accumulation depends.

As the real of capital, value can never appear without its veil. The dream of an immediate value, undistorted and unconcealed, is precisely the limit of any possible overcoming. Proudhon's "time chits" treat value as natural, and propose that capital's real can be made to stand before us, can be known, without simply affirming capitalism sans capitalists (hence Marx's eventual dismissal: "petty bourgeois"). But we must recall that communism does not arrive as a revelation but as abolition. Communism is "real" precisely to the extent that it has done away with the value form (this is why Lacan's is a psychoanalysis of capitalism in particular). And this then is our last *real*, the one that doesn't appear in *Capital* except as a horizon. Communism achieves its realism by doing away with the real of capital; this is the real movement, *die wirkliche Bewegung*. Its aesthetic would be what must be called, if only to provoke, *communist realism*.

It is generally overlooked, or treated as a sort of jape, that Malevich's "Red Square," with its reduction to a lone geometrical form, is in truth titled "Pictorial Realism of a Peasant Woman in Two Dimensions, Called Red Square."

But this is not to suggest that the complex aesthetic regime of Soviet modernism, from *zaum* to the abstraction of the Vitebsk atelier and beyond, should thereby be understood according to a real communism. For one thing, we must attend to Ukrainian anarchism, surviving briefly in the space carved out by Makhno's black army; for this moment in art history, T. J. Clark's chapter in *Farewell to an Idea*, "God Is Not Cast Down," remains the decisive account.[4] Reflecting on that moment, we recall that anarchism itself is no friend to the value form. But, neither in Huliaipole nor Moscow was the overcoming of the value form finally achieved; that is the dolorous truth of things. Still, for a moment the world must have seemed to obey different laws of gravity, a different physics altogether, freed even provisionally from the dead weight of abstract labor. How else does Malevich's airplane climb above those of Apollinaire and Delaunay? How else Khlebnikov's imagined languages of gods and birds, his victory over the sun?

Mayakovsky called Khlebnikov "a poet for producers." Surely he meant production of another kind, production beyond value. This would be the ground for a non-capitalist realism; it is the soil of Mayakovsky's 1917 manifesto. "The past is too tight. The Academy and Pushkin are less intelligible than hieroglyphics. Throw Pushkin, Dostoevsky, Tolstoy, etc., etc. overboard from the Ship of Modernity."[5] Impossible not to hear Marx's enigmatic formulation here: "Value, therefore, does not have its description branded on its forehead; it rather transforms every product of labour into a social hieroglyphic. Later on, men try to decipher the hieroglyphic, to get behind the secret of their own social product: for the characteristic which objects of utility have of being values is as much men's social product as is their language."[6] The failure of communism to get behind the secret, to replace the hieroglyphic with a language beyond the value form—this is the story narrated by the tumbling descent from the new sun down to socialist realism. Mayakovsky, it is always worth recalling, wrote and died precisely within this period. We are told with shocking frequency that he was a victim of communism's brutality. That error itself is redolent of capitalist realism, with its placid hostility toward any extreme. Mayakovsky died not of revolution but of its failure. He died of blood loss during the reinscription by edict of the social hieroglyphic. "He who does not forget his *first* love will not recognize his last"; this is realism too. Realism's first love was capital itself; how could we forget?

NOTES

1   Simon During, *Exit Capitalism: Literary Culture, Theory and Post-Secular Modernity* (New York: Taylor & Francis, 2010), v.

2   Karl Marx and Friedrich Engels, *The German Ideology* (New York: International Publishers 1970), 57.

3   Karl Marx, *Grundrisse: Foundations of the Critique of Political Economy*, trans. Martin Nicolaus (London: Penguin, 1993), 706.

4   T. J. Clark, *Farewell to an Idea: Episodes from a History of Modernism* (New Haven, CT: Yale University Press, 2001), 15–54.

5   Anna Lawton, *Words in Revolution: Russian Futurist Manifestoes, 1912–1928* (Washington, DC: New Academia Publishing, 2005), 51.

6   Karl Marx, *Capital*, 3 vols. (London: Penguin, 1992–1993), 167.

Afterword

Unreal Criticism

RICHARD DIENST

"Capitalist realism"—is this an old joke or a new, serious concept? Is it a useful category or an ideological insult? There's an uneasiness about this phrase throughout this collection, a feeling that it names something both important and elusive about the current situation and our critical tasks. That uncertainty should be our first clue. Which comes first: capitalism or realism? How do they fit together? Is the phrase redundant (because all realism is somehow capitalist) or contradictory (because capitalism is always more real than any realism)? Should we use the phrase in the narrowest way, at the level of individual texts or subgeneric signals? Or does it rather force us to frame our analyses in the broadest historical or even ontological terms? From the very start, then, this vaguely funny and strangely unsettling phrase prompts us to think about how our critical and theoretical work tries to grasp the circumstances in which we find ourselves today.

The expression "capitalist realism" did not come from out of nowhere. Gerhard Richter is credited with making the phrase famous in April 1963, although it is hard to imagine that it had not been uttered many times before. The timing is significant. Richter, recently arrived from the DDR, was trying to claim a share of the Pop Art juggernaut. In a statement he sent to the press to drum up business for a Happening he was staging in Dusseldorf, Richter boasts that the painters of Germany (he did not say "West Germany") were now producing "Pop Art, Junk Culture, Imperialist or Capitalist Realism, New Objectivity, Naturalism" that could rival America.[1] The press seized on the phrase "capitalist realism" and continued to apply it to Richter even after he had shrugged it off. Like all things Pop, it was a throwaway item whose time had come.

But we should pause over the original formulation—"Imperialist or Capitalist Realism"—as a time-capsule surprise. It marks the confluence of several chronologies: the generational exhaustion of "socialist realism" as an official policy in the East, the early rebranding of capitalism in the West in its new consumerist guises, and the early-1960s tension between the blocs, when the socialist camp confronted the imperialist camp at the height of European division and global decolonization. So the phrase "capitalism realism" returns after fifty years to a changed world—and we will need to think carefully about what has really changed. Whatever the ruling order may call itself these days, it no longer worries about being called "imperialism." That does not mean that we should not have been talking about "imperialist realism" all along.

Meanwhile there is another term that has a prior claim to address these complexities: "postmodernism." In its now-canonical construction by Fredric Jameson, postmodernism is the third term in a three-stage model of the dialectical relationships between culture and capitalism. In the first phase, market or liberal capitalism corresponds to the dominance of nineteenth-century realism; in the second phase, monopoly capitalism and high imperialism correspond to the dominance of modernism; finally, the third stage of late or multinational capitalism corresponds to postmodernism proper.[2] Jameson's scheme, first articulated in the early 1980s, apparently strikes many contemporary literary critics as a hopelessly antiquated or démodé piece of periodizing machinery. Yet it poses, with a great deal more complexity than my sketch indicates, precisely the set of questions with which we are concerned here. It helps us to understand how realist techniques, once taken to their limits and dismantled by modernism (magnificently evoked above by Joshua Clover), have to be reinvented for a new, postmodern era, splitting into both commercial brand names and subversive experiments in the process. What is "capitalist realism" other than a strong variant of postmodernism, precisely the one that corresponds to the economic and ideological dominance of neoliberalism?

In this volume we can find both dimensions of the problem at work. On one hand, we find a series of critical appraisals of realist texts, which offer indispensible evidence of the way realist motifs and methods are being reinvented in order to grapple with their putative object, the life-world of contemporary capitalism. On the other hand—especially in the dialogue between Mark Fisher and Jodi Dean but in fact signaled throughout—we find reflections on the specific operations of neoliberalism as a capitalist system. This part of the analysis also draws inspiration from Jameson's work, where he emphasizes the difficulties of locating ourselves historically in postmodern times.

In Fisher's hands, Jameson's famous statement that "it seems to be easier for us today to imagine the thoroughgoing deterioration of the earth and of nature than the breakdown of late capitalism"[3] becomes not so much a verdict on the weakness of our collective imagination as a statement about the strength of the contemporary capitalist world-picture.

In its most current sense, then, "capitalist realism" is no longer a literary category or a genre, but an attitude and disposition so pervasive that we could hardly expect to locate it—let alone to dispel it—through the critical analysis of a few key examples. It would be more like the framework or set-up in which reality itself always appears, and appears always to confirm the necessity and naturalness of capitalism. It might be another name for Debord's spectacle, "[spreading] itself to the point where it now permeates all reality," and thereby falsifying "the whole of production and perception."[4] In a worst-case scenario, radicals would be the last people who could talk realistically about the monopolization of reality—they know too much. All that would be left is lucid compromise or ironic withdrawal, both dead ends. Are things really as bad as that? The contributors to this volume do not take the road of pessimism, either of the intellect or the will. Fisher, Dean, and others argue that both leftist pessimism and neoliberal triumphalism are now obsolete, owing to the 2008 financial crisis or the 2011 season of revolutionary uprisings from Tunis to Occupy. In the wake of these systemic crises, it has become possible to peel the trappings of "capitalist realism" away from messy capitalist reality (or from a reality no longer seen as completely capitalist), and strike out in new critical and political directions.

At this point it may seem that we are very far from anything that might be called "reality." As soon as the word "realism" is uttered, we start to erect a scaffolding of definitions and periodizations to keep the problem of reality at a distance. It is quite possible, and in fact it is often preferable, to build this scaffolding entirely out of the differentia of aesthetic forms, without having to judge the truth-value of each element in relation to some supposedly objective reality. Critical work on realism can proceed a long way without having to adjudicate the metaphysical status of representation in general. We proceed as if every realist text deploys a particular jargon of the particular: no grander claims are necessary. When Georgia O'Keeffe said that "there is nothing less real than realism," she was merely stating the obvious in a form slightly less obvious than usual, a tactic perfectly in keeping with the realistic method.

On the other hand, as soon as we talk about "capitalism" as a historical system, we take our distance from so-called reality in another way. Historical materialism repeatedly insists that we cannot understand the functioning of this immense and ever-changing system using the perceptual and cognitive tools with which we situate ourselves in our existential surroundings. The "ruthless critique of everything that exists" (Marx) happens somewhere besides the realm of existing things. In order for this critical operation to succeed, our grasp of the capitalist system must exceed the reach of our own lived experience. In this context what we call "theory," then, is the special, provisional discourse in which we try to grasp what reality fails or refuses to give us.

The phrase "capitalist realism" makes us think that we must combine these two operations—the formal or nominalist reduction of realism and the dialectical leap toward capitalism—into a single descriptive and hermeneutic system. More than that, it tempts us to think that there is something about the present moment that actually calls upon us to do so. But what motivates the exercises and experiments in the present volume is not *fidelity to reality*, but rather a *commitment to history*. These attitudes are not at all the same: in fact, they are often engaged in outright hostilities. Whereas the first organizes its critical interventions as a rectification of errors and a reconciliation with what is already established, the second is always attentive to what goes unrecognized and unrealized—for better and for worse—in whatever presents itself to us. (The first tends toward the privileges of philosophy, the second toward the haecceities of narrative.) It would be fair to say that only this restless historical attitude deserves to be called realistic. Alexander Kluge has expressed this paradox in the strongest terms:

> The root of a realistic attitude, its motivation, is *opposition* to the misery present in real circumstances; it is, therefore, an Anti-realism of motivation, a denial of the pure reality-principle, an *anti-realistic* attitude, which alone enables one to look realistically and attentively.[5]

We already know that capitalism itself is not realistic: it is composed of countless incomplete processes, floating values, half-baked schemes. No doubt this is its strength as a representational system: individual agents must bear, to very different degrees, the risks of failed representation (bad money, bad deals) without endangering the structural mechanisms that allow the accumulation of value (capital as such) to continue. As we trace and retrace the working of this system, we should remember that our motives, as Kluge reminds us, always spring from a kind of protest, whether that is expressed in anger or hope, refusals or wishes. Critical reading is nothing other than the practice whereby we keep learning how to tap into this reservoir of psychic and social energies. It may turn out that nothing is less realistic than capitalism, except history itself.

NOTES

1   Gerhard Richter, "Letter to a Newsreel Company, 29 April, 1963," in *The Daily Practice of Painting: Writings and Interviews, 1962–1993*, ed. Hans-Ulrich Obrist, trans. David Britt (Cambridge, MA: MIT Press, 1995), 16.

2   Fredric Jameson, *Postmodernism, or, The Cultural Logic of Late Capitalism* (Durham, NC: Duke University Press, 1991), 35–36.

3   Fredric Jameson, *The Seeds of Time* (New York: Columbia University Press, 1994), xii.

4   Guy Debord, *Comments on the Society of the Spectacle*, trans. Malcolm Imrie (London: Verso Books, 1998), 9, 10.

5   Alexander Kluge, "The Political as Intensity of Everyday Feelings," trans.
    Andrew Bowie, *Cultural Critique* 4 (Fall 1986), 121. Kluge explores this
    point in "Die schärfste Ideologie: daß die Realität sich auf ihren realist-
    ischen Charakter beruft," in *In Gefahr und größter Not bringt der Mittelweg
    den Tod: Texte zu Kino, Film, Politik*, ed. Christian Schulte (Berlin: Verlag
    Vorwerk 8), 127–134.

Timothy Bewes is professor of English at Brown University. He is the author of *The Event of Postcolonial Shame* (2011), *Reification, or The Anxiety of Late Capitalism* (2002), and *Cynicism and Postmodernity* (1997). He has also co-edited several collections of essays. He has served on the editorial board of the journal *New Formations* since 1998, and as an editor of *Novel* since 2005.

Joshua Clover is professor of English at the University of California Davis. He is the author of *1989: Bob Dylan Didn't Have This to Sing About* (2009), *The Totality for Kids* (2006), and *The Matrix* (2005). He is currently at work on a book tentatively titled *The Transformation Problem*, concerning the unraveling of hegemony within the current cycle of global accumulation.

Michael W. Clune is assistant professor of English at Case Western Reserve University. His books include *Writing against Time* (2013), *White Out* (2013), and *American Literature and the Free Market* (2010).

J. D. Connor is assistant professor of art history at Yale University. He works on the interplay of art and industry in the Hollywood system, particularly its contemporary version. He is currently completing *The Studios after the Studios: Hollywood in the Neoclassical Era, 1970–2005*. He is a member of the steering committee for Post45, a collective of scholars working on American literature and culture since 1945.

Jodi Dean is professor of political science at Hobart and William Smith Colleges. She is the author of *Democracy and Other Neoliberal Fantasies* (2009), *Žižek's Politics* (2006), *Publicity's Secret: How Tech-*

noculture Capitalizes on Democracy (2002), *Aliens in America: Conspiracy Cultures from Outerspace to Cyberspace* (1998), and several edited book collections. She is co-editor of *Theory and Event.*

Richard Dienst is the author of *The Bonds of Debt: Borrowing against the Common Good* (2011) and *Still Life in Real Time: Theory after Television* (1994). He teaches theory in the Department of English at Rutgers University, New Brunswick, NJ.

Mark Fisher is the author of *Capitalist Realism* (2009) and the forthcoming *Ghosts of My Life: Writings on Depression, Hauntology and Lost Futures.* He is a commissioning editor at Zero Books. His writing has appeared in a wide variety of publications, including *Film Quarterly, The Wire, The Guardian,* and *Frieze.* He is programme leader of the MA in aural and visual cultures at Goldsmiths, University of London, and a lecturer at the University of East London. His weblog can be found at http://k-punk.abstractdynamics.org.

Andrew Hoberek is associate professor of English and director of graduate studies at the University of Missouri, Columbia. He is the author of *The Twilight of the Middle Class: Post–World War II American Fiction and White-Collar Work* (2005) and has begun work on a book called *Mission to Mankind: Post-1960 US Fiction and US Foreign Policy.* He is a member of the steering committee for Post45.

Caren Irr is professor of English at Brandeis University. She is the author of *Pink Pirates: Contemporary American Women Writers and Copyright* (2010) and *The Suburb of Dissent: Cultural Politics in the United States and Canada during the 1930s* (1998).

Alissa G. Karl is assistant professor of English at the State University of New York, Brockport, and author of *Modernism and the Marketplace: Literary Culture and Consumer Capitalism in Rhys, Woolf, Stein, and Nella Larsen* (2009).

Phillip E. Wegner is a University Research Foundation Professor and coordinator of the graduate program in the Department of English at the University of Florida. He is the author of *Life between Two Deaths, 1989–2001: U.S. Culture in the Long Nineties* (2009), *Imaginary Communities: Utopia, the Nation, and the Spatial Histories of Modernity* (2002), and the forthcoming *Periodizing Jameson; or, The Adventures of Theory in Post-Contemporary Times* and *Ontologies of the Possible: Utopia, Science Fiction, and Globalization*. He is also president of the Society for Utopian Studies.